mlr

Marxist Left Review

Number 22 – Winter 2021

Editor
Omar Hassan

Editorial Committee
Mick Armstrong
Sandra Bloodworth
Omar Hassan
Louise O'Shea

Reviews Editor
Alexis Vassiley

© Social Research Institute

Published by Socialist Alternative
Melbourne, August 2021

PO Box 4354
Melbourne University, VIC 3052

www.marxistleftreview.org
marxistleftreview@gmail.com

Contributions to *Marxist Left Review* are peer-reviewed

ISSN 1838–2932
rrp. $17

Subediting and proofreading
Tess Lee Ack
Diane Fieldes
Tom Bramble

Layout and production
Oscar Sterner

Cover
James Plested

Printed by IngramSpark

Marxist Left Review is a theoretical journal published twice-yearly by Socialist Alternative, a revolutionary organisation based in Australia.

We aim to engage with theoretical and political debates on the Australian and international left, making a rigorous yet accessible case for Marxist politics. We also seek to provide analysis of the social, political and economic dynamics shaping Australian capitalism.

Unless indicated otherwise all articles published reflect the views of the individual author(s).

We rely on our readers' support to continue publication.

Subscribe at *marxistleftreview.org*

mlr

Marxist Left Review

Number 22 – Winter 2021

FEATURES

REVIEWS

OMAR HASSAN

Diverging destinies in a global crisis

Omar Hassan is an editor of *Marxist Left Review*. He has been active in anti-fascist and Palestine solidarity work, and has written extensively on the Middle East.

THOUGH COVID REMAINS the key factor shaping world politics, its social and political impacts are increasingly uneven. From New York to Delhi, Shanghai to Melbourne, discussions remain focused on COVID casualties, healthcare systems, the quantity and quality of government welfare and, of course, lockdowns. But the conditions from country to country vary wildly. The central debate continues to be whether to prioritise profits over public health. The editorial in the previous edition of this journal surveyed many of these issues, and made a strong case for the elimination of the virus.[1] The subsequent experience of countries that achieved this goal has vindicated this argument. The *Lancet* medical journal has reported that countries that acted aggressively against the virus have experienced fewer limits on civil liberties, stronger economic outcomes, and most importantly, fewer deaths.[2]

Yet despite these partial achievements, the virus remains out of control, and many countries have no realistic prospect of accessing sufficient vaccines for the indefinite future. As a result, much of the analysis of the pandemic presented in the last edition of this journal remains applicable to the majority of the world's population,

1. Hassan 2021.
2. Oliu-Barton et al 2021.

including large parts of Latin America, the Middle East, South-East Asia and Africa. According to official statistics, deaths in the first six months of 2021 have surpassed the first year of the pandemic.[3] Yet we know that this data is deeply flawed, and in some cases entirely worthless. Indonesia has reported roughly 50,000 deaths, but an independent investigation by the University of Washington assessed the real tally – as of May 6 – to be over 110,000. According to the same research the real figure for worldwide deaths at that time was an astonishing 6.9 million, more than double the official figure of three million.[4]

Countries like India offer us a terrifying insight into the devastating impact the virus can have in the underdeveloped world. In early May new daily diagnoses peaked at over 400,000, and at the time of writing more than 400,000 people had died. Some have sought to dismiss the Indian catastrophe as a product of Modi's hard-right administration, a regime similar in style and substance to the authoritarian neoliberalism of Trump and Bolsonaro. It would be spurious to totally discount the impact of conspiracism, machismo, and pro-business leanings of right-wing populist administrations the world over. But such an explanation acts as a cover for the broader Indian ruling class, with little difference in outcomes in states controlled by Congress or even the Communist Party (M). This fits with the earlier experience in Europe and the US, where governments across the political spectrum all tended to prioritise profits over public health. The problem in India and much of the underdeveloped world is capitalism, regardless of whether it presents in neoliberal, authoritarian or proto-fascist guises.

Many commentators have used the horrors seen in India and other poor nations to highlight inequities facing the Global South in terms of their fiscal capacity, social development and pre-existing healthcare infrastructure. Yet it would be a mistake not to also emphasise the role of class divisions *within* such societies. Despite being home to unimaginable poverty, India now possesses the world's third largest number of billionaires. These parasites saw

---

3.   Kamp et al 2021.
4.   Institute for Health Metrics and Evaluation 2021.

their fortunes grow by over $230 billion last year.[5] While essential workers and slum dwellers had their emaciated bodies burnt in the streets, the wealthy took private jets to overseas safehouses.[6] A *Wall Street Journal* report on the pandemic in the underdeveloped world found similar stories everywhere. In Peru, where the public health system has collapsed due to one of the world's worst per capita death rates, the middle class and wealthy can purchase oxygen for more than $1,000 a canister. In a society where the monthly average income is US$420, the combination of poor healthcare and a thriving black market turned the pandemic into a form of social cleansing, a targeted massacre of workers and the poor.[7]

In a similar vein, Western governments and pharmaceutical companies have been rightly denounced for failing to ensure access to vaccines for poorer nations. Capitalists have shown once again that they prioritise intellectual property and profits more than human life. Yet the division between rich and poor nations is not the only or even the most important one. For instance, in Lebanon politicians and their cronies gained early access to vaccines back in February. With that vital task completed, it has taken the government another five months to fully vaccinate just 6 percent of the public. This experience is repeated in a number of underdeveloped nations where vaccine scarcity is exacerbated by corruption and class privilege.

In the face of such catastrophes, governments have increasingly turned to repression to maintain their rule. Following a request by the Indian government, Twitter took the shameful step of censoring posts criticising Modi's handling of the pandemic.[8] In a range of countries, police and executive powers have been strengthened in order to manage dissent. Some of these measures prefigure the pandemic, but have been pushed through in the context of the absolute failure to deal with the virus. The insensitive use of police and military forces to enforce public health measures has rightly aroused opposition everywhere, but is particularly a problem in

---

5.   IANS 2021.
6.   Kotoky 2021.
7.   Dube and Agarwal 2021.
8.   Madhok and Suri 2021; for the free speech argument see Bates 2021.

underdeveloped nations where democratic freedoms tend to be more fragile.

Looking ahead, the situation in the underdeveloped world remains grim. Southern Africa, South-East Asia and most of Latin America are still being ravaged by the virus. Eastern Europe has also been hit extraordinarily hard this year, and there's no reason to think they will avoid new waves. Given the ongoing issues of vaccine scarcity, weak healthcare systems and enormous slums, it is only a matter of time before other poor countries have deadly new outbreaks for which they are totally unprepared. The scale of the global outbreak also means that the emergence of new variants that increase the contagiousness and severity of the virus is increasingly likely. Such variants act as threat multipliers, making prevention, containment and treatment more difficult.

This terrible state of affairs has produced a deep economic slump in much of the underdeveloped world. Even before the pandemic a range of countries were struggling, most prominently Lebanon, Argentina, South Africa and Mexico. The pandemic has multiplied the misery of these nations, while also damaging those that were previously doing better. India's economy for instance, contracted by 7.3 percent in the 2020–21 fiscal year, its worst outcome since independence.[9] Peru's plummeted by 11.6 percent, and negative growth rates were seen in most of Africa, the Middle East and Latin America. Countries that are heavily reliant on tourism and migration have seen some of the worst drops, while those involved in resource extraction have benefited from high prices generated by supply shortages. While the IMF has consistently revised up economic predictions overall, it expects a number of countries – especially among those it describes as "emerging and developing" – to suffer reduced growth rates and increased poverty for years to come. The problem is, as Martin Wolf has pointed out in a series of strong pieces on this issue in the *Financial Times*, two-thirds of humanity live in this category of nations.[10]

The pandemic is clearly the major factor explaining the difficult situation facing much of the Global South. But the virus has exposed

---

9.   Misra 2021.
10.   Wolf 2021.

existing fragilities. Decades of structural poverty and underinvestment in health and welfare have made the social and economic impact of the pandemic worse. As well, poorer nations tend to rely on more restrictive and expensive credit lines for borrowing. So although budget deficits were seen in almost every country in the world last year, the details reflect big divergences in policies. In the advanced capitalist nations, much of the deficit was produced by a boost in discretionary spending, whereas in much of the Global South, it was a result of collapsing revenues.[11] Compounding these difficulties are a series of other factors, including the dearth of white-collar jobs that could sustain themselves through the pandemic, a large informal sector, the lack of social infrastructure to lockdown humanely, the absence of tourists, and a 30 percent collapse in foreign direct investment.[12] While growth is expected to pick up again this year, inevitable new waves of the virus and underlying economic weaknesses mean that a strong recovery in the Global South seems some time away.

Many of these arguments will be familiar to readers of this journal. Indeed they were the focus of my editorial in the last issue, with one key difference. Back then, it was the West that was responsible for the bulk of the world's casualties, especially the US and western Europe. It was Western nations which saw the most calamitous drops in economic growth due to strict lockdowns and out of control caseloads.

Today, the situation is reversed, as the last six months of the pandemic have seen a sharp reversal of fortunes in the parts of the world. A handful of countries such as China, Australia, New Zealand and Singapore have emerged nearly unscathed, after deploying rigorous health measures early on. Strict border closures and lockdowns were vital to achieving these good outcomes, and remain vital to preserving this situation alongside further investment in health and quarantine facilities. But even Western countries that initially failed to control the virus are emerging from the worst of the pandemic and are rebuilding their economies faster than expected.

This bulk of this piece will focus on explaining how the situation

---

11. Wolf 2021 and Díaz-Bonilla 2020.
12. World Bank 2021.

has changed so dramatically, as well as assessing the consequences of recent developments for the world system.

Economic rebound

At the peak of the health crisis in 2020, many economists – bourgeois and Marxist – believed that this would be a multi-year event akin to the Great Depression. The IMF concurred, predicting that it would take years before economies returned to their pre-pandemic state, let alone saw new growth. As it turns out, these early predictions were wrong. Notwithstanding the incredible destruction documented above and elsewhere, the Global North has now rebounded from one of the deepest recessions of all time via an historic surge in economic activity. What happened?

Firstly, wealthy governments have provided seemingly endless fiscal and monetary support for businesses across the board. The state opened its pockets to big business in the form of cheap credit, low interest rates, and myriad other handouts. The US saw the most pro-business approach, the centrepiece being Trump's creation of a $500 billion slush fund for distressed businesses.[13] On top of this and other fiscal measures, the Federal Reserve took the extraordinary measure of purchasing $120 billion in corporate bonds each month, providing corporations with essentially unlimited credit at low cost. Similar measures were undertaken elsewhere, though to a lesser extent. As well as propping up businesses, wealthy nations also substantially increased their expenditure on welfare by implementing a range of furlough schemes. The UK is spending around $66 billion on its furlough program, the figure for Germany is $42 billion, while Australia – a much smaller country which suffered less from the pandemic than most – spent a whopping $90 billion on the JobKeeper program alone.[14] Unemployment benefits also expanded dramatically, the US heading the pack with close to $800 billion spent on federal unemployment benefits.[15] These figures not only prevented a collapse in consumer demand but actually increased it. Household savings in Australia, the US and the UK are substantially

---

13. Hirsch 2020.

14. BBC 2021, Ziffer 2020, Economist 2020.

15. PGP Foundation 2021.

up, facilitating purchases on big ticket items such as cars, home renovations and consumer electronics. As a result of these substantial interventions, both individual and corporate bankruptcies are at historic lows. Reuters reported that while bankruptcies linked to corporate restructuring increased slightly during the pandemic,

> overall filings, including all personal and other business bankruptcies, for the year were 529,068, compared to nearly 800,000 annually in recent years, and triple that in 2010 at the end of the last recession.[16]

The second factor limiting the collapse is that corporations – especially the largest – have found ways of adapting and restructuring faster than previously expected. The closure of shopping malls and big retailers has led to an unprecedented explosion in online shopping and delivery services, fast-tracking the shift towards e-commerce already underway. This burst of activity – supercharged by the stimulus payments – generated a surge in the logistics and manufacturing sectors, with Amazon nearly doubling its global workforce last year.[17] At the same time, a range of industries have found ways to reorganise to continue and indeed expand production. Outdoor and takeaway dining options have blossomed as one of the few experiences available to health-conscious citizens, taking the edge off some of the initial collapse in hospitality. Delivery services like UberEats and DoorDash have also multiplied and expanded, enjoying bizarrely high valuations despite never making a sustainable profit.[18] Of course, the growth in new areas comes at the expense of others, but the impact so far has been positive for the economy as a whole.

Thirdly, after a relatively short hiatus, a range of major industries have continued to function through the pandemic. Manufacturing output has been building since the middle of last year. Australian manufacturing has been growing steadily since June of last year, as reflected in the Purchasing Managers' Index (PMI)

---

16. Reuters 2021a.
17. Soper 2021.
18. McKinnon 2021.

which measures business activity in the sector.[19] The US situation is similar, and though German, Italian and French manufacturing lagged for much of last year, they're now heading in the same direction.[20] Services are tracking similarly, despite the overall category being weighed down by the relatively poor performance of restaurants and, even more, hotels and tourism. The construction sector is also booming, driven by rising house prices pushed along by cheap interest rates and a savings glut. Mining and agriculture are reaping the benefits of a surge in the price of commodities driven by growth in manufacturing.

These factors explain why the economic activity of major nations was far less impacted by the lockdowns introduced in the first months of 2021 than those early in the pandemic. In fact, the main factor constraining output in a range of industries is no longer COVID but shortages of industrial inputs and overwhelmed logistics networks.[21] Faced with nearly universal lockdowns and a possible economic depression, companies opted to hoard cash to shore up their position early in the pandemic. They thus sold down their existing inventories and avoided restocking, let alone investing in new production capacity. Just a few months later, the explosion in online shopping suddenly created enormous demand for goods that were now out of stock. Across the world, factories producing cars, computers, chips and other consumer goods were suddenly trying to place orders for parts for which they had no reserves. This scarcity of inputs has forced slowdowns and temporary closures in a range of facilities, as well as increased the prices of goods across the board. It has also produced a crisis in international shipping, with freight prices increasing substantially due to both shortages and misallocations of containers and ships.[22] In these circumstances, shipping workers have been exploited to extreme extents, often ending up stranded at sea in conditions described by the International Transport Workers Federation as akin to slavery.[23]

---

19. Investing 2021a.
20. See Investing 2021b for the US and other nations.
21. Goodman and Chokshi 2021.
22. Dempsey and Hume 2021.
23. Thompson and Sveen 2020.

It is significant to note that these processes have overwhelmingly benefited big capital at the expense of their smaller rivals.[24] The former have reaped the rewards of government stimulus, cheaper and more accessible credit, and greater brand recognition that is vital for online shopping. Large supermarkets and liquor distribution centres boomed at the expense of bars, restaurants and cafes.[25] The shift to working from home also generated growth in a range of industries, including tech companies such as Zoom, pharmaceutical industries, furniture manufacturers and retailers, electronic manufacturing and retailers, and so on. This was accompanied by a boost in spending on home entertainment, including streaming services such as Netflix and Disney+ as well as home gaming consoles. Overall, as with all capitalist crises, the shock generated by the pandemic forced through a substantial reorganisation of industry on new and – for now – highly profitable lines.

The fourth element shaping the economic rebound is the acquisition and distribution of COVID vaccines. The development and rollout of the vaccine – in the advanced capitalist world at least – has exceeded the most optimistic expectations imaginable twelve months ago. A range of countries have now achieved quite high rates of vaccination, headed up by Israel, the UK and the US, with a number of countries in western and northern Europe following close behind. Of course, the political leaders of these nations should not be forgiven for allowing some of the worst death tolls on the planet. Nevertheless, up until the Delta variant cases were trending down, despite the substantial – and in some cases, irresponsible – easing of health measures. What happens going forward is unclear, but it seems likely that casualties will not return to previous levels. In some cases their advantageous access to vaccines is a product of an advanced domestic pharmaceutical sector, while for others it reflects their capacity to pay a premium in order to guarantee early doses. While it is too soon to know whether the vaccines will be enough to stave off waves of new strains, the capacity of mRNA technology in particular to be quickly adapted to new variants is promising. Again, this only applies to those who can access them.

---

24. See Taylor K 2021 and Arora 2020.
25. Greenblat 2021 and Wells et al 2021.

Together, these factors mean that while the world remained in recession in the first quarter of 2021, the prospects for immediate growth are strong if the vaccines hold. Unlike the slow recovery following the global financial crisis (GFC), the IMF has gleefully announced that the advanced economies and China will emerge from the crisis economically unscathed, notwithstanding the comparatively minor fact of hundreds of thousands of dead bodies. Indeed, Australia has already surpassed its pre-COVID GDP levels, with the US and Europe not far behind. The US is predicted to exceed their pre-pandemic position by the time this article is published, with the EU a few months behind. The IMF's quarterly World Economic Outlook report in April predicted global GDP growth of 6 percent, which would be the highest since 1973.[26]

So capitalism has survived, and some sectors have thrived. But the impact has been highly uneven. Even as many workers and the poor temporarily benefited from improved welfare, the year saw a major distribution of wealth towards the rich, as important sections of capital grew enormously. The Forbes rich list reflects this reality: the wealthiest people on earth overwhelmingly increased the size of their already unimaginable fortunes despite the broader economic collapse.[27] It is horrifying to think that a year that saw so much misery and death could be so profitable. One is reminded of Trotsky's bitter account of the barbarism of World War One, where "enormous fortunes arose out of the bloody foam".[28]

Before moving on, it is worth briefly exploring in more detail the conditions in some of the key centres of capital accumulation.

China
China is in a unique situation among the major powers. Despite being the source of the virus, it has subsequently managed to keep it under control. Less affected by the pandemic than most, China was the only major economy to grow in 2020, albeit at a weak 2.3 percent.[29] This has accelerated the rate at which the Chinese economy is catching

26. International Monetary Fund 2021.
27. Dolan et al 2021.
28. Trotsky 2008, p.22.
29. Cheng 2021.

up to the US, with experts predicting that it will now take place by 2030 rather than 2032. While China's per capita GDP remains one-sixth of the US figure, the absolute size of its economy gives it a growing geopolitical and economic weight in the world system. According to officially surveyed data – which excludes around 300 million migrant workers and 149 million self-employed – unemployment peaked at just 6.2 percent last year, and has since receded back to 5 percent.[30] Its relative success in handling the health crisis has given China the freedom to engage in proactive vaccine diplomacy. A spokesperson for China's foreign ministry claimed on 2 June that China had exported more than 350 million doses to over 40 countries around the world, before the US had exported a single dose.[31] Many of these doses have been directed towards counties with which it has growing relations, with a strong focus on Asia and Latin America. In an era where great power competition is front and centre, all of this is an indication of real strength.

On the back of these factors, it would be tempting to assume China will once again drive global growth, much as it did in the aftermath of the GFC. Yet China is in a challenging phase of its economic development, and has indicated it has no desire to take on this responsibility. In 2020 China showed no interest in replicating the substantial stimulus and monetary loosening it deployed in 2008, which amounted to one-sixth of national GDP. In fact, after a brief stimulatory phase, China has for months been cracking down on lending and trying to reduce financial liquidity. In particular, they've been imposing fines and restrictions on the shadow banking and finance sectors, which have enjoyed a boom in the past decade. Partly this reflects sincere concerns about the instability and inflationary dynamics that loose monetary policy can breed, most tangibly manifest in the property boom in China's coastal cities. As well, the high reliance of Chinese corporations on debt – valued at around 160 percent of national GDP – means they are under less pressure to modernise and streamline their operations. The tightening of credit is thus also an attempt to force through a rationalisation and consolidation of capital, and has had

---

30. Peach and Leng 2020.
31. Wenbin 2021.

the effect of sending a number of state-owned enterprises bankrupt in recent months.[32]

The other element of this crackdown relates to more directly political concerns. A small number of Chinese corporations have grown incredibly powerful in recent years, leveraging their near monopoly over local markets to produce billions in profits. In the process, a layer of celebrity billionaires has emerged, with independent minds, interests and capacities that do not always align with those of the ruling Communist Party. In December last year, the Chinese government announced it would prioritise "anti-trust efforts and prevent the disorderly expansion of capital". Just weeks later it launched an anti-trust probe into Jack Ma, at the time China's richest man. It has since blocked his attempt to float his company Ant on the Shanghai and Hong Kong stock markets as well as pushed to curtail its financial activities, costing the man and his company billions. This unfolding clash between Jack Ma and Xi Jinping, now supplemented by government crackdowns on a range of tech giants, is illustrative of the inevitable tensions of China's unique form of capitalist development. A recent World Economic Forum report, albeit produced by a highly ideological and pro-market body, documented the substantial role played by the private sector:

> China's private sector – which has been revving up since the global financial crisis – is now serving as the main driver of China's economic growth...they contribute 60% of China's GDP, and are responsible for 70% of innovation, 80% of urban employment and provide 90% of new jobs. Private wealth is also responsible for 70% of investment and 90% of exports.[33]

While welcoming this dynamism, the central government is concerned to maintain its unquestioned dominance over all sectors of society, including the economy. How this contradiction plays out in the medium term is yet to be seen.

---

32. Somasundaram 2020.
33. Guluzade 2019.

The US

Unlike China, the US allowed the virus to tear through its population as the government failed to take necessary health measures. Nevertheless, it was able to ride out the pandemic with fewer negative economic effects than most. Partly this reflected its status as a nation with deep pockets and access to high-end research and manufacturing capacities. In addition to the figures referenced earlier, according to an estimate by macroeconomist Ceyhun Elgin from Boğaziçi University in Turkey, the US has spent more on COVID stimulus measures than any country other than Japan. The figure he gives for the total stimulus introduced by Trump and Biden is equivalent to 27 percent of national GDP.[34] It also spent over $12 billion on research, development, manufacturing subsidies and early contracts to support the development of vaccines.[35] This has all been crucial to propping up the US economy and allowing it to reopen quickly. The other key factor in America's success has been its preparedness to let the virus rip, whatever the human cost. Not once did Trump or Biden impose a national lockdown, more fearful of the economic impact than the loss of lives. Nor did states – including Democrat-run ones – take sufficient measures to protect lives.

Regardless of the health impacts, these policies have placed the US in a commanding economic situation. It has lifted most of its health restrictions, and has not yet suffered terrible new waves. The economic benefits of getting the virus under control have been significant. The US has enjoyed a sharp bounceback following the historic contraction in the first half of 2020. US GDP has now exceeded its pre-pandemic heights following consecutive quarters of strong growth since June last year of 7.5, 1.1 and 1.6 percent.[36] Solid figures for job creation suggest the recovery is far from over, with tourism, hospitality and retail driving the creation of over 850,000 jobs in June. Despite this better than expected news, both unemployment rates and overall labour market participation are 2 points worse compared to pre-pandemic levels, at 5.9 percent and 61.6 percent

---

34. Taylor A 2021.
35. Barone 2020.
36. OECD 2021.

respectively.[37] Predictably, the political class has bitterly fought over the interpretations of these mixed results, with Republicans blaming generous unemployment payments for the elevated unemployment levels and corresponding labor shortages, while Democrats insist that stimulus measures are helping to drive consumer demand and broader growth.

The strong recovery has placed the US in a position of driving the global economy not seen since the early years of the Cold War. For comparison, while the US has consistently outperformed its rivals in the UK, Germany, France and Japan since the GFC, its growth rates averaged a relatively anaemic 2.3 percent from 2010–2019 and never exceeded 3 percent.[38] It was the rise of China that drove global expansion and capital accumulation across that decade. Now the condition of the US economy is such that it is America that is straining the capacity of the world market and lifting others in its wake, with a predicted growth rate of well over 6 percent this year. This dynamic will entrench its economic leadership over the advanced capitalist world going forward. Another advantage the US economy has over comparable rivals is the relative youth of its population, maintained by relatively high immigration and fertility rates. This has multiple benefits, the most immediate of which are increasing the tax base and lowering the cost of social spending, both of which increase the amount of surplus value that can be deployed by the government.

Europe

On both public health and economic measures, Europe has been one of the big losers from the pandemic so far. Along with the US, the region suffered terribly from the virus. As of 3 July, European countries make up a staggering 15 of the top 20 places worst hit as measured by deaths per capita.[39] Central and eastern Europe in particular are a disaster zone, with countries such as Hungary, the Czech Republic, Slovakia and the various Balkan states high on the list. Elevated poverty levels paired with decades of attacks on social

---

37. Bartash and Robb 2021.
38. World Bank 2020.
39. Johns Hopkins Coronavirus Resource Centre 2021.

services and marketisation of their economies left these nations especially vulnerable. But it is not simply Europe's periphery where the damage has been done. Governments in the UK, Italy, Sweden, France, Belgium, Germany and Spain have badly failed their populations, resulting in death counts not seen since the world wars.

Unlike the US, however, European governments have in many cases been prepared to engage in nation-wide lockdowns. Thus most citizens of western Europe spent last winter in isolation, as governments were forced to reimpose social distancing measures to stop the second wave. Even today, some restrictions remain in place in most countries. Though to some extent this reflects a higher value on human life produced by historically stronger working-class movements, these lockdowns have been limited by the desire to prop up capitalism to the greatest possible extent. They were thus imposed reluctantly, belatedly, and totally inadequately across the board. In many cases personal and political freedoms were significantly curtailed even as the economy was overwhelmingly kept open. The transparent hypocrisy of this approach, and its subsequent failure to control the virus, fuelled substantial opposition to public health measures. In every case, the lockdowns ended prematurely even as thousands of daily cases were reported; even now countries are opening up despite the Delta strain sweeping through.

Of primary concern to socialists is the fact that these half-hearted policies have been a disaster for public health. But they've also severely undermined the broader economy, and with it the lives of working-class people. The damage caused by the pandemic put them at a disadvantage compared to China and others that controlled it more successfully. Yet their repeated imposition of partial lockdowns meant that, unlike the US, their economies have been slow to rebound. While China and US economies expanded consistently from mid-2020, the European Union had a brief respite of positive growth in the July quarter before collapsing back into recession.[40] Britain has achieved marginally better results, though it remains impacted by its catastrophic 19.5 percent contraction in the second quarter of 2020 and the difficulties associated with Brexit. European

---

40. OECD 2021.

unemployment figures remain higher than in the US, at 7.3 percent across the EU and 4.7 percent in the UK. The overall figure for the EU masks stark differences; Germany sits on just 3.7 percent, France on 7.5, while Italy, Spain and Greece languish on over 10 percent each. There is no one reason behind this divergence, though the centrality of tourism and travel in southern Europe is clearly a factor.

Aside from the UK and Germany, Europe was also slow to utilise its manufacturing and pharmaceutical expertise to develop and roll out vaccines, especially when compared to the US and China. Some have blamed the slow moving bureaucracies of the EU for the insipid response, a factor which can't be totally discounted. But Europe has actually produced well over 400 million doses, of which around half have been exported around the world. This willingness to trade has been presented by French President Emanuel Macron as evidence of their global civic mindedness. But in a relatively generous assessment of Europe's vaccine failures, Professor of European Law Gareth Davies suggests a very different explanation:

> The vaccine shortage now demands that market processes be subordinated – at least to some extent – to state planning and supervision, in a switch that is common in times of war or emergency, but alien to the practices of the EU.[41]

Thus the exports of desperately needed vaccines reflects the embedded neoliberalism in European institutions. One farcical example of this is that Australia – a country that has nearly eliminated COVID – was allowed to purchase one millions of doses of AstraZeneca from an Italian manufacturer, even as that country struggled with tens of thousands of cases. Sensing an opportunity in this unfolding disaster, China has provided desperately needed vaccines and PPE to eastern Europe, most notably Orban's Hungary.

Overall, Europe presents a mixed picture. In the short term, the vaccine rollout is now accelerating and the region seems set for a period of somewhat healthy growth. Yet it remains hampered by a series of fundamental weaknesses, not least of which are a long-term

---

41. Davis 2021.

failure to generate a rival to America's Silicon Valley, and the social and economic fragility of its southern and eastern fringes.

Australia

While Australia is not a major site of capital accumulation, it is the most important example of a Western nation that has managed to practically eliminate the virus. Apart from the journal being produced here, it is therefore also worth discussing because Australia's handling of the pandemic in 2020 – though inadequate in many ways – could and should have been a model for the rest of the world to follow.

As one of the wealthiest nations in the world, Australia had a number of advantages that have thus far seen it through the pandemic in good stead.

The first and fundamental factor has been the success in containing the virus. Unlike in most advanced nations, government policies were relatively proactive and far-sighted in containing the virus, with a number of strict lockdowns implemented that have successfully eliminated the virus after small outbreaks. At the same time, it implemented a relatively generous welfare scheme in the form of JobSeeker – which temporarily doubled previous unemployment benefits – and JobKeeper – a furlough scheme that guaranteed workers up to $750 a week in income. These policies made Australia one of the countries least affected by COVID in the advanced capitalist world. Aside from Victoria, which endured a painful though necessary three-month lockdown late last year, most of the economy has been open for the last 12 months. Increased welfare payments provided a boost to domestic industries of all kinds, including the significant property market where sales, the construction of new homes and renovations of existing properties are all on the rise.[42] The overall health of the economy is reflected in unemployment figures, which peaked at 7.4 percent in July last year before dropping to 5.1 percent in May 2021. The gravity of the crisis was hidden by the JobKeeper furlough scheme, which makes the information regarding overall participation in the labour market a better measure. Here

---

42. Dowling 2021.

too the data is positive, back up above the pre-pandemic trend to 66.2 points.[43] Other sectors have also benefited from the strong management of the pandemic; Australia was one of the few places in the world where film and television could be produced last year. Scandalous (though largely unreported) exemptions to the travel ban for celebrities and the sector more broadly allowed it to take advantage of this situation.[44]

The second factor that contributed positively to the economy, contrary to early expectations, was the ban on tourists and immigration. Economists had been nervous about the impact of the loss of tourists and international students, who together contribute around $22 billion to the national economy according to independent economist Saul Eslake.[45] It is true that the revenues of higher education and the hospitality industries have suffered, and there has been downward pressure on rental properties in inner city Melbourne and Sydney. At the same time, Australian citizens have been forced to cancel their annual trips to Bali, Europe and other hotspots; instead their tourism dollars have been spent at home. The figures are substantial: Eslake estimates Australian overseas spending on holidays at an annual $55 billion, much of which will have been redeployed in other ways that benefit the local economy.[46] So the net effect has been positive. Writing for the *Sydney Morning Herald*, Shane Wright presents data that reinforces this conclusion:

> Australians are a nation of travellers. In the 12 months to January last year, more than 11.3 million Australians returned to the country after a trip overseas. The average length of time overseas was about 17 days. By contrast, the country welcomed 9.5 million tourists into the country.[47]

The loss of international students is a different phenomenon. Saddled with absurdly high education costs and restrictive visa

---

43. ABS 2021.
44. Williams 2021.
45. Gittens 2021.
46. Gittens 2021.
47. Wright 2021.

conditions that force them into informal employment scenarios, the roughly 700,000 international students Australia welcomes annually bring with them more long-lasting revenues. This explains why governments and universities are so desperate to allow them in; their absence is an unambiguous loss. From a boss's perspective, the best of all worlds would involve supplementing the spending of trapped citizens with hundreds of thousands of incoming tourists and international students. In contrast, the left should insist that international travel should be subordinated to the interests of workers and the poor. Expanded and specially designed quarantine facilities are vital to allow safe and humane travel between nations. Yet the scarcity of places means they should be filled by the most needy – refugees and migrants fleeing poor and dangerous conditions – not on those who can afford to pay the most.

The third factor strengthening the Australian economy is the boom in prices for primary goods such as iron ore, copper, coal and gas, which represent a substantial chunk of Australia's economy. The prices of these essential commodities are through the roof, spurred on by the higher demand driven by the global economic rebound. This has given the Australian economy – and government revenues – a massive boost. Estimates for the 2021/2022 budget assumed iron ore prices of $55 a tonne, while global shortages have driven prices well over $200. A writer for the *Australian Financial Review* estimates that the boom will provide the Coalition government with an extra $36 billion in revenues in the 2021/22 financial year.[48] Tucked away in rural areas that have barely noticed the pandemic, the agricultural sector has also reaped mega-profits due to soaring prices for wheat, barley and beef.

Downside risks

While the positive signs are there for all to see, there remain a number of economic headwinds. The pandemic remains the single biggest factor shaping the world economy. Tourism, trade and a range of industries cannot fully recover until borders and economies are open as before. As a result, new waves – even in the Global South

---

48. Mizen and Ker 2021.

– endanger the social and economic prospects of all by limiting the capacity to fully reopen. It is not simply or mainly that economic disruption in underdeveloped nations could undermine growth more broadly. Evidence and probability suggest that when a virus is given the freedom to move through large populations, it will generate mutations that pose greater risks to the world. The example of the Delta and Lambda variants, which arose from huge outbreaks in India and Peru respectively, are a warning. These strains are now producing new outbreaks and waves, even in countries with relatively high vaccination rates. This then increases the nightmare scenario of a variant emerging that can bypass the protection provided by existing vaccines, as such a mutation would have a strong adaptive advantage in a highly immunised population.[49]

The slow rollout of vaccines remains a risk factor in most countries. Herd immunity is a laudable goal, but new variants mean that experts have had to keep revising up their estimates regarding the proportion of the population that needs to be vaccinated to achieve it. Some now believe that it would take more than 90 percent of citizens being fully immunised.[50] Yet in some countries there has been a tendency for vaccine rollouts to slow well before that level. The US for instance peaked at four million doses per day in April, but is now averaging well below one million a day, despite just 58 percent of people being fully vaccinated. At this rate, the *New York Times* estimates the population will not be fully vaccinated until July 2022.[51]

How do we explain this seemingly reckless failure to take up a life- and economy-saving opportunity? The self-satisfied middle-class commentariat would have us blame deranged anti-vaxxers, many of whom sincerely believe Bill Gates is planting microchips in our brains via the COVID vaccine. The influence of reactionary anti-science conspiracism is undeniably a factor here, exacerbated by the growth and radicalisation of the hard right. But while this angle generates reliable clickbait and has some truth,[52] it does not

49.   Grover 2021.
50.   Cohen 2021.
51.   *New York Times* 2021.
52.   Pepinksy 2021.

fully explain the challenges of widespread vaccine take-up; which is not primarily constrained by conspiracism but by the daily realities of working-class oppression. A recent poll by the Kaiser Family Foundation found that almost half of all American adults yet to be vaccinated cite fear of missing work as an important factor in their decision.[53] A *New York Times* report on the topic identified a range of structural factors that make it harder for working-class Americans to access vaccines.[54] Here in Australia, vaccine hesitancy has become a stalking horse for a government that has proven incapable of organising a logical and accessible rollout. By launching a cynical debate about mandatory vaccination for healthcare and aged-care workers, the government hopes to distract from its failure to grant paid vaccine leave or organise workplace distribution at key sites.

The second risk factor is the issue of public debt and its relationship with inflation. An enormous amount of debt has been accumulated through this crisis. The US saw its debt-to-GDP ratio increase by around 25 percentage points in 2020, up to 129 percent as of December of that year.[55] The Eurozone, countries that use the Euro currency, increased its debt by 14 points to 98 percent of GDP in the same period, while Australian government debt sat on 30 percent, up from 20 percent a year earlier.[56] The figures for China are difficult to untangle, due to complexities surrounding state-owned enterprises and the opacity of the system broadly. However, debt levels in China have been trending up for years, hence the attempt to curb liquidity discussed earlier.[57]

This situation is sustainable as long as interest rates remain low. But as the recovery gains steam there will be a growing pressure on central banks to tighten monetary policy and increase interest rates. Ultra-low – in some cases negative – interest rates and bond-purchasing programs have allowed governments and corporations to engage in relatively risk-free spending. Even corporations that do not make enough money to cover their debt payments – referred

---

53. Hamel et al 2021.
54. Harman and Holder 2021.
55. FRED 2021.
56. Reuters 2021b, Parliamentary Budget Office 2021.
57. Lee 2021.

to as zombie corporations – have managed to survive. A Bloomberg study in November of last year found that a quarter of the wealthiest 3,000 American companies can be classified as zombie companies. This group added more than $1 trillion in debt between them last year, bringing their total to almost $2 trillion.[58] The survival of these essentially bankrupt corporations drags down the profitability and efficiency of global capitalism. While placing a floor under the depth of the economic crisis, the availability of cheap credit props up inefficient capitals and prevents the kind of thorough cleaning out of dead labour that would be necessary to restore profit rates and lower the organic composition of capital. This doesn't preclude growth in the short term, but remains a long-term issue that can exacerbate future crises.

Cheap credit has also fuelled rampant speculation on the stock, bond, real estate, cryptocurrency and commodity markets. Prices have risen substantially across the board, which in turn has increased the production costs of inputs and finished products. A shortage of labour supply has also forced up wages in a number of countries, led by Amazon and other sections of big capital in the US.[59]

Some bourgeois economists believe that these developments will lead to a vicious cycle of wage and price growth akin to the 1970s, and some on the right are sounding the alarm, calling for an end to stimulus measures and an increase in interest rates. The difficulty is that raising interest rates would substantially increase the cost of debt repayments. In a world so heavily reliant on debt, such a move could drive many companies into bankruptcy and destabilise entire economies. While the US is somewhat shielded by the unique position of the dollar in the world financial system, a range of heavily indebted mid-level countries such as Argentina and Turkey could be ruined by any substantial increases to interest rates.

Others insist that the current spike in inflation is temporary. Janet Yellen, US Treasury Secretary, spoke at the G7 to dismiss inflation concerns as premature. She argued that recent inflation is the product of contingent and temporary factors such as logistical

---

58. Lee and Contiliano 2020.
59. See Rockemen and Pickert 2021 for US data, Charlish and Than 2021 for Eastern Europe, and Strauss 2021 for a comparison between Europe and the US.

bottlenecks and material shortages.[60] Yellen and her co-thinkers believe these pressures will ease as the world economy gets going and a surge in capital investment comes online. While it is too soon to be definitive there are good reasons to support this view; even prior to the pandemic growth rates were anaemic in the advanced capitalist world.[61]

The final risk to the world economy would be a premature return to austerity and fiscal normality. Everyone agrees that enormous stimulus spending was vital to propping up the economies through the last 12 months. Yet there is much debate about what to do next. The OECD and IMF have put out numerous reports warning against premature austerity, and calling for extended government support. Yet given the political makeup of parliaments and the weak state of the unions, it seems highly unlikely that a sustained era of generous welfare expenditure is upon us. In Australia welfare payments returned to poverty-inducing levels months ago, and the budget was far more in line with previous Liberal offerings than was reported by the media.[62] In the US, Biden has made clear that the top-up of regular unemployment benefits will end in September, though 25 states – not all controlled by Republicans – will have already phased them out by the end of July.

An important caveat to raise is that welfare expenditure and government spending are not necessarily synonymous. It is often assumed by centre-left economists that government expenditure and stimulus measures are beneficial to both workers and bosses. Yet it is possible for governments to spend enormous sums without there being any gain for workers, as for instance with Trump's tax cuts for the wealthy or the Australian government's subsidies for business investment. Thus even as the Morrison government phased out emergency welfare programs, it has been prepared to run enormous deficits to prop up big business. Even protectionism, often presented as pro-working class, is really just a mechanism to support capital, with workers shouldering the burden of higher prices. Thus the rise of a more interventionist and economically stimulatory state

---

60. Bruce and Lawder 2021.
61. Smith 2020.
62. Hillier, 2021.

following the pandemic does not inherently entail a better situation for workers. Only the class struggle can ensure that.

Biden has attempted to win Republican backing for a range of stimulatory policies by portraying them as part of America's competition with China. To this point, he has had little success. With negotiations over a number of his packages ongoing at the time of writing, it is too soon to predict the outcome of this important debate among the US ruling class. But the result could be of global significance, given the centrality of the US to the economic fortunes and political trends of the world system.

Political reverberations

All of these developments have taken place in a world that was already being shaken by three profound developments: a new cold war between US and China, the rise of a new hard right, and an explosion of radical protest movements, particularly (though not only) in the Global South. The social and economic crises triggered by the pandemic have interacted with and deepened all three of these phenomena.

A new cold war

Though there have always been tensions, the US-China relationship is in its worst state for decades. Under Premier Xi Jinping, China has consciously sought to project itself as a regional and world power. This has involved adopting a more assertive foreign policy; manifest in the violent absorption of Hong Kong, the threats aimed at Taiwan, and the massive expenditure on the Belt and Road Initiative. At the same time, China's domestic economy has transcended the sweatshop model, deploying technical expertise in a range of fields from digital finance through to 5G. Though it remains decades behind the US in a range of fields, most notably the design and fabrication of semi-conductors, it is determined to catch up. Xi has unleashed the famous "Made in China 2025" program, a national industrial policy which combines careful forward planning and subsidies to develop key industries necessary for military and industrial competition with the US.

This growing Chinese self-confidence has been responded to

aggressively by consecutive US administrations. Though Obama made gestures in this direction, it was Trump and now Biden, who have most clearly articulated the American determination to contain China's rise and to retain its dominant position in the Asia-Pacific region. Trump was decisive in forcing the issue of China to the heart of US politics. Although crude and in some ways counterproductive, Trump's aggressive mercantilist approach to global politics – "America First" – successfully reshaped discussions on the US role in global affairs. There have been some shifts from the Trump to the Biden administrations, but the general parameters have remained consistent. Biden's policy is best understood as Trumpism with liberal characteristics: preserving the rational core of Trump's obsessive hostility towards China while taking a range of steps to renew America's capacity to compete and repair relations with important allies. Tom Bramble's piece in this edition is a crucial attempt to make sense of this unfolding situation; he explores the past, present and potential future of these complex and era-defining issues.

Political polarisation

One destabilising factor common to countries on both sides of the Atlantic is the growth of the hard and extreme right. The radicalisation of the Republican party threatens to undermine the entire US empire. Its economic agenda is somewhat in flux; caught between traditional neoliberal hostility to tax and spend policies and a more recent flirtation with right-wing populism. Lacking a clear argument on this issue, it chooses to fight instead around obsessive culture wars and a more or less open hostility to voting rights for Blacks. This agenda runs totally counter to the progressive common sense of the country's urban centres, and risks further destabilisation of US society and politics. All things being equal, this irrationalist organisation – in which two-thirds of the members do not believe the president of the United States is legitimate – stands a good chance of taking control of the House next year.[63] Such a victory would paralyse key elements of Biden's agenda and further undermine US prestige among its allies.

---

63. Mastrangelo 2021.

The situation in Italy and France is approaching catastrophic proportions, with fascist or proto-fascist parties receiving high levels of support. If things are not so bad elsewhere, the hardening and strengthening of the political right – albeit in different forms – is an identifiable trend across the continent.[64] Some commentators have tried to argue that liberal democracy has proven a successful barrier to fascism, and that the institutionalisation of the extreme right has neutralised it as a force.[65] In reality, the major constraint on the right is that in the absence of serious class struggle, no major section of capital is prepared to back a fascist overthrow. Yet short of that, their consolidation as a major force in European politics is an urgent challenge for the left and the oppressed, who are the targets of their violence and bigotry. If unchallenged, the hard right will enter future contests from a position of substantial strength.

Meanwhile, it is no exaggeration to say that the European parliamentary left is close to collapse. Three decades after the collapse of world Stalinism, it appears that social democracy is now in a terminal decline. The polls are consistently bad. In Germany, the Social Democratic Party that was once the flagship of the world's socialist movement has just 15 percent support from the public, just a few points clear of the neo-fascist AfD. In France, the Socialist Party is on an embarrassing 6 percent, while its sister party in Belgium sits on 16 percent. In Italy the Democratic Party – which can only generously be described as reformist – has the loyalty of 20 percent of the electorate. In each of these countries – with the partial exception of Italy – liberal centrism in various forms has claimed the mantle of opposition to the conservative and hard right. It is hard to overstate the significance of this historic retreat towards the bourgeois politics of the nineteenth century, in which liberal progressives confronted conservatives with no independent class position manifested in the polls. The situation is different in the UK, Australia and New Zealand, where less representative election systems help to artificially prop up the reformist parties. But with the Corbyn experiment well and truly over, there is little prospect of anything left-wing emerging from these organisations in the foreseeable future.

---

64. Callinicos 2021.
65. Rachman 2021.

Of course, politics cannot be read directly off elite machinations and electoral results. In France, for instance, the working class and radical left retain a substantial capacity for explosive mobilisation that is absent in most other European nations. It wasn't long ago that the Yellow Vests owned the streets with their courageous resistance, and strikes in defence of pensions by railway workers and other public servants in 2019 suggest that the working class is far from defeated. More broadly, the volatility of the general situation and the rise of a shallow but broad anti-capitalist sentiment among young people means there are constant opportunities for unions and the revolutionary left to rebuild their forces.

Mass resistance
The final feature of world politics is that we continue to live in an era of mass social struggles, of which Myanmar and Colombia are just the most recent examples. Some of the grievances driving these movements predated the pandemic, produced by weak economic development and a lack of democratic rights. But in many countries the pandemic has exacerbated existing grievances, with high mortality counts and a growth in poverty, factors that have further discredited vulnerable governments. Given the theme of this piece, it is notable that it has been underdeveloped countries where the most explosive and sustained struggles have taken place. While the short-lived Black Lives Matter movement was the most publicised event of the last twelve months, it was an exception to this broader pattern. The remaining countries that have seen the most substantial protests and strikes have been in the Global South: Iran, Myanmar, Belarus, Colombia, Paraguay, Thailand, Poland, Lebanon and Palestine.

Of these, it is the latter that has had the largest international impact so far. While the Palestinian movement was not a product of the current crises but a longstanding struggle, it manifested many of the similar dynamics seen elsewhere. Furious at the ethnic cleansing of East Jerusalem, Palestinian youths displayed incredible determination in resisting incursions into their community by Zionist thugs. Protests quickly spread to all parts of the Palestinian population, most notably those within so-called Israel who had previously been more quiescent. This movement – culminating in what seems to have been a successful two day general strike – spontaneously created a long sought after unity across all of historic Palestine. This stands in stark contrast to the repeated attempts to patch together a bureaucratic coalition government between the bankrupt leaderships in Gaza and the West Bank.[66] In trying to impose a traditional military paradigm onto a popular rebellion, Hamas hoped to claim leadership over the mobilisations, which electorally at least, seems to have been somewhat successful. A new generation of freedom fighters will need to organise a new resistance project that sees international revolution as the key to Palestinian liberation, though arriving at this necessary conclusion is hampered by the quiescence of the Arab world in the recent round of protest. Meanwhile the Israeli parliament has crowned the fascistic Naftali Bennett as the new prime minister. His bizarre coalition included sections of the Israeli "left", as well as the Palestinian Islamist group connected to the Muslim Brotherhood, Ra'am. In a sign of what to expect from the incoming administration, Bennett started his term with an assault on Gaza and approved a Zionist march through East Jerusalem that chanted "death to Arabs".[67]

Though motivated by specific concerns and grievances, each of the movements in the last twelve months display features consistent with those seen since the wave of rebellions in 2011. They continue to be highly decentralised: lacking institutional or political cohesion and even the basic civic infrastructure needed to get to that point. Social discontent has often been refracted through pre-existing social fractures, including various national questions as well as specific social oppressions. The relative involvement of organised workers varies from place to place, but nowhere are they consciously acting as the vanguard. This is true even when they act as one in practice, as for instance with textile and health workers in Myanmar. As well, nowhere have we yet seen a left that can lead or even seriously recruit from these incredible uprisings. On the other hand, nor have we seen governments able to co-opt them by offering reforms and substantial changes to the ruling strategy. Brute repression has been the preferred policy, a tactic that can succeed temporarily, but does not

66. Bullimore 2014.
67. Johnson 2021.

resolve underlying issues in a lasting way. The urgency of rebuilding a left that can intervene into such a circumstance remains clear.

Latin America looks like it will continue to be a focal point for left-wing struggles. The continent has suffered some of the worst impacts of the pandemic, producing severe social and economic dislocations. This compounded the pre-existing tensions generated by highly politicised polities, where sizeable left-nationalist blocs face off against a violent and well-rooted anti-democratic right. In particular, many Latin American countries possess small but serious revolutionary organisations, and a strong history of broader left organisation, which can provide important lessons for the international left as events unfold. Recent developments in Colombia, Brazil and Chile are of particular interest, being some of the largest, wealthiest and most influential countries in the region. Colombia in particular has been one of the key props of the US empire and has had a ruthlessly oppressive and rightist regime for decades. In Brazil, opposition to Bolsonaro appears to be gaining momentum, as protests against his appalling COVID response grow in size and scope. In addition to mass struggles, nine Latin American nations will be holding elections this year. Given the dire conditions across the continent, it's likely that voters will seek to punish incumbents. The result in Peru, where a left-nationalist leader looks to have won a closely fought election, may be a sign of things to come. We should not exaggerate the radical potential of any new pink tide-style governments, given their well-documented failures.[68] Nonetheless, a regional defeat for the right would be a positive sign and could result in more offensive struggles for social reforms. For an international left that is struggling to impose itself on events, these precious signs of hope should be studied and cherished as a reminder of what is possible.

---

68. For the best critique see Webber 2016.

References

ABS 2021, "Labour force, Australia, May 2021", Australian Bureau of Statistics, 17 June. www.abs.gov.au/statistics/labour/employment-and-unemployment/labour-force-australia/latest-release#participation

Arora, Rohit 2020, "Which companies did well during the coronavirus pandemic?", Forbes, 30 June. www.forbes.com/sites/rohitarora/2020/06/30/which-companies-did-well-during-the-coronavirus-pandemic/

Barone, Emily 2020, "The Trump Administration's 'Operation Warp Speed' Has Spent $12.4 Billion on Vaccines. How Much Is That, Really?", *Time*, 14 December. www.time.com/5921360/operation-warp-speed-vaccine-spending/

Bartash, Jeffry and Greg Robb 2021, "US gains 850,000 new jobs in June in sign of strength for the economy", *Market Watch*, 2 July. www.marketwatch.com/story/u-s-gains-850–000-new-jobs-in-june-in-sign-of-strength-for-the-economy-11625230019

Bates, Sarah 2021, "The social media bosses are not on our side", *Socialist Worker*, 17 January. www.socialistworker.co.uk/art/51164/The+social+media+bosses+are+not+on+our+side

BBC 2021, "Covid: How is furlough changing and when will it end?", BBC News, 2 July. www.bbc.com/news/explainers-52135342

Bruce, Andy and David Lawder 2021, "Yellen tells G7 to keep spending, says inflation will pass", *Australian Financial Review*, 6 June. www.afr.com/world/north-america/yellen-tells-g7-to-keep-spending-says-inflation-will-pass-20210606-p57ygq

Bullimore, Kim 2014, "Palestinian unity government no step towards justice", *Red Flag*, 16 June. www.redflag.org.au/article/palestinian-unity-government-no-step-towards-justice

Callinicos, Alex 2021, "Neoliberal capitalism implodes: global catastrophe and the far right today", *International Socialism*, 170, Spring. www.isj.org.uk/implodes-catastrophe/

Charlish, Alan and Kriztina Than 2021, "Analysis: Remember me? With fast recovery, labour shortage haunts Eastern Europe", Reuters, 8 June. www.reuters.com/world/europe/remember-me-with-fast-recovery-labour-shortage-haunts-eastern-europe-2021–06–08/

Cheng, Jonathan 2021, "China is the only major economy to report economic growth for 2020", *Wall Street Journal*, 18 January. www.wsj.com/articles/china-is-the-only-major-economy-to-report-economic-growth-for-2020–11610936187

Cohen, Joshua 2021, "Covid-19 herd immunity looks like a mirage, but is worth pursuing", Forbes, 8 May. www.forbes.com/sites/joshuacohen/2021/05/08/COVID-19-herd-immunity-looks-like-a-mirage-but-is-worth-pursuing/

Davis, Gareth 2021, "Principled generosity mixed with unmanaged market", Verfassungsblog, 31 March. www.verfassungsblog.de/principled-generosity-mixed-with-unmanaged-market/

Dempsey, Harry and Neil Hume 2021, "Commodities boom sends bulk shipping costs to decade highs", *Financial Times*, 11 May. www.ft.com/content/849434bb-1311–4d89-bc13–3e6c5dc7111a

Díaz-Bonilla, Eugenio 2020, "Fiscal and monetary responses to the COVID-19 pandemic: Some thoughts for developing countries and the international community", International Food Policy Research Institute, 5 April. www.ifpri.org/blog/fiscal-and-monetary-responses-COVID-19-pandemic-some-thoughts-developing-countries-and

Dolan, Kerry A, Jennifer Wang and Chase Peterson-Withorn 2021, "World's billionaires list: The richest in 2021", Forbes. www.forbes.com/billionaires/

Dowling, Sarah 2021, "Homeowners use savings war chest to fund home renovations", *Smartline*, 16 April. www.smartline.com.au/mortgage-news/homeowners-use-savings-war-chest-to-fund-home-renovations/

Dube, Ryan and Vibhuti Agarwal 2021, "The cost of COVID-19 treatment has left families destitute around the world", *Wall Street Journal*, 29 May. www.wsj.com/articles/the-cost-of-COVID-19-treatment-has-left-families-destitute-around-the-world-11622280600

Economist, The 2020, "German firms are conflicted about the Kurzarbeit furlough scheme", *The Economist*, 26 June. www.economist.com/business/2021/06/26/german-firms-are-conflicted-about-the-kurzarbeit-furlough-scheme

FRED 2020, "Federal debt: Total public debt as percent of gross domestic product [GFDEGDQ188S]", US Office of Management and Budget and Federal Reserve Bank of St. Louis, 24 June. https://fred.stlouisfed.org/series/GFDEGDQ188S

Gittens, Ross 2021, "Our closed borders have turbo-charged the economy's recovery", *Sydney Morning Herald*, 7 May. www.smh.com.au/business/the-economy/our-closed-borders-have-turbo-charged-the-economy-s-recovery-20210506-p57pl2.html

Goodman, Peter and Nijar Chokshi 2021, "How the world ran out of everything", *New York Times*, 1 June. www.nytimes.com/2021/06/01/business/coronavirus-global-shortages.html

Greenblat, Eli 2021, "Woolworths posts weaker sales in March quarter after pandemic shopping boom", *The Australian*, 29 April. www.theaustralian.com.au/business/retail/woolworths-posts-weaker-sales-in-march-quarter-after-pandemic-shopping-boom/news-story/05d645b20196ef36db831299b4b6dce0

Grover, Natalie 2021, "Surging Covid and unlocking: does England risk being a variant factory?", *The Guardian*, 6 July. www.theguardian.com/world/2021/jul/05/will-uk-rising-COVID-cases-increase-risk-of-vaccine-evasive-variants

Guluzade, Amir 2019, "The role of China's state-owned companies explained", World Economic Forum, 17 May. www.weforum.org/agenda/2019/05/why-chinas-state-owned-companies-still-have-a-key-role-to-play/

Hamel, Liz, Lunna Lopes, Grace Sparks, Mellisha Stokes and Mollyann Brodie 2021, "KFF COVID-19 Vaccine Monitor – April 2021", KFF, 6 May. www.kff.org/coronavirus-COVID-19/poll-finding/kff-COVID-19-vaccine-monitor-april-2021/

Harman, Amy and Josh Holder 2021, "They haven't gotten a COVID vaccine yet. But they aren't 'hesitant' either", *New York Times*, 12 May. https://www.nytimes.com/2021/05/12/us/covid-vaccines-vulnerable.html

Hassan, Omar 2021, "Pandemic politics: 2020 in hindsight, and a perspective on 2021", *Marxist Left Review*, 21, Summer. www.marxistleftreview.org/articles/2020-in-hindsight-and-a-perspective-on-2021/

Hirsch, Lauren 2020, "Trump pushes back against congressional oversight for $500 billion bailout fund", CNBC, March 28. www.cnbc.com/2020/03/28/trump-pushes-back-against-congressional-oversight-for-500-billion-bailout-fund.html

Hillier, Ben 2021, "Calling bullshit on the budget", *Red Flag*, 14 May. www.redflag.org.au/article/calling-bullshit-budget

IANS 2021, "Indian billionaires saw there [sic] wealth go up by Rs 12.97 trn during Covid-19", *Business Standard*, 25 January. www.business-standard. com/article/current-affairs/indian-billionaires-saw-there-wealth-go-up-by-12–97-trillon-during-COVID-19–121012500423_1.html

Institute for Health Metrics and Evaluation 2021, "COVID-19 has caused 6.9 million deaths globally, more than double what official reports show", 6 May. www.healthdata.org/news-release/COVID-19-has-caused-69-million-deaths-globally-more-double-what-official-reports-show

International Monetary Fund 2021, "Global economy on firmer ground, but with divergent recoveries amid high uncertainty", April. https://www.imf.org/en/Publications/WEO/Issues/2021/03/23/world-economic-outlook-april-2021

Investing 2021a, "Australia manufacturing purchasing managers index (PMI)", Investing. www.au.investing.com/economic-calendar/manufacturing-pmi-1838

Investing 2021b, "U.S. manufacturing purchasing managers index (PMI)", Investing. www.au.investing.com/economic-calendar/manufacturing-pmi-829

Johns Hopkins Coronavirus Resource Center 2021, "Mortality analysis", Johns Hopkins University & Medicine, accessed 3 July. www.coronavirus.jhu.edu/data/mortality

Johnson, Jake 2021, "New Israeli government bombs Gaza after far right chants "Death to Arabs", Truthout, 16 June. www.truthout.org/articles/new-israeli-government-bombs-gaza-after-far-right-chants-death-to-arabs/

Kamp, Jon, Jason Douglas and Juan Forero 2021, "Covid-19 deaths this year have already eclipsed 2020's toll", *Wall Street Journal*, 10 June. www.wsj.com/articles/COVID-19-deaths-this-year-have-already-eclipsed-2020s-toll-11623350773

Kotoky, Anurag 2021, "Rich Indians flee by private jet as virus infections spiral", Bloomberg Quint, 27 April. www.bloombergquint.com/business/wealthy-indians-flee-by-private-jet-as-virus-infections-spiral

Lee, Amanda 2021 "China debt: has it changed in 2021 and how big is it now?", *South China Morning Post*, 5 June. www.scmp.com/economy/china-economy/article/3135883/china-debt-has-it-changed-2021-and-how-big-it-now

Lee, Lisa and Tom Contiliano 2020, "America's zombie companies rack up $2 trillion of debt", Bloomberg, 17 November. www.bloomberg.com/news/articles/2020–11–17/america-s-zombie-companies-have-racked-up-1–4-trillion-of-debt

Madhok, Diksha and Manveena Suri 2021, "Twitter blocks posts in India critical of Narendra Modi's Covid-19 response", CNN Business, 26 April. www.edition.cnn.com/2021/04/26/tech/twitter-COVID-india-modi-facebook/index.html

Mastrangelo, Dominick 2021, "Two-thirds of Republicans think Biden's victory was not legitimate: poll", The Hill, 26 May. thehill.com/homenews/administration/555584-two-thirds-or-republicans-think-bidens-victory-was-not-legitimate

McKinnon, Tricia 2021, "Why DoorDash & other delivery apps struggle with profitability", 16 March. www.indigo9digital.com/blog/fooddeliveryappprofitability

Misra, Udit 2021, "Explained: India's GDP fall, in perspective", *Indian Express*, 8 June. www.indianexpress.com/article/explained/india-gdp-gdp-fall-7–3-per-cent-in-perspective-modi-govt-coronavirus-economy-7338852/

Mizen, Ronald and Peter Ker 2021, "Iron ore boom to bolster Frydenberg's war chest by $36b", *Australian Financial Review*, 3 May. www.afr.com/politics/federal/iron-ore-boom-to-bolster-frydenberg-s-war-chest-by-36b-20210429-p57ndk

New York Times 2021, "See how vaccinations are going in your county and state", *New York Times*, accessed 3 July. www.nytimes.com/interactive/2020/us/COVID-19-vaccine-doses.html

OECD, 2021, "Quarterly national accounts: Quarterly growth rates of real GDP, change over previous quarter", Organisation for Economic Co-operation and Development, https://stats.oecd.org/index.aspx?queryid=350

Oliu-Barton, Miquel, Bary Pradelski, Philippe Aghion, Patrick Artus, Ilona Kickbusch, Jeffrey Lazarus, Devi Sridhar and Samantha Vanderslott 2021, "SARS-CoV-2 elimination, not mitigation, creates best outcomes for health, the economy, and civil liberties", *The Lancet*, Volume 397, Issue 10291, 12 June. www.thelancet.com/journals/lancet/article/PIIS0140–6736(21)00978–8/fulltext#articleInformation

Parliamentary Budget Office 2021, "Government finances – December quarter 2020", 11 February. www.aph.gov.au/-/media/05_About_Parliament/54_Parliamentary_Depts/548_Parliamentary_Budget_Office/Reports/2020–21/Government_finances_-_December_quarter_2020/Government_finances_-_December_quarter_2020_PDF.pdf

Peach, Brian and Sidney Leng 2020, "China unemployment rate: how is it measured and why is it important?", *South China Morning Post*, 17 November. www.scmp.com/economy/china-economy/article/3110193/china-unemployment-rate-how-it-measured-and-why-it-important

Pepinsky, Tom 2021 "Trump support and vaccination rates: some hypotheses and some data", Tom Pepinsky Blog, 24 June. www.tompepinsky.com/2021/06/24/trump-support-and-vaccination-rates-some-hypotheses-and-some-data/

PGP Foundation 2021, "The coronavirus has led to a surge in spending on unemployment compensation", Peter G Peterson Foundation, 11 June. www.pgpf.org/blog/2021/06/the-coronavirus-has-led-to-a-surge-in-spending-on-unemployment-compensation

Rachman, Gideon 2021, "Democracy in Europe adjusts to the far right", *Financial Times*, 28 June. www.ft.com/content/8dded432–2d6d-4ee7-ad5f-1f8e7b6448f1

Reuters 2021a, "U.S. bankruptcy filings hit 35-year low thanks to government pandemic aid", 6 January. www.reuters.com/article/us-usa-economy-bankruptcy-idUSKBN29A264

Reuters 2021b, "Euro zone debt surges in 2020 on pandemic spending", Reuters, 22 April. www.reuters.com/article/eurozone-debt-idUSL8N2MF2ZC

Rockemen, Olivia and Reade Pickart 2021, "Surprise jump in U.S. wages gives inflation debate a new twist", Bloomberg, 9 June. www.bloomberg.com/news/articles/2021–06–09/surprise-jump-in-u-s-wages-gives-inflation-debate-a-new-twist

Smith, Ashley 2020, "The virus, capitalism, and the long depression: Interview with Michael Roberts", *Spectre*, 24 March. www.spectrejournal.com/the-virus-capitalism-and-the-long-depression/

Somasundaram, Narayanan 2020, "China debt fears grow amid wave of corporate defaults", *Nikkei Asia*, 23 December. www.asia.nikkei.com/Business/Markets/China-debt-crunch/China-debt-fears-grow-amid-wave-of-corporate-defaults

Soper, Taylor 2021, "Amazon now employs nearly 1.3 million people worldwide after adding 500,000 workers in 2020", GeekWire, 2 February. www.geekwire.com/2021/amazon-now-employs-nearly-1–3-million-people-worldwide-adding-500000-workers-2020

Strauss, Delphine 2021, "Labour shortages hit advanced economies despite many people still out of work", *Financial Times*, 26 May. www.ft.com/content/12361ab6-dc39–4345-b756–1a8c788b3345

Taylor, Adam 2021, "How the $1.9 trillion U.S. stimulus package compares with other countries' coronavirus spending", *Washington Post*, 6 April. www.washingtonpost.com/world/2021/03/10/coronavirus-stimulus-international-comparison/

Taylor, Kate 2021 "In 2020, big businesses got bigger and small businesses died. The vicious cycle won't stop until we take action", Business Insider Australia, 4 January. www.businessinsider.com.au/in-2020-big-businesses-got-bigger-small-businesses-died-2020–12?r=US&IR=T

Thompson, Geoff and Benjamin Sveen 2020, "Border controls leave an army of invisible workers trapped on floating sweatshops", ABC News, 21 November. www.abc.net.au/news/2020–11–21/maritime-workers-left-floating-in-a-sea-of-red-tape/12899040

Trotsky, Leon 2008, *History of the Russian Revolution: Volume 1 – The Overthrow of Tsarism*, Haymarket Books.

Webber, Jeffery 2016, *The Last Day of Oppression, and the First Day of the Same: The Politics and Economics of the New Latin American Left*, Haymarket Books.

Wells, Jeff, Sam Silverstein and Catherine Douglas Moran 2021, "8 trends that will shape the grocery industry in 2021", Grocery Dive, 4 January. www.grocerydive.com/news/8-trends-that-will-shape-the-grocery-industry-in-2021/592574/

Wenbin, Wang 2021, "Foreign ministry spokesperson Wang Wenbin's regular press conference on June 2, 2021", Ministry of Foreign Affairs of the People's Republic of China. www.fmprc.gov.cn/mfa_eng/xwfw_665399/s2510_665401/2511_665403/t1880861.shtml

Williams, Leah 2021, "How COVID-19 reshaped Australia's film industry", Gizmodo, 26 March. www.gizmodo.com.au/2021/03/australian-film-tv-industry-COVID-19/

Wolf, Martin 2021, "Economic recovery masks the dangers of a divided world", *Financial Times*, 21 April. www.ft.com/content/0be32ec5–8a75–48f2–99f3-eb5bcd055287

World Bank 2020, "GDP growth (annual %) – United States", accessed 27 June. www.data.worldbank.org/indicator/NY.GDP.MKTP.KD.ZG?end=2020&locations=US&start=1961&view=chart

World Bank 2021, "Defying predictions, remittance flows remain strong during COVID-19 crisis", World Bank, 12 May. www.worldbank.org/en/news/press-release/2021/05/12/defying-predictions-remittance-flows-remain-strong-during-COVID-19-crisis

Wright, Shane 2021, "The unexpected stimulus: How the closed border helped save the economy", *Sydney Morning Herald*, 8 May. www.smh.com.au/politics/federal/the-unexpected-stimulus-how-the-closed-border-helped-save-the-economy-20210505-p57p7m.html

Ziffer, Daniel 2020, "JobKeeper supports nearly a million workers. It's over…so what happens now?", ABC News, 29 March. www.abc.net.au/news/2021–03–29/jobkeeper-ends-what-now-for-australian-businesses/100031668

TOM BRAMBLE

The Biden administration's plan for US imperialism

Tom Bramble has published widely on political economy and the labour movement in Australia and overseas and is a regular contributor to *Marxist Left Review*. His recent books include *Labor's Conflict: Big Business, Workers and the Politics of Class* (with Rick Kuhn), *Introducing Marxism: A Theory of Social Change*, and *The Fight for Workers' Power: Revolution and Counter-Revolution in the 20th Century* (with Mick Armstrong).

J OE BIDEN'S FIRST 100 DAYS as US president were met with enthusiasm by many of those who regarded Donald Trump's four years in office as an unmitigated nightmare. *Financial Times* columnist Rana Foroohar told her readers: "Most Democrats I know are positively giddy about Joe Biden's presidency".[1] "Transformational" was the word most commonly used to describe the early days of the new presidency.[2] Leading liberal Democrats who had denounced Biden during the presidential nominations contest as an uninspiring, out of touch conservative joined the praise.[3] In Australia, progressives of various stripes in the Greens and the ALP, who had alternated between treating the Trump administration as circus clowns and dangerous madmen, fell swooning over the new-look Biden. This response was not restricted to those in professional political circles. In Trump's last year in office, just one in six of the public in a dozen US allies had confidence that the US president would do the right thing in world affairs; in 2021, with Biden occupying the White House, that figure rose to three-quarters. Biden helped to give the US fresh appeal: those

---

1. Foroohar 2021a.
2. Taibbi 2021.
3. Pengelly 2021.

with a favourable view of the US jumped from 37 percent in 2020 to 61 percent in 2021.[4]

We must be blunt. This response is wrong-headed. It may be understandable that leading Democrats in the US and "progressive circles" in Australia would be breathing a sigh of relief that the US under President Biden is now in safe hands. Such people may now with clear consciences once again swear their allegiance to the world's biggest imperialist power. But what may be welcome to them should be resisted by socialists. Far from constituting a sharp break with the Trump administration, the Biden presidency is in some important respects only consolidating Trump's program, in particular its attempt to prepare the country for conflict with its new imperialist rival, China.

For all the social, political and other divisions in the US, the ruling establishment –Republican and Democratic alike – is united on one thing: a concern to outcompete China and contain its rise. China has been growing in the twenty-first century while the US has been beset by a string of crises, several of them self-inflicted, which have undermined its own standing in the world. While previous US administrations have recognised and attempted to respond to Beijing's increasing global influence, the Biden administration is trying to develop a more cohesive strategy to deal with relative US decline and to confront China. Some elements of this strategy appear to offer workers a break from the policies of successive administrations that only rewarded the rich at the expense of the poor. But the fundamental purpose of the strategy is to defend US global hegemony. In what follows, I spell out the Biden administration's plans to protect the US's place at the top of the imperialist heap, along with some limits and contradictions.

The evolving US response to the rise of China
The US response to China's rise has evolved considerably over the past five decades.[5] During the 1970s and 1980s, Washington looked to Beijing to balance against the Soviet Union, and the two nations worked together on several fronts. The collapse of the USSR removed

4.   Wike et al 2021.
5.   Tellis 2020.

this as a factor in relations between the two and raised the potential for China to at some point become a threat to the US. But with China's economy one-ninth the size of America's in 2000 (expressed in US dollars) and with no ability to project power far from its shores, there were few in Washington who regarded China as a serious threat.

The Clinton and George W Bush administrations operated on the assumption that China would expand its economy under the auspices of the US-led global framework of commerce, much as Germany and Japan had done earlier. There were great advantages for the US to promote China's development because of the complementarity of the two economies: China offered US corporations a low-wage platform to offshore their factory operations, along with a rapidly growing market. China ran a large trade surplus with the US but was willing to invest its foreign currency reserves in US Treasury bonds, thereby underwriting US government debt and preventing the US dollar from sliding. On the basis of this complementarity, the US sponsored China's admission to the World Trade Organization (WTO) in 2001.

Although there were occasional attempts to elevate China as a threat, as when George W Bush criticised President Clinton in 1999 for his treatment of China as a "partner" not a competitor, in practice successive administrations, including that of Bush himself, pursued what they called "comprehensive engagement" with China. In 2002, Bush, now president, told an audience at Beijing's Tsinghua University that "My nation offers you our respect and our friendship". The changes underway in China would, Bush argued, "lead to a stronger, more confident China – a China that can astonish and enrich the world".[6] As late as 2014, President Barack Obama could declare to an audience of Asia-Pacific Economic Community (APEC) business leaders that:

> The United States welcomes the rise of China as a prosperous, peaceful and stable state... Over recent decades, the United States has worked to help integrate China into the global economy – not only because it's in China's best interest, but because it's in

---

6.   Tellis 2020, p.5.

America's best interest, and the world's best interest. We want China to do well.[7]

China enjoyed nearly two decades without any significant US pushback. It helped that the US was distracted by the War on Terror. And then from 2008, the Obama administration was occupied for several years in dealing with the global financial crisis, a period when China played a big role in lifting the world economy out of a deep recession.

Obama's "Pivot to Asia" in 2011, with its commitment to deploy 60 percent of US naval and aerial power to the Asia-Pacific, was the first real sign that the US ruling class had begun to regard China as a serious threat, but the continuing pull of dramas and conflicts in the Middle East and Central Asia, including the challenge from a revived Russia, prevented the administration from focusing its efforts on containing China.

China, meanwhile, continued to grow from strength to strength. In 2008, it surpassed Japan to become the world's second largest economy and by 2015 its economy was 60 percent of that of the US, a more than sixfold increase in its relative size in just 15 years. The Chinese ruling class used these years to leverage its booming economy into geostrategic power through its Belt and Road Initiative. Its "Made in China 2025" program spells out China's ambitions to develop a leading role in a wide range of advanced industries. Its military and strategic power accumulated in proportion from the mid-1990s onwards. As China grew, it made clear that it had no intention of remaining in America's shadow and was now striving for great power status itself.

The 2016 presidential contest between Democrat candidate Hillary Clinton and the Republican Donald Trump marked something of a turning point. Clinton ran hard marking out China as a threat to US hegemony and positioned a White House under her leadership as one that would aggressively take on its new rival. Trump made much of China's huge trade surplus with the US which, he alleged, was the result of China cheating, manipulating

---

7.   Tellis 2020, p.5.

its currency and stealing from America. For too long, Trump argued, China had taken the US for a ride, and it was time to "put America first". China, however, was not America's only adversary. In Trump's view, the whole international order was stacked against the US. America's willingness to oversee world trade, commerce and governance via institutions such as the International Monetary Fund (IMF), World Bank, WTO and the United Nations had allowed its rivals, China included, to rise at its expense.

In office, Trump maintained his inflammatory rhetoric against the international system of trade and diplomacy that the US had helped create and, using the rhetoric of "national sovereignty" and "Make America Great Again", downgraded US support for the international liberal order.[8] This involved undercutting the operations of the WTO, which Trump described as "a disaster", reducing funding to the United Nations, withdrawing from the Trans Pacific Partnership (TPP) and the Paris Climate Accord and renegotiating the North American Free Trade Agreement (NAFTA). Multilateral trade negotiations were put aside in favour of bilateral trade deals. The US also exited the Iran nuclear deal, the Intermediate Nuclear Forces Treaty and the Global Compact on Migration and threatened to withdraw from the North Atlantic Treaty Organisation (NATO), with Trump declaring the military alliance "obsolete". Trump was, however, nothing if not inconsistent, on the one hand blasting China for its alleged economic crimes and appointing noted China hawks to key positions, on the other making much of his meetings with Chinese leader Xi Jinping, describing their allegedly warm personal relations and the good deals the two leaders had struck.

While Trump blew hot and cold about China in his first year in office, leading elements in the state apparatus resolved that the US had to shift to a much more aggressive approach. The main changes, when they came, came quickly. In December 2017, the White House released its new National Security Strategy. This was followed one month later by the Pentagon's National Defense Strategy and that in turn one month later by the US Strategic Framework for the Indo-Pacific. These were followed with a little gap by the US Asia

---

8. See, for example, Trump 2017.

Reassurance Initiative Act (December 2018) and the State Department's US Indo-Pacific Strategy (November 2019).

These were not primarily the work of Trump and his closest ideologues. In some domains, in particular US relations with Russia, the documents ran directly counter to Trump's stance. These strategy documents were described by the head of the Australian National University's (ANU) National Security College and a leading China hawk, Professor Rory Medcalf, as "one of the few achievements of an otherwise grim era in American foreign policy":

> The slightly reassuring news is that beneath President Donald Trump's unpredictability, conceit and unilateralism, the policy professionals were striving to advance a more serious and coherent agenda. There was a plan after all, however incomplete and insufficiently resourced its implementation.[9]

The significance of the Strategic Framework for the Indo-Pacific was that, in Medcalf's view, it represented "the beginning of a whole-of-government blueprint for handling strategic rivalry with China".[10]

What might be called the "China pivot" had several components. First was the US ruling class's clear acknowledgement that its domination of the world, unchallenged since the fall of the Soviet Union, was now at risk. "Today, we are emerging from a period of strategic atrophy, aware that our competitive military advantage has been eroding", the Defense Strategy read. Four rivals to US power were identified: two "rogue regimes", Iran and North Korea, and two "revisionist powers", Russia and China. Very significantly, China was no longer a "strategic partner" but a "strategic competitor":

> China is leveraging military modernization, influence operations and predatory economics to coerce neighbouring countries to reorder the Indo-Pacific region to their advantage...displacing the United States to achieve global pre-eminence in the future.[11]

---

9.   Medcalf 2021.
10. Medcalf 2021.
11. Department of Defense 2018.

Like the first Cold War, there was a clear ideological aspect to this struggle:

> Inter-state strategic competition, defined by geopolitical rivalry between free and repressive world order visions, is the primary concern for U.S. national security.[12]

Specifically,

> [i]t is increasingly clear that China and Russia want to shape a world consistent with their authoritarian model – gaining veto authority over other nations' economic, diplomatic and security decisions.[13]

Second, those responsible for the China pivot recognised that the existing strategies towards the "revisionist powers" had not reined them in. The US must therefore change course:

> These competitions [with China and Russia] require the United States to rethink the policies of the past two decades – policies based on the assumption that engagement with rivals and their inclusion in international institutions and global commerce would turn them into benign actors and trustworthy partners. For the most part, this premise turned out to be false.[14]

Urgent action was needed to deal with the threat China represented in its region because "US security and prosperity depend on free and open access to the Indo-Pacific region, which will remain an engine of US regional and global economic growth".[15]

One element of the response involved expanding US military capacity. In his State of the Union address on 31 January 2018, Trump announced his determination to "modernise and rebuild our nuclear arsenal" to build "unmatched power" as "the surest means

---

12. National Security Council 2018.
13. Department of Defense 2018.
14. White House 2017.
15. National Security Council 2018.

to our true and great defence".[16] On top of more ballistic missiles and bombs, the Trump administration increased investments in long range and stealth weapons, upgraded US bases around the Asian periphery, enlarged the inventory of sophisticated munitions and developed technologies such as hypersonic systems, unmanned systems and new advanced missiles. The US also began to step up its so-called "freedom of navigation" patrols, challenging Chinese claims in the South China Sea.

Despite Trump's erratic behaviour, the US under his watch opened negotiations to restart the Quad, a pact involving the US, India, Japan and Australia whose main purpose was to combat China. The US began to sell allies more sophisticated defence systems. The US also expanded the role of the Five Eyes intelligence sharing pact which in 2019–20 issued statements denouncing China's crushing of democracy in Hong Kong.

The Trump administration's bid to forestall China's threat to US power also included economic measures. The Security Strategy stated that "the United States will no longer turn a blind eye to violations, cheating or economic aggression" by its trading partners. Of particular concern to the Pentagon was the notion that US military capability had been undermined by the run-down in US manufacturing capacity. In January 2018, the president announced new tariffs on imports of washing machines and solar panels, and this was followed later in the year by the imposition of tariffs on Chinese steel and aluminium, justified on national security grounds; the US wanted to ensure it had the capacity to produce the steel for the big new orders coming through for missiles, bombers and ships.

While Silicon Valley capitalists are a Democratic Party stronghold, they nonetheless cheered the Trump administration's commitment to what the Security Strategy called the "national security innovation base" – the companies and research institutions that provide the information technology that guides and powers US weapons systems. The Trump administration imposed export controls, limiting Chinese high tech firms' ability to procure a variety of US goods and components, tightened the constraints on China's

---

16. Trump 2018.

ability to invest in the US (including the ability to acquire US firms), restricted the enrolment of Chinese students in advanced science and technology programs at the best US universities, and placed limits on Chinese high tech firms' ability to do business in the US. Confrontations over Huawei's 5G technology and the "digital Silk Road" were manifestations of the deeper danger that China might use its national champions to build new electronic infrastructure networks that the Chinese government could exploit. Pressure by the Trump administration on this front eventually succeeded in forcing the British government to renege on an earlier agreement with Huawei to operate Britain's 5G network.

Even though the Trump administration undertook a definite shift in US policy towards China, many elements in the US state apparatus tasked with developing imperialist strategy, most obviously the CIA, State Department and Pentagon, were not convinced that Trump was the leader who could carry this through. They shared several concerns.

First, Trump jeopardised vital US alliances on which the China pivot depended. The key policy documents endorsed close relations with allies, but Trump did the opposite, trashing international agreements and abusing important US partners. In what was meant to be America's main region of concern, East and South East Asia, Trump was missing in action. Trump attended only one Association of South East Nations (ASEAN) summit during his four years in office and ignored the APEC leaders' meeting in 2018 and the East Asian Summits in 2018 and 2019. In Europe, Trump described the European Union as an "economic foe" and did not hide his disdain for many of America's NATO partners.

Trump's economic warfare was scattergun, imposing tariffs on goods from China but also on key US allies such as Australia, Japan, South Korea, the EU, Brazil, Mexico and Canada. Only under pressure did Trump relent on some of these measures. Trump's support for bilateral trade deals in place of WTO multilateral trade rounds threatened to make America's trade relations with other countries significantly more complicated. By rejecting the Paris Climate Accord, Trump also signalled that the US had no interest in leading the international effort to respond to global warming.

Trump's support for Brexit concerned the State Department, since Britain had been the US's wedge in the European Union. With Britain out of the EU, the balance of power would tilt further to the rather less pliant Germany. Trump also supported the far right in Europe whom established figures in the State Department regarded as dangerous irritants.

Trump's undermining of alliances gave China the opportunity to pose as a player in international affairs. There were already concerns in Brussels and Washington following China's establishment of the "17+1" arrangement in 2013 which involved China drawing Central and Eastern European governments into its Belt and Road program, undermining the EU's ability to present a united front in negotiations with China. But it was not just the minnows; no European government wanted to be left behind in the China goldrush. The Conservative government in Britain boasted that the UK was "China's best partner in the West". Britain was the first G7 country to join the Chinese-sponsored Asian Infrastructure Investment Bank (AIIB) and lobbied within the EU for China-friendly trade policies. In 2019, Boris Johnson, just before becoming prime minister, insisted that the government would be very "pro-China" and that he was "very enthusiastic about the Belt and Road Initiative". Germany, too, was an enthusiast for closer links with China, its biggest trading partner, and Chancellor Angela Merkel was an early champion of a new investment pact between the EU and China, the Comprehensive Agreement on Investment. German companies, in particular the car manufacturers, were big investors in China. In Asia, China engineered the Regional Comprehensive Economic Program in 2019 to draw Asian nations towards China, while excluding the US. Such developments appeared increasingly threatening to US strategists who could sense that traditional allies might be swayed by their new economic partner.

While antagonising partners, Trump appeared to his detractors in the State Department and Pentagon too friendly to US rivals. His pronouncements about his good relations with Xi and North Korean leader Kim Jong-un caused palpitations in foreign policy circles, something the Democrats were happy to run with. After the president had described Xi as "an incredible guy" and "a friend of mine" at a time when the Chinese government was cracking down on Hong Kong democracy protests, Senate Minority leader Chuck Schumer told the press: "For a guy who promised to be tough on China, President Trump's reliable deference to President Xi is all the more bewildering".[17] Close relations between Trump's team and the Kremlin during the 2016 presidential election campaign caused the *New York Times* and *Washington Post* to campaign hard against Trump on the basis that he represented a national security threat to the US. That was the significance of Russia's inclusion as a "revisionist power" in the National Security Strategy, a slap-down of Trump and his relations with Putin.

Finally, Trump's fostering of right-wing extremism at home worried some elements of the state apparatus. The growing preparedness of the hard right to bomb and murder its targets, with a nod and wink from the president (and forbearance by many police departments), raised alarm within the FBI, which began to describe such actions as "domestic terrorism".[18] The military top brass also grew concerned. Following the November 2020 presidential election, chairman of the Joint Chiefs of Staff, General Mark A Milley, prepared to head off any attempt by Trump to use what he called the president's "Brownshirts" and "Nazis" to overturn the election result. The January 6 attack on the Capitol building only confirmed the fears of Milley and his colleagues.[19] The political polarisation which Trump thrived upon did not suit the Pentagon's desire to project US power overseas because it highlighted US political dysfunction at a time when the Chinese regime appeared competent and stable by comparison.[20] In 2021, just one in six people in America's major allies believed that "US democracy is a good example for others to follow", while nearly six in ten believed that this was once the case but is no longer.[21]

In summary, the Trump administration signalled a clear shift in the US approach to relations with China. Nonetheless, by alienating

---

17. Swanson and Crowley 2019.
18. Bergengruen and Hennigan 2019.
19. Thebault 2021.
20. Bennhold and Myers 2021.
21. Wike et al 2021.

US allies and destabilising American politics the Trump administration created opportunities for China to expand its influence, thereby undermining America's ability to contain its new imperialist rival.

Biden's program

The Biden administration has continued and intensified the China pivot set in motion by its predecessor, what *The Economist* has described as "the most dramatic break in American foreign policy in the five decades since Richard Nixon went to China".[22] Before outlining the main themes of Biden's policy towards China, it is important to confirm that the primary factor in the development of a more aggressive response to China is not the presidents themselves. As vice president during the Obama administration, Biden had not marked himself out as a China hawk. As late as May 2019 he ridiculed the idea that China represented a threat to the US.[23] But as his bid for the presidency gathered steam later in the year, Biden shifted tack. An important role in this transition was played by key advisers, almost all China hawks, including Jake Sullivan and Kurt Campbell who, as Obama's Assistant Secretary of State for East Asia, had been largely responsible for the administration's "pivot to Asia" in 2011.

The first indication that Biden had embraced an aggressive approach to China was his article in the March/April 2020 issue of *Foreign Affairs*, the premier journal of the US foreign policy community. "The United States does need to get tough with China", he wrote.[24] The new imperialist rival was mentioned 17 times in the article. By the time of the presidential debates in September 2020, Biden was as bullish on challenging China as Trump.

Following his victory in the November 2020 elections, Biden appointed Sullivan his national security adviser, and Campbell as National Security Council Coordinator for the Indo-Pacific. Rush Doshi, author of newly published *The Long Game: China's Grand Strategy to Displace American Order*, works under Campbell as China director on the National Security Council. Biden also appointed Anthony Blinken, another longstanding China hawk,

22. *The Economist*, 2021a.
23. Associated Press 2019.
24. Biden 2020.

Secretary of State. Biden's maiden speech as president to Congress spelled out the priority of the new administration: "We can't stop now – we are in competition with China and other countries to win the 21st century".[25]

The following are the main elements of the Biden administration's policy towards China, some which continue where Trump left off, some which represent a distinctive shift.

Linking domestic economic policy to imperial geo-policy

One area where Biden is very much following in the footsteps of Trump is by explicitly linking economic and industrial policy to imperial policy. America's ramshackle infrastructure has increasingly been thrown into the spotlight as a competitive failing when compared to the rapid steps that China has taken to improve its ports, highways, airports, fast rail and in particular its internet capacity.

The ability of the US to run a war economy is further challenged by the very measures that successive US administrations encouraged to boost the profits of US corporations over many decades, namely, outsourcing of manufacturing to low-wage countries through extended international supply chains. Such business practices helped US corporations cut costs but they have also exposed the country to danger in the event of war, especially since many of these supply chains originate in China itself. One important area where the US has fallen behind is in semiconductors, a vital component in both civilian and military industries and the subject of ongoing tension between the US and Asian producers since the 1980s. US imports of semiconductors tripled in value between 2010 and 2020.[26]

Trump's campaign to "Make America Great Again" promised to rebuild infrastructure and recreate a robust manufacturing base. Nonetheless, the administration's regular announcements of a new "infrastructure week" became a running joke; "like Samuel Beckett's Godot, it was perennially promised and never arrived", as *The Economist* put it.[27] Trump's main economic achievement in office was to

---

25. White House 2021a.
26. Trading Economics 2021.
27. *The Economist*, 2021b.

push through tax cuts for big business and the wealthy and to remove environmental regulations, rather than pumping public money into rebuilding the physical capacity of the nation to transport goods and people effectively.

The Trump administration had boasted of its ambition to bring industry "back home" by cutting corporate taxes and imposing tariffs on imports. Trump targeted companies that had offshored operations to China. Nonetheless, there is no evidence that his policies had much success. In Trump's last year in office, the US still ran a massive deficit on its balance of trade on goods and services with China – $679 billion, up by $100 billion on 2019.[28] Merchandise imports from China continue to run ahead of exports to China by four to one.[29]

COVID-19 has proven brutal in exposing problems in the US. Leaving aside the initial denialism by the Trump administration, the US response in 2020 suffered from disrupted supply chains in PPE, ventilators and pharmaceuticals, along with longstanding problems in the public health system. This situation was particularly embarrassing when China, let alone countries much poorer, smaller or weaker than the US such as Vietnam and Cambodia, were initially able to take decisive action to stop the spread of the pandemic. China's rapid response in tackling the pandemic has been compared to a new "Sputnik moment", the moment when the successes of the US's chief imperialist rival cast doubts about its own, at least in the early stages.[30]

"Economic security is national security" sums up much of Biden's response to these problems.[31] Prior to his election, Biden identified China as "a special challenge" in terms that could have been lifted from Trump's campaign speeches:

> If China has its way, it will keep robbing the United States

---

28. US Census Bureau 2020.
29. US Census Bureau 2021.
30. Subsequently, the poorer track record of China's vaccines compared to those developed in the US now calls for some reassessment of this early judgement. Wee 2021.
31. Biden 2020.

and American companies of their technology and intellectual property. It will also keep using subsidies to give its state-owned enterprises an unfair advantage – and a leg up on dominating the technologies and industries of the future.[32]

Years of neoliberal economic mismanagement, which had weakened America's domestic manufacturing capacity, had now become a matter of national security, argued his adviser Sullivan and fellow former State Department adviser Jennifer Harris:

> While military power will still matter, the emerging great-power competition between the United States and China will ultimately turn on how effectively each country stewards its national economy and shapes the global economy.[33]

For too long, Harris and Sullivan argued, US trade policy had pandered to companies which offshored most of their manufacturing, avoided paying tax and charged US consumers extortionate prices. Such practices had to end if the US was to recover its dominant position. Harris and Sullivan argued that a big program of investment in infrastructure, technology, innovation and education was needed to improve US competitiveness with China. While Trump had promised much, his corporate and personal tax cuts had only piled up "bad debt".

Economic security was a theme that ran through several of Biden's early major statements – the American Rescue Plan, the American Jobs Plan, the American Families Plan and the president's first speech to Congress on 28 April. The initial version of the Jobs Plan involved major outlays on so-called "hard infrastructure", including $621 billion on transport infrastructure, including rail, bridges, roads, airports, mass transit and electric vehicle development, $300 billion for assisting manufacturers and small business and improving access to capital for green energy, $100 billion for workforce training and billions more for expanding broadband access and upgrading electrical grids.

---

32. Biden 2020.
33. Harris and Sullivan 2020.

While some elements of Biden's agenda, such as his tax hikes on big business and increased social spending, drew strident Republican opposition, Republicans have been more open to some of Biden's proposals to expand spending on infrastructure. On 8 June, in a bipartisan vote, Congress passed the US Innovation and Competition Act, which provided for $52 billion added spending on US semiconductor manufacturing. The Endless Frontier Act, which was also passed with support on both sides of Congress, significantly increases federal investment in domestic science and technology research in key areas. The Act provides for the establishment of ten regional technology hubs to help US companies exit the Chinese market, relocate production facilities outside of China, and to diversify sources to locations outside of China.

The Biden administration also maintained Trump's sanctions against Chinese IT and semiconductor businesses, adding five Chinese companies to a US government blacklist on national security grounds and expanding a Trump-era order that banned US investment in Chinese companies that work with China's military.

Biden made clear in his address to Congress that the main motivation for spending on infrastructure and semiconductors is the new Cold War. Why should the US renew and upgrade its investment in high tech research? Because, Biden told his audience, "China and other countries are closing in fast. We have to develop and dominate the products and technologies of the future". Why should rival politicians accept Biden's plan? Because "we can't be so busy competing with one another that we forget the competition that we have with the rest of the world".[34]

What has been called the return of industry policy is not counterposed to the Biden administration's rhetorical commitment to free markets and international trade. The bipartisan Strategic Competition Bill states that the US must "lead in the advancement of international rules and norms that foster free and reciprocal trade and open and integrated markets". As the fastest growing region of the world economy, the Indo-Pacific is of particular concern to Congress and "free trade" therefore inevitably draws in the power of the US

---

34. White House 2021a.

state, including its military arm, to defeat threats to US interests. The Strategic Competition Bill enjoins Biden to ensure that:

> the United States and its allies maintain unfettered access to the region, including through freedom of navigation and the free flow of commerce, consistent with international law and practice, and the PRC neither dominates the region nor coerces its neighbors.[35]

While supposedly fostering "free and reciprocal trade", the Biden administration has maintained the tariffs imposed by the Trump administration on trade with China and continues Trump's "America First" rhetoric. As Biden told Congress: "All the investments in the American Jobs Plan will be guided by one principle: Buy American".[36]

Military policy

The Biden administration is also maintaining Trump's program of military expansion. The US, which spends three times as much as its Asian rival, enjoys an overwhelming military advantage over China on a global scale. It has about 20 times the number of nuclear warheads as China. It has twice the tonnage of warships at sea, including 11 nuclear-powered aircraft carriers compared with China's two carriers (which are much less advanced). Washington has more than 2,000 modern fighter jets compared with Beijing's roughly 600. And the United States deploys this power using a vast network of some 800 overseas bases; China by contrast has only three.

The problem for the US is that China's spending is primarily focused on expanding its reach in the Western Pacific, while that of the US is spread across the world. Given the troubles the US experienced in Iraq and Afghanistan, the longstanding principle that the US should be able to fight and win wars in two different regions at once is now in question. A simultaneous conflict with Russia in Ukraine and with China in the Pacific, for example, could easily overwhelm US military capabilities.

Biden has been responding on several fronts. First, by lifting the Pentagon budget in 2021–22 to $715 billion, an $11 billion

---

35. Senate Foreign Relations Committee 2021, p.19.
36. White House 2021a.

raise on Trump's last military outlays. The administration is now winding back spending on fighter jets such as the F35 but devoting more money to hypersonic missiles, new generation warships and space-related projects. Second, the administration is rapidly expanding research and development spending on the technologies needed to guide weapons systems and disrupt those of America's enemies, including China's ability to deploy electronic warfare against vital US infrastructure and battlefield communications. And third, Biden is continuing the Trump administration's program of more aggressive positioning of US navy and air force in contested areas.

China has in recent years been building a military presence in the South China Sea, establishing military facilities on island atolls and rapidly expanding its blue-water navy, while also increasing its capacity to strike the US Pacific fleet with land-based missiles. In response, the US has maintained and expanded so-called "freedom of navigation operations", displays of US naval power in regions claimed by China – the so-called first and second island-lines. On 9 February, two nuclear-powered carrier groups conducted joint exercises in the South China Sea.

The major test for the US is Taiwan, situated just 160km off the coast of mainland China and a key US partner for 70 years. Leaving aside its value as a Western ally on China's doorstep, Taiwan is home to 92 percent of advanced semiconductor manufacturing capacity. Were China to capture it, this would leave the US in a very vulnerable position. In recent months, Chinese fighter jets, navy ships and surveillance planes have conducted dozens of missions around and over Taiwanese territory. The US has also increased its presence. Since Biden's inauguration, US warships have transited the Taiwan Strait on five occasions, heavily shadowed by Chinese aircraft which, on some reports, conducted mock attack runs on a US aircraft carrier.

There are mixed understandings in the US about how quickly such shadow-boxing with China might develop into something much larger. In March, Admiral Philip Davidson, commander of the US Indo-Pacific Command, told Congress that:

> There is a fundamental understanding that the period between now and 2026, this decade, is the time horizon in which China

is positioned to achieve overmatch in its capacity, and when Beijing could...widely choose to forcibly change the status quo in the region. And I would say the change in that status quo could be permanent.[37]

His successor at the head of the Indo-Pacific Command, Admiral John Aquilino, told the Senate Armed Services Committee later that month: "My opinion is this problem is much closer to us". He added that the US needs to field weapons and capabilities to deter China "in the near term and with urgency". Other US generals dispute this assessment, arguing that China is a long way away from being able to take aggressive action against Taiwan.[38]

US relations with its allies

To sum up the argument so far: the Biden administration's program in response to the threat to US hegemony represented by China involves substantial areas of continuity – a focus on rebuilding domestic manufacturing capability and infrastructure alongside escalation of military pressure in the South China Sea and Taiwan. Biden's approaches to US allies and to domestic politics are, however, two areas of clear differentiation.

Biden recognises that America's ability to challenge China relies on support from its allies. Such support, Biden contends, was jeopardised by Trump. In his 2020 *Foreign Affairs* article, Biden argued:

> By nearly every measure, the credibility and influence of the United States in the world have diminished since President Barack Obama and I left office on January 20, 2017. President Donald Trump has belittled, undermined, and in some cases abandoned U.S. allies and partners.[39]

Biden promoted instead "a united front of U.S. allies and partners to

---

37. Nakamura 2021.
38. Hille 2021.
39. Biden 2020.

confront China's abusive behaviors and human rights violations".[40] Biden promised to hold a global Summit for Democracy within his first year in office "to renew the spirit and shared purpose of the nations of the free world".[41]

On announcing his new national security and foreign policy team in the days after his election, Biden said:

> It's a team that reflects the fact that America is back, ready to lead the world, not retreat from it. Once again sit at the head of the table. Ready to confront our adversaries and not reject our allies. Ready to stand up for our values.[42]

Very soon after his inauguration, Biden indicated the main themes of his approach. At his first speech at the State Department in February 2021, Biden stated:

> We will compete from a position of strength by building back better at home, working with our allies and partners, renewing our role in international institutions, and reclaiming our credibility and moral authority, much of which has been lost.[43]

Early moves have included halting US withdrawal from the World Health Organization. The US took steps to rejoin the Paris Climate Accord and to extend the New Strategic Arms Reduction Treaty.

The administration's priority in its first weeks in office were US allies in the Indo-Pacific. After his confirmation by the Senate at the end of January, Secretary of State Blinken held video calls with the leaders of the Philippines and Thailand, two important US allies in Asia. On 12 March, Biden convened the first meeting of leaders of Quad nations as a video conference. While the resulting communique by the Quad does not mention China directly, the first statement of what is sometimes called the "Asian NATO" states the commitment of its signatories to maintain the Indo-Pacific as a

---

40. Biden 2020.
41. Biden 2020.
42. Manson and Weaver 2020.
43. White House 2021b.

region that is "free, open, inclusive, healthy, anchored by democratic values and unconstrained by coercion". In April and May, Biden held his first in-person meetings in Washington with foreign leaders – Prime Minister Yoshihide Suga, representing Japan, the US's most important ally in Asia, and President Moon Jae-in of South Korea. The three leaders pledged to strengthen their alliance to combat China's rise and condemned what they called its threats to Taiwan.[44] The Biden administration also declared its support for another key US ally, Australia, which had been undergoing low-level economic warfare with China since 2019. On 23 May the US president attended the virtual ASEAN ministerial meeting, repairing a rift with the Asian bloc.

With the US's main allies in Asia giving verbal support to a more aggressive position in relation to China, in June, the president and his ministers met European and other leaders to convince them to join the US's anti-China bandwagon. On 13 June, Biden attended the G7 conference in England. Here the main priority was to overcome traditional European hostility to US attempts to foster enmity towards China. Even though the EU would not agree to broad anti-China joint statements proposed by the US, the G7 did issue a communique denouncing China for its treatment of Hong Kong and Xinjiang. The G7 also agreed in the communique to adopt "collective approaches to challenging non-market policies and practices which undermine the fair and transparent operation of the global economy", clearly aimed at China. One such measure included a commitment to boost international investment in developing countries ("Build Back Better World") in an attempt to push back against China's Belt and Road program.

On the day after G7 meeting concluded, Biden attended the annual NATO summit in Brussels. NATO had been designed to contain Russia in Europe, whereas now the US's major strategic concern was the Indo-Pacific, a region where the US's European allies were of little use. Nonetheless, Biden was keen that NATO orient not just to Russia's continuing challenges in Ukraine and its hacking of European and US infrastructure, but also to China. While many of

---

44. White House 2021c.

America's NATO allies had at best cool relations with Trump, they warmly welcomed Biden. For the first time, NATO declared China a "global security risk".

The third leg of Biden's European trip involved a meeting with Vladimir Putin in Geneva. The US security and foreign policy apparatus is keen to hold Russia in check. Biden sought to set down certain red lines that must not be crossed by Russia, but the overall tone of the meeting was not one of confrontation. While the US regards Russia as a threat to US interests in Europe, its chief concern is China. In what may be conceived of as a "reverse Kissinger", harking back to Secretary of State Henry Kissinger's successful negotiations to pull China into an anti-Soviet bloc in 1971, Biden and his advisers want to "turn" Russia against China in the new Great Game in Eurasia. In June, the administration announced that it was dropping sanctions on the Russian company building the Nord Stream 2 gas pipeline to Germany. Although there is no unanimity in the US state apparatus on this score, with accusations of "appeasement" lobbed at Biden by some in the Republican camp,[45] it seems likely that the US is doing what it can to at least avoid driving Russia closer to China and to play up points of tension between the two, as for example over competing claims in the Arctic.

The Biden administration's approach to climate change is an extension of its foreign policy. Trump's decision to abandon the Paris Climate Accord weakened US prestige. In a signal that the US is back in the game, the Biden administration organised a virtual climate summit on 22–23 April. It used the weeks leading up to the summit to embarrass China, which is deeply invested in coal mining and coal-fired power stations both at home and abroad. The summit failed to generate any serious commitments to reduce global warming, and the Biden administration demonstrated the seriousness of its climate credentials by granting hundreds of permits to drill on federal land and pressing ahead with a Trump-era oil project in Northern Alaska. Despite the US's lack of commitment to climate action, the summit had served Biden's purpose.[46]

The COVID-19 pandemic is another arena where the Biden

---

45. Nelson et al 2021.
46. Friedman 2021.

administration has sought to do battle with China. Following China's donation of vaccines to developing countries, the Biden administration announced in May that it would support a waiver of World Trade Organization's intellectual property restrictions on COVID-19 vaccines. In his first speech to Congress in April Biden drew the clear link between vaccine distribution and foreign policy: "We will become an arsenal for vaccines for other countries, just as America is an arsenal for democracy for the world".[47] In late May, Biden ordered an investigation into the origins of COVID-19 and whether it might have emerged as the result of a lab leak in Wuhan, bringing into the mainstream what had been dismissed up until this point by most Democrats as a right-wing conspiracy theory encouraged by the Trump administration.

The attempt to create an anti-China bloc among US allies is embedded in a clear ideological framework. Far more than Trump had done, the Biden administration is instrumentalising democracy as a weapon in the new Cold War. The Trump administration had pitched its foreign policy as a battle between "free and repressive world orders"[48] and cynically used Xinjiang and Hong Kong as cudgels to beat Beijing. Nonetheless, Trump's cordial relationships with figures such as Brazil's Bolsonaro, Russia's Putin, Turkey's Erdogan and the Philippines' Duterte, let alone his disdain for democracy in the US itself, meant that the president could hardly make a convincing case that the White House could wage a global defence of democracy. Biden, who is trying to position the US as the head of the world's liberal democracies, at least appears more consistent. At the virtual Munich Security conference on 19 February, Biden framed the issue as follows:

> We are in the midst of a fundamental debate about the future and direction of our world. We're at an inflection point between those who argue that...autocracy is the best way forward...and those who understand that democracy is essential.[49]

---

47. White House 2021a.
48. National Security Council 2018.
49. White House 2021d.

Like Trump, however, Biden used human rights rhetoric very selectively. China was the target. In his speech to Congress, Biden argued that the US must prove that democratic governance can work, because Xi Jinping "and others, autocrats, think that democracy can't compete in the twenty-first century with autocracies, because it takes too long to get consensus".[50] But the US under Biden continues close relations with friendly autocrats such Duterte, Thai Prime Minister Prayut Chan-o-cha and Indian Prime Minister Narendra Modi, all of whom Biden wants to join the US in the fight against China.[51] Hypocrisy never stands in the way of the main game.

Social policy, electoral considerations and the US's image

Another area where Biden has broken with Trump concerns social policy. Partisan Democratic Party electoral considerations and a desire for a united front at home as the US gears up for a clash with China are the main drivers of the administration's switch.

In his first 100 days in office, the Biden administration announced several major spending plans: the $1.9 trillion Rescue Plan, comprising for the most part short-term emergency welfare relief in the midst of the COVID-19 pandemic; the $2.3 trillion American Jobs Plan, involving big outlays not just on the "hard infrastructure" already discussed but also on "human infrastructure", including public housing, public schools, aged care and assistance for African American college students; and the $1.8 trillion American Families Plan which includes childcare subsidies, assistance for health insurance, new education funding, paid family leave and family tax credits. To pay for these spending measures, Biden proposed tax hikes on business and the wealthy.

Despite the gushing by liberals, these packages if passed are far from "transformational". They are nothing like as substantial as the New Deal of the 1930s or the Great Society program of the 1960s which created social security, Medicare and Medicaid. The existing proposals will not fundamentally transform the lives of the tens of millions of Americans destitute and saddled with debt in the richest country on earth, and do not bring US social welfare even close

---

50. White House 2021a.
51. Chowdhury 2021.

to the provisions in many European countries. Further, the Biden administration removed from the Rescue Plan an earlier plan to lift the federal minimum wage.

Nonetheless, Biden's social and economic policies do stand out compared to the standard budget measures of the past 40 years. It is true that the Trump administration oversaw huge fiscal stimulus in 2020 but much of that was for tax cuts to the rich and handouts to big business, whereas Biden is flagging modest tax hikes for the rich. The Biden administration is trying to position the government very differently to its predecessors. Ronald Reagan's argument that "Government is not the solution to our problem; government is the problem", is clearly rejected by Biden. Instead, Biden wants Americans to have confidence in a government that can deliver for the mass of people as well as the billionaires; that can make services, that can deliver water, transport, ports, electricity, and can respond effectively to climate change.

Electoral considerations are clearly a factor in Biden's proposals. The conventional wisdom in the Democrats is that the Obama presidency was wasted. They believe now that his administration (which of course included Vice President Biden) was too cautious and too concerned to seek compromise with the Republicans for its own sake. The fiscal stimulus during the 2008–09 global financial crisis was too small and too quickly wound back, meaning most workers saw nothing from Obama's budgets while profits soared. For evidence, Democrat strategists can point to the big swing against the party in the 2010 Congressional mid-term elections, ensuring that Obama served the remaining six years of his presidency without a clear majority in Congress.

Political polarisation means that while Biden rates very highly among Democrat supporters, he has little support among Republicans. The administration wants to give the Democratic base a reason to vote for the party in the mid-term elections next year so as to secure clear majorities in both houses. If Biden's spending packages are passed in full, they would definitely help in this regard, as all three are electorally popular.

Biden is also appealing to other sections of the ruling class. The 6 January riot at Congress was a boon for Biden and the Democrats since it allowed them to present themselves as the party of stability and order, able to govern the country competently without encouraging the far right or left. A substantial section of the US state apparatus and big capitalists do not want to see Trump return in 2024 with all the associated political instability that this might entail and are willing to see the Democrats pass some minor reforms if these will enhance the party's chances in the coming federal elections. Notably, US stock markets rose at the fastest rate since the weeks following Franklin Delano Roosevelt's inauguration in Biden's first 100 days in office.[52]

Biden's social programs could also potentially play a role in firming up the home front in preparation for war with China. Every imperialist power from Britain and Germany before World War I to the United States during the Cold War has understood that imperialist success depends in part on social stability at home. After the political polarisation and instability of the Trump years, Biden hopes that social reforms can settle things down again. As the ANU's Rory Medcalf put it on the eve of Biden's inauguration:

> If the US is serious about that long-term contest [strategic rivalry with China], it will not be able to choose between getting its house in order domestically and projecting power in the Indo-Pacific. It will need to do both at once.[53]

Biden's project thus shares with Trump the nationalist project of "making America great again", building America's industrial base and military capacity and turning popular sentiment against China. It differs in that it appeals to college students, liberals, Black middle-class professionals, swathes of the big city working class, along with many big capitalists. This helps explain why Biden can adopt some of the language of Black Lives Matter and the climate movement, even as he champions the police and the oil industry. It is also why he appointed a tamed Bernie Sanders to chair his economic subcommittee and selected the most multicultural Cabinet in American history. These gestures should not, however, obscure the fact that Biden's

52. Sraders 2021.
53. Medcalf 2021.

project is to rebuild the cohesion, prestige and fighting capacity of the most destructive imperialist power the world has ever known.

For a Democrat president to pitch themselves to the ruling class as the most competent champion of US imperialism is hardly unusual. It was Woodrow Wilson who took America to war in Europe in 1917. It was Roosevelt who in 1937 began to ramp up US military spending in preparation for a new world war in Europe and Asia at a time when many big capitalists were isolationists. It was Harry Truman who started the Cold War in the late 1940s and the shooting war in Korea, and it was John F Kennedy who started and Lyndon Baines Johnson who sharply escalated the war in Vietnam. The Democrats have repeatedly proven themselves the best imperialist warmongers.

Democratic presidents also tend to improve the US's image in the eyes of its allies. So long as Trump was president, the US would have struggled to win widespread public support abroad for a major US-led war, such was his unpopularity in much of the world, in particular among key US allies and partners. But, as mentioned at the start of this article, Biden has done much to restore America's prestige among international audiences.

Some questions

Biden is developing a program to deal with the threat of China; but whether he succeeds or not depends on the answers to several questions, four of which we highlight here.

How realistic is it for the US to decouple from China?

Trump and Biden's economic nationalist project of winding back international supply chains and promoting the country's domestic manufacturing base through tariffs and "Buy American" programs threaten significant sections of American capitalists who have prospered from international trade. For example, the higher steel prices and supply shortages resulting from tariffs on imports of Chinese steel are eating into the profits of the far more numerous and economically significant industrial users of steel.[54]

---

54. Letter to the President 2021.

Building new domestic supply chains is problematic because manufacturing capacity in some areas has already dwindled so far that reviving it will be difficult. The Biden administration is, for example, promoting uptake of solar power to reduce carbon emissions, but Chinese companies now account for 80 percent of all solar panels on world markets, and the US industry has largely collapsed. The first effect of greater solar panel use by the US will be to widen its trade deficit with China. Even if US companies move into manufacturing solar panels, one-half of the silicon used to produce solar panels originates from China's Xinjiang province by enterprises now targeted by Congress sanctions for their use of forced labour.

As for semiconductor production, a priority for the US ruling class, three-quarters of current capacity is concentrated in East Asia. US efforts to boost domestic semiconductor production will take a decade or more, and even then, the US will need partners to create enough demand to make the economics of scale for an industry like semiconductors work.[55]

Then there are cases where US business, far from "onshoring", is seeking still deeper engagement with China. Wall Street banks, for example, are seeking to break into China's domestic market, as the *Financial Times* reports:

> In an era that is increasingly defined by geopolitical competition and a push towards economic "decoupling", American finance has never been closer to Chinese wealth. Seduced by untapped savings and a growing asset management market, worth an estimated Rmb121.6tn ($18.9tn) last year, Wall Street's most storied firms are embedding themselves more deeply than ever into the country.[56]

At the same time, overseas investors' holdings of Chinese equities and bonds are also rising sharply, up by 40 percent in 2020.[57]

In short, it appears highly unlikely that the US will simply abandon trade and investment with China, but rather more likely that the US government under Biden and his successors will seek to

---

55. Foroohar 2021b.
56. Hale et al 2021.
57. Lockett 2021.

more tightly guard key industries that are integral to the US military and to insulate them from pressures that China might be able to use against them.

How enthusiastic are the US's allies to join in a new Cold War with China?
While the Biden administration is seeking help from its allies in confronting China, their response has been mixed. *The Economist* magazine summarises the situation as follows:

> European and Asian democracies alike are wary of joining America in anything resembling a cold-war effort to check China's aggression – especially if it jeopardises profitable trade relationships.[58]

Consider America's Asian allies. Japan is the staunchest US military partner in Asia, but it remains reliant on China, its biggest trading partner, for its economic prosperity.[59] While some Korean companies have shifted manufacturing from China to Vietnam and India as Chinese production costs rise, the South Korean government has been careful not to join the US in confronting Chinese technology companies or condemning China's Asian Infrastructure Investment Bank or Belt and Road Initiative. Trump and Biden have both tried to foster closer relations with Taiwan, but Taiwanese companies remain critical sources of advanced electronic components for Chinese industry – Taiwan cannot pursue policies that antagonise China without threatening its own economic security. South East Asian nations have also prospered by deeper integration with the Chinese, Japanese and US economies and are reluctant to narrow their economic options such as might be required by more antagonistic relations with China.

The situation is similar in Europe. China is rapidly catching up with the US as the EU's major trading partner.[60] Few European governments want to have to choose one against the other and nor are their electorates keen to do so: three-quarters of German citizens

---

58. *The Economist* 2021c.
59. World Bank 2019a.
60. World Bank 2019b.

believe that their government should take a neutral position in the event of a dispute between the US and China; only one in six believe that Germany should back the US, albeit this survey was done while Trump was still US president.[61]

The EU also has its own disputes with the US, chiefly concerning information technology patent rules, and who gets what share of the digital economy. The EU is doing its best to introduce regulations to force US companies such as Alphabet, Apple, Facebook and Amazon to pay tax on their European operations. These create ongoing tensions in transatlantic relations.

The Biden administration's ability to pull its allies around it and to promote their collective international influence in competition with China is also held back by the paltry resources the US has dedicated to its new initiatives. Mention has already been made of the administration's refusal to follow through on its rhetoric with measures that will actually slow down the rate of global warming. Western half-heartedness is also apparent with the G7's new Build Back Better World program, which so far lacks any firm commitment of funding by member governments or even a framework through which to deliver it. The G7's commitment of one billion vaccines to poorer countries unable to afford expensive vaccines, in part a response to China's international efforts, is woefully inadequate. And nor can the US offer its allies effective substitutes for many Chinese products. An unnamed "Middle Eastern ambassador" told the *Financial Times* in April:

> America tells us to ban Huawei. But when we ask the name of America's Huawei there is no answer. America has no Huawei. So what are we supposed to do?[62]

It does not help Biden that many European and Asian leaders are hedging their bets on his attempt to draw them close to the US. They fear a return to American unilateralism should Trump regain the presidency in 2024, a not unlikely prospect.

Nonetheless, we should not exaggerate America's difficulties.

61. Infratest dimap 2021.
62. Luce 2021.

Japan and South Korea may trade with China, but their giant neighbour is their primary security threat. The two countries still host US bases housing tens of thousands of US soldiers that could well be mobilised in the event of conflict with China. The Biden administration has secured their support for a united approach in the event of war over Taiwan and, the *Financial Times* reports, the US and Japan are already conducting war games and joint military exercises.[63] Then there is India which shares a contested border with China that has already been the subject of one war between the two powers and threatens to trigger another. Were the US and China to go to war, the US might expect support from India, which could force China to fight on two fronts.

Nor is European hesitancy to throw its lot in with the United States a given. There have been recent signs of a more aggressive approach by the EU towards China. A diplomatic row between the EU and China over China's treatment of Uyghurs has led to a serious cooling of relations this year, resulting in the scrapping of the proposed investment pact between the two. Other indications of Europe adopting more aggressive measures against China include more rigorous investment-screening laws, investigations into "foreign influence" operations in domestic policies and blocking foreign bidders suspected of jeopardising national security. The European Commission is also proposing new curbs on state-subsidised firms wanting to compete in European markets, which will target Chinese companies. The European Union's decision this year to join the US in establishing common internet protocols, a critical issue that will determine the shape of the internet as much as international product and service standards do for trade in goods and services, also reduces China's opportunity to play the EU off against the US. Such developments may be extended if national elections in Germany in September put the Greens in a powerful position; the party is probably the most aggressive party in the German parliament towards China. While most Germans prefer neutrality in a clash between the US and China, they, like most in Europe, exhibit growing hostility towards China; the arrival of Biden as US president

---

63. Sevastopulo and Hille 2021.

may boost support for the US in the event of a clash between the two sides.[64]

That close trading relations with China need be no barrier to US allies backing the US is evident in the case of Britain and Australia. The British government continues to explore opportunities to expand trade with China, but in June dispatched what the Ministry of Defence called "the largest concentration of maritime and air power to leave Britain in a generation".[65] The strike group will visit 40 countries, but its ultimate destination is the South and East China Seas. The commander of the strike group described the presence of the US Air Force flying combat missions from a Royal Navy ship for the first time since World War II as a "significant moment":

> To date we have delivered diplomatic influence on behalf of the UK through a series of exercises and engagements with our partners. Now we are ready to deliver the hard punch of maritime-based air power against a shared enemy.[66]

The same combination is evident in Australia. China accounts for close to 40 percent of the country's exports but under both Labor and Coalition governments Australia has openly backed the US's increasingly aggressive posture towards its imperialist rival. Far from holding back out of concern for damage to trade, Australia has frequently been to the fore in preparing for conflict with China. Successive Australian Defence White Papers have focused on competition with China as the country's main priority, and the military budget will increase by hundreds of billions of dollars over the decade to 2028. The US now maintains a Marines base in Northern Australia, and also enjoys the use of port facilities in WA and air strips in the Northern Territory. Australian Defence Forces regularly participate in joint military exercises both in Australia and in the wider Asia-Pacific region.

Australia has joined America's diplomatic offensive in the Asia-Pacific and South Asia, encouraging India, South Korea, Japan

---

64. Silver et al 2020.
65. Lendon 2021.
66. Lendon 2021.

and New Zealand to embrace the US's project of containing China. At home, the federal government has also passed legislation targeting "foreign influence" and has specifically targeted Chinese investments in any "strategic" sectors of the economy, including vetoing the Victorian government's involvement in China's Belt and Road Initiative. The Australian government was one of the first US allies to ban Huawei from the country's 5G network.

Since the beginning of 2020, there has been a significant escalation of propaganda aimed at preparing the Australian population for a war with China. Government ministers and senior public servants have led the way, and Australia was one of the first countries to join the Trump administration's call for an "independent inquiry" into the origins of COVID-19. While the Murdoch press has carried the government's hawkish line, if anything it is outdone by the ABC and the Nine Entertainment press, which now includes the *Age* and *Sydney Morning Herald*, which report in detail the latest stories from the Australian Strategic Policy Institute, one of the main conduits for Cold War propaganda in Australia. The propaganda barrage is certainly influencing popular opinions. In 2017, one-third of Australians held "unfavourable" attitudes towards China; three years later, the figure had jumped to 81 percent, making Australians only marginally less hostile to China than Japan (86 percent), historically always the most hostile, and Sweden (85 percent).[67]

If Labor wins the next federal election, Australian government policy will not change. The ALP is as committed as the Coalition to US domination of the Asia-Pacific. Labor may complain about some of the Coalition's hostile rhetoric towards China, but it shares the same concern to support the US in what will be a battle to determine the future of the Asia-Pacific.

This brief review suggests that the hesitancy that some US allies currently express towards US escalation of tension with China might give way to support as a definite clash takes firmer shape. And, ultimately, while support from the US's European NATO partners might be appreciated, its absence would not significantly impair America's military capacity to wage war in the Asia-Pacific.

---

67. Silver et al 2020.

Will Congress gut Biden's plans, and how serious is he anyway?

Much of the economic program proposed by Biden in his first 100 days in office faces opposition. The first obstacle is Republican opposition in the Senate, where the Democrats hold only a wafer-thin majority. Weeks of negotiations with the Republicans saw the initial infrastructure budget proposed in the Jobs Plan cut from $2 trillion to less than $600 billion, with any references to tax increases eliminated and only scant reference to climate expenditures. At less than $300 billion a year for eight years, the original Jobs Plan did not cover even maintenance of existing US infrastructure, let alone improve it. Now that it is significantly smaller, the Plan will do even less to fix problems and ensures US government spending on infrastructure will lag even further behind that of the Chinese.

On 13 July, Schumer, now Senate Majority Leader, announced plans for a revised $3.5 billion omnibus bill that will incorporate much of the "human infrastructure", healthcare and social welfare provisions that featured in the original Jobs Plan and Families Plan, including measures to combat climate change and raise business taxes.[68] Because of Republican opposition, the revised bill will be moved through the reconciliation process that does not require Republican support but does require all 50 Democratic Senators to vote in favour.

The administration's revised legislative program is fraught with danger. It requires, first, that the Republicans do not walk away from the compromise infrastructure deal they have agreed to in response to the Democrats pressing ahead with the omnibus bill. Republicans looking to rally their base in preparation for the 2022 mid-term elections have so far obstructed most attempts by the Biden administration to win bipartisan support for any bills except those that are directly aimed at fighting China. There is a strong chance the compromise will collapse. Second, it requires that the conservative bloc of Democratic Congress representatives, most prominently Joe Manchin and Kyrsten Sinema, back Schumer's proposed omnibus bill. They have already signalled their opposition to tax increases

---

68. Kim et al 2021.

and their preference for bipartisan deals. The longer the process drags on, the more likely that Biden's plans will be stripped further back, and at the time of writing (July 2021), neither bill had even been drafted.

Congressional pressure on the Biden administration is overwhelmingly from the right. Liberal Democratic Congress representatives have not shown the same kind of intransigence as the right-wing Democrats. With no significant left outside the Democrats and few signs of rising working-class struggle in the US, only the prospect of failing in the mid-term elections is likely to push the Democrats to persevere with even token reforms to deal with the dire condition faced by many millions of American workers.

If Biden's social and economic programs face Congressional opposition, the only pressure on the administration over its military budget will be to increase it. Republican and Democrat representatives will not balk at spending money on the wherewithal to do battle with China.

What does it mean for the US to "beat China"?

The final question is perhaps the crux of the matter: what does "beating China" in the new Cold War look like from the point of view of US imperialism? China is not going to collapse like the USSR in 1991, nor is regime change likely in Beijing in the foreseeable future. Nor will China accept a subordinate role in a US-led world order in the way past great powers, such as Britain, or resurgent powers, such as Germany and Japan, did in the 1950s and 1960s. Much more likely is that it will continue to try to build its own sphere of influence in the Asia-Pacific and elsewhere to the detriment of the US. Factors such as an ageing population and environmental degradation may well lower China's rate of economic growth in coming decades but will not in themselves prevent its consolidation as a big power. China now has the largest domestic market in the world and a population that still has a long way to go before reaching high-income status, suggesting that sooner rather than later it will outrank the US. As it begins to overhaul the US, so it will exert an ever stronger gravitational pull far beyond its borders.

Militarily, it is difficult to see how the US could eke out victory in this new Cold War. China's immediate priority is not global hegemony but control over the sea lanes to its immediate south and the ability to deny access to the US Navy and Air Force to sensitive areas in the region. The US, by contrast, is burdened with maintaining military hegemony across the planet and must spread its military assets accordingly. Nor does the US have the capacity to invade and conquer China, no matter how many allies it can call on.

Taiwan may be the first test for the US. China may not be capable of invading and holding Taiwan, but it could certainly conduct cyber-warfare operations aimed at jamming the operation of military communications and civilian infrastructure in preparation for a missile attack and a blockade of the island. And whatever may be the current balance of military force, China can afford to wait until the military calculus more clearly favours it. What resources would the US send to defend Taiwan if China attacked it? A conventional military response is one option, but China may now have the capacity to sink US aircraft carriers coming to Taiwan's aid. It is possible, then, that the US might turn to "tactical" nuclear weapons. Would the US be prepared to use these to defend Taiwan if it risked provoking a Chinese nuclear attack on Guam, Hawaii or the US West Coast? On the other hand, the US's failure to respond, or an intervention in which it clearly came off the worse, would cause immense reputational damage to US imperialism in the region and risk US allies breaking away and making individual deals with China. The wide range of possible military outcomes are such as to give the Pentagon reason for caution.

Wars also throw up the question of the preparedness of the population at home to fund them and to tolerate casualties. A serious war with China would involve the loss of many lives, both military and civilian. How many naval ships sunk would the US public be prepared to accept? Would the population continue to support a war with China if China mounted electronic attacks on the US, much as Russia has already done, to shut down oil pipelines, power stations, air traffic control, banks, transport infrastructure and hospitals? The American people are clearly being sensitised by their government to accept a conflict with China in coming years, but how much sacrifice they are willing to tolerate to save Taiwan cannot be determined ahead of time.[69]

To conclude: Biden's project to contain China may not succeed; several obstacles lie in its path. But its main purpose should not be in doubt. The Biden administration aims to put America in the best position to engage and defeat the challenge to US domination posed by China. The Australian government understands this and is fully backing the Biden administration in pursuing a strategy that, in the context of China's parallel attempts to increase its sway in the Asia-Pacific, may lead to the first major inter-imperialist war since 1945. To the extent that progressives and the left let their guard down with Biden as president, this will only handicap our ability to create an anti-war movement now that the shape of a new battle between the two great powers is clearly coming into view.

References

Associated Press 2019, "Joe Biden: China not economic threat to U.S.", 7 May. www.youtube.com/watch?v=dew9qqoAM9A.

Bennhold, Katrin and Steven Lee Myers, 2021, "America's Friends and Foes Express Horror as Capitol Attack 'Shakes the World'", *New York Times*, 6 January. https://www.nytimes.com/2021/01/06/world/europe/trump-capitol-2020-election-mob.html

Bergengruen, Vera and WJ Hennigan 2019, "'We are being eaten from within.' Why America is losing the battle against white nationalist terrorism", *Time*, 8 August. https://time.com/5647304/white-nationalist-terrorism-united-states/?utm_source=reddit.com

Biden, Joe 2020, "Why America Must Lead Again: Rescuing US Foreign Policy After Trump", *Foreign Affairs*, March/April 2020. https://www.foreignaffairs.com/articles/united-states/2020–01–23/why-america-must-lead-again

Chowdhury, Debasish Roy 2021, "How Long Will Joe Biden Pretend Narendra Modi's India Is a Democratic Ally?", *Time*, 15 February. https://time.com/5939510/joe-biden-india-democracy/

---

69. Silver et al 2021.

Department of Defense 2018, *Summary of the 2018 National Defense Strategy of the United States of America: Sharpening American Military's Competitive Edge*, January 2018. https://dod.defense.gov/Portals/1/Documents/pubs/2018-National-Defense-Strategy-Summary.pdf

Economist, The 2021a, "Biden's new China doctrine", 17 July. https://www.economist.com/leaders/2021/07/17/bidens-new-china-doctrine

Economist, The 2021b, "Joe Biden's agenda depends on steering two trains at once", 17 July. https://www.economist.com/united-states/2021/07/17/joe-bidens-agenda-depends-on-steering-two-trains-at-once

Economist, The 2021c, "China wants the world to know that resistance to its rise is futile", 8 May. https://www.economist.com/china/2021/05/08/china-wants-the-world-to-know-that-resistance-to-its-rise-is-futile

Foroohar, Rana 2021a, "Joe Biden's battles have just begun", *Financial Times*, 2 May. https://www.ft.com/content/d5664613-dc05–425d-8ac4-f52a044a70a9

Foroohar, Rana, 2021b, "America and the EU are stronger together", *Financial Times*, 27 June. https://www.ft.com/content/0f50071d-08e4–4857–9c58–1429a2dad057

Friedman Lisa 2021, "Biden Administration Defends Huge Alaska Oil Drilling Project", *New York Times*, 26 May. https://www.nytimes.com/2021/05/26/climate/biden-alaska-drilling.html

Hale, Thomas, Harriet Agnew, Michael Mackenzie and Demetri Sevastopulo 2021, "Wall Street's new love affair with China", *Financial Times*, 29 May. https://www.ft.com/content/d5e09db3–549e-4a0b-8dbf-e499d0606df4

Harris, Jennifer and Jake Sullivan 2020, "America needs a new economic philosophy. Foreign policy experts can help", *Foreign Policy*, 7 February 2020. https://foreignpolicy.com/2020/02/07/america-needs-a-new-economic-philosophy-foreign-policy-experts-can-help/

Hille, Kathrin 2021, "Top US general dismisses warnings of imminent Chinese invasion of Taiwan", *Financial Times*, 18 June. https://www.ft.com/content/f68c3fdf-5f3b-4cd3–9fcf-03b7a19ea7ee

Infratest dimap 2021, "Possible conflict USA-China: majority for neutral position of Germany", 10 January. www.infratest-dimap.de/umfragen-analysen/bundesweit/umfragen/aktuell/moeglicher-konflikt-usa-china-mehrheit-fuer-neutrale-position-deutschlands/

Kim, Seung Min, Tony Romm, Mike DeBonis and Marianna Sotomayor 2021, "Biden rallies Democrats on Capitol Hill for his spending plans", *Washington Post*, 14 July. https://www.washingtonpost.com/politics/2021/07/14/biden-congress-spending-bill/

Lendon, Brad 2021, "US warplanes fly first combat missions off foreign aircraft carrier since World War II", CNN, 23 June. https://edition.cnn.com/2021/06/22/middleeast/us-fighter-jets-uk-aircraft-carrier-intl-hnk-ml-scli/index.html

Letter to the President by US manufacturing companies, 6 May 2021, www.tariffsaretaxes.org/sites/default/files/2021–05/FINAL_Business%20Letter%20to%20Presiden%20Biden%20232%20Business.pdf

Lockett, Hudson 2021, "Global investors' exposure to Chinese assets surges to $800 billion", *Financial Times*, 14 July. https://www.ft.com/content/f0c71c66-b386–4f3c-8796–4384e7378a56

Luce Edward 2021, "The First 100 days: just how radical is Joe Biden?", *Financial Times*, 29 April. https://www.ft.com/content/47eb1c2d-eb25–4591-a27c-9b8a1d25ff3f

Manson, Katrina and Courtney Weaver 2020, "America is back and ready to lead world, says Joe Biden", *Financial Times*, 25 November. https://www.ft.com/content/e9f7fc88–7f08–43af-976c-9b164cf32ed8

Medcalf, Rory 2021, "Declassification of secret document reveals US strategy in the Indo-Pacific", *The Strategist*, 13 January 2021. https://www.aspistrategist.org.au/declassification-of-secret-document-reveals-real-us-strategy-in-the-indo-pacific/

Nakamura, Ryo 2021, "US to build anti-China missile network along first island chain", *Nikkei Asia*, 5 March. https://asia.nikkei.com/Politics/International-relations/Indo-Pacific/US-to-build-anti-China-missile-network-along-first-island-chain

National Security Council 2018, *U.S. Strategic Framework for the Indo-Pacific*, https://trumpwhitehouse.archives.gov/wp-content/uploads/2021/01/IPS-Final-Declass.pdf

Nelson, Steven, Juliegrace Brufke and Bruce Golding 2021, "Biden let Putin 'spout Russian propaganda' unchallenged at summit: critics", *New York Post*, 16 June. https://nypost.com/2021/06/16/biden-let-putin-spout-russian-propaganda-unchallenged-at-summit-critics/

Pengelly, Martin 2021, "Ocasio-Cortez says Biden exceeded progressives' expectations", *The Guardian*, 24 April. https://www.theguardian.com/us-news/2021/apr/24/aoc-joe-biden-exceeded-progressive-expectations

Senate Foreign Relations Committee 2021, *Strategic Competition Bill*, www.foreign.senate.gov/imo/media/doc/DAV21598%20-%20Strategic%20Competition%20Act%20of%202021.pdf

Sevastopulo, Demetri and Kathrin Hille 2021, "US and Japan conduct war games amid rising China-Taiwan tension", *Financial Times*, 1 July. https://www.ft.com/content/54b0db59-a403–493e-b715–7b63c9c39093

Silver, Laura, Kat Devlin and Christine Huang 2020, "Unfavorable Views of China Reach Historic Highs in Many Countries", Pew Research Center, 6 October. www.pewresearch.org/global/2020/10/06/unfavorable-views-of-china-reach-historic-highs-in-many-countries/

Silver, Laura, Kat Devlin and Christine Huang 2021, "Most Americans Support Tough Stance Toward China on Human Rights, Economic Issues", Pew Research Center, 4 March. https://www.pewresearch.org/global/2021/03/04/most-americans-support-tough-stance-toward-china-on-human-rights-economic-issues/

Sraders, Anne 2021, "The stock market's performance during Biden's first 100 days has officially bested everyone from Trump back through Truman", *Fortune*, 30 April. https://fortune.com/2021/04/29/stock-market-performance-under-biden-first-100-days-sp-500-spx-nasdaq-dow-jones-djia-april-2021-update/

Swanson, Ana and Michael Crowley 2019, "Trump Says He's 'Standing' With Xi (and With Hong Kong's Protesters)", *New York Times*, 22 November. https://www.nytimes.com/2019/11/22/us/politics/trump-hong-kong-protests-xi.html

Taibbi, Matt 2021, "So much for 'transformational' Joe Biden", 28 May. https://taibbi.substack.com/p/so-much-for-transformational-joe

Tellis, Ashley J. 2020, "The return of US-China strategic competition", in Ashley J Tellis, Alison Szalwinski, and Michael Wills (eds), *Strategic Asia 2020: U.S.-China Competition for Global Influence*, National Bureau of Asian Research.

Thebault, Reis 2021, "Joint Chiefs feared potential 'Reichstag moment' aimed at keeping Trump in power", *Washington Post*, 14 July. https://www.washingtonpost.com/politics/joint-chiefs-chairman-feared-potential-reichstag-moment-aimed-at-keeping-trump-in-power/2021/07/14/a326f5fe-e4ec-11eb-a41e-c8442c213fa8_story.html

Trading Economics 2021, "United States Imports of Semiconductors". https://tradingeconomics.com/united-states/imports-of-semiconductors.

Trump, Donald 2017, "US President Donald Trump's inauguration speech transcript", *Sydney Morning Herald*, 21 January. https://www.smh.com.au/world/north-america/us-president-donald-trumps-inauguration-speech-transcript-20170121-gtvwes.html

Trump, Donald 2018, "State of the Union Address", 30 January. www.npr.org/2018/01/30/580378279/trumps-state-of-the-union-address-annotated

US Census Bureau 2020, "Foreign Trade: Annual 2020 Press Highlights". www.census.gov/foreign-trade/statistics/highlights/AnnualPressHighlights.pdf

US Census Bureau 2021, "Trade in Goods with China", data series. www.census.gov/foreign-trade/balance/c5700.html

Wee, Sui-Lee 2021, "They Relied on Chinese Vaccines. Now They're Battling Outbreaks", *New York Times*, 22 June. https://www.nytimes.com/2021/06/22/business/economy/china-vaccines-covid-outbreak.html

White House 2017, *National Security Strategy of the United States of America*. https://trumpwhitehouse.archives.gov/wp-content/uploads/2017/12/NSS-Final-12–18–2017–0905.pdf

White House 2021a, "Remarks by President Biden in Address to a Joint Session of Congress", 28 April. www.whitehouse.gov/briefing-room/speeches-remarks/2021/04/29/remarks-by-president-biden-in-address-to-a-joint-session-of-congress/

White House 2021b, "Remarks by President Biden on America's place in the world", 4 February. www.whitehouse.gov/briefing-room/speeches-remarks/2021/02/04/remarks-by-president-biden-on-americas-place-in-the-world/

White House 2021c, "Quad Leaders' Joint Statement: The Spirit of the Quad", 12 March. www.whitehouse.gov/briefing-room/statements-releases/2021/03/12/quad-leaders-joint-statement-the-spirit-of-the-quad/

White House 2021d "Remarks by President Biden at the 2021 Virtual Munich Security Conference", 19 February. www.whitehouse.gov/briefing-room/speeches-remarks/2021/02/19/remarks-by-president-biden-at-the-2021-virtual-munich-security-conference/

Wike, Richard, Jacob Poushter, Laura Silver, Janell Fetterolf and Mara Mordecai 2021, "America's Image Abroad Rebounds with Transition from Trump to Biden", Pew Research Center, 10 June. www.pewresearch.org/global/2021/06/10/ americas-image-abroad-rebounds-with-transition-from-trump-to-biden/

World Bank 2019a, "Japan trade balance, exports and imports by country and region 2019", *World Integrated Trading Statistics*. https://wits. worldbank.org/CountryProfile/en/Country/JPN/Year/2019/TradeFlow/ EXPIMP

World Bank 2019b, "European Union Trade", *World Integrated Trading Statistics*. https://wits.worldbank.org/countrysnapshot/en/EUN

SARAH GARNHAM

The failure of identity politics:
A Marxist analysis

Sarah Garnham is a regular contributor to
Red Flag newspaper and a member of Socialist
Alternative's national executive.

"UNION JACK", AN ANTI-IMPERIALIST ARTWORK by Spanish
artist Santiago Sierra, was pulled from the 2021 Dark Mofo
festival amidst a storm of controversy. The plan for the
artwork was to drench the flag in the blood of the victims of British
colonisation. Sierra invited groups colonised by Britain, including
Aboriginal people, to donate their blood to the project.

This clearly anti-colonial piece was met with widespread outrage,
manifested in a Twitter storm and flurry of denunciatory articles
in the liberal media. For these critics, there was no generosity; no
attempt to recognise that, while something may be misguided or
in bad taste, it should be understood in the spirit it was intended.
Instead Sierra was denounced as racist and his work as an exercise
in colonisation.

Artist Jamie Graham-Blair wrote on Instagram: "Indigenous
bodies are not tools to be used by colonisers. We are not props for
your white guilt art".[1] Caz Lynch argued in *Overland* journal that the
piece could easily be interpreted as *"celebrating* the domination of
Indigenous people by the British empire" and as leaning into "the
glorification of the gore and violence of colonisation". She even

---

1.   Jefferson 2021.

compared the artist's request for voluntary blood donations from supporters of the work with invasion and genocide itself, claiming that it was "an extractive exercise that *repeats* the loss of blood suffered as a result of colonisation".[2] The very commissioning of the artwork "drives home how racist this country still is when a progressive arts festival can't even get this right", according to Kira Puru, while Rachael Sarra branded the gallery hosting the festival as "culturally unsafe".[3]

An honourable few, including the chairman of the Tasmanian Aboriginal Land Council Michael Mansell, disagreed, arguing that: "The artist challenges Tasmanians about whether Aboriginal lands were peacefully or violently taken, and uses the blood-smattered Union Jack to express his view".[4] Mansell also argued in response to the backlash that "people have every right to disagree with the artist's depiction of the discussion and may be offended by his methods, but they are not sound reasons to stifle the artist's freedom of thought".[5]

But it was the former voices that won out. Museum of Old and New Art founder David Walsh and Dark Mofo creative director Leigh Carmichael apologised profusely for the supposed inappropriateness of the art. Other institutions have now cut ties with Sierra and removed his other work from their galleries.

Episodes like this are typical of discussions of oppression today. There are strict moral codes about who can express an opinion and how they may do it. Breaches lead to condemnation and sometimes censorship, often couched in terms of "cultural safety" or preventing harm. It is difficult, however, to see how the withdrawal of this anti-racist artwork has advanced the struggle against Aboriginal oppression. The flag that was going to be symbolically drenched in blood will presumably now remain dry and unsullied, like the Australian flags proudly flown atop hundreds of courthouses, parliaments and other government buildings. These ostentatious displays of support for the empire are so normalised they barely provoke comment, let alone outrage. Yet an artist seeking to draw attention

---

2.   Lynch 2021.
3.   Ross 2021.
4.   Ross 2021.
5.   Ross 2021.

to the barbarism concealed by this familiar symbol has had his reputation destroyed.

Even if Sierra's work was inadvertently racist, drawing an equivalence between a work of art and the actual genocide of Indigenous people invariably trivialises the history of Aboriginal oppression. In a similar vein, one of the main demands made in this debate was for Aboriginal voices to be centred and for their opinions to prevail. The problem here, however, is deciding which Aboriginal voices should take precedence, as they were on both sides of the debate.

This episode provides a snapshot of modern identity politics, and the issues it raises are widespread. These ideas inform the political assumptions and strategies that have come to dominate discussions of oppression across the cultural sphere, the academy, the public sector, and the NGO industry, through to activist milieus and even the socialist left. This article is an attempt to critique this liberal common sense from a Marxist perspective, one that sees oppression as a central feature of capitalist society and that aims for the overthrow of both.

What is identity politics?

Identity politics is a set of ideas and practices that aim to build recognition of and expand representation for particular identity groups. It reflects the social, political and career aspirations of a particular layer within these groups, who seek to hegemonise their political approach to oppression among all those concerned with challenging it. The starting point is the elevation of select identity groups to moral and political pre-eminence, while implicitly or explicitly subordinating others. Different advocates of identity politics see the world through different identity lenses, usually the ones that they are personally connected to.

To the extent other issues are incorporated, it is not because the framework demands an understanding of and sensitivity to all forms of oppression and exploitation, but rather in order to deflect potential criticism from equivalent advocates claiming to represent other identity groups. The popularity of the concept of "intersectionality", for example, can partly be explained by the eagerness of many modern feminists to demonstrate they are not racist or transphobic. But despite the apparent prevalence of intersectionality, it is usually one or two categories of oppression that are prioritised in liberal discourse at any one time. These can change, but the general effect is to create a highly moralistic attitude towards particular favoured categories and their anointed spokespeople, regardless of the political context.

There are some general theoretical and political assumptions about the organisation of society that underpin identity politics. The first and most important of these is an essentialist view of identity, in relation to both social identity categories and personal identity. The second is the assumption that those with "lived experience" of oppression are automatically, and exclusively, political authorities on challenging it. Related to this is the assumption that the subjective experience of marginalisation is the defining feature of oppression. Two other concepts at the heart of identity politics are intersectionality and privilege, which are used, to varying degrees, to justify the political tactics associated with identity politics.

Identity essentialism

Though it is difficult to imagine, the concept of identity was barely used prior to the 1960s and '70s. Marie Moran, who has researched the history of the term, reports that a survey of popular literature and political texts written before that time reveals barely any references to it. It came into use during the social movements in the late 1960s, and by the 1980s and '90s, "identity was completely embedded in the popular, political and academic lexicon". This shift indicated not only a massive increase in the popular usage of the term, but also a change to its meaning. As Moran points out, identity once referred to an "abstract formal property of an entity (any entity), namely, its 'oneness' or sameness to itself". It now references "a substantive human property or attribute – something which may be personally or collectively possessed, or indeed, lost".[6] These two interwoven concepts, of collective and personal identity, warrant some explanation.

---

6. Moran 2018.

Collective identity refers to social categories of people defined by their race, gender, nationality, sexuality, class, or a number of other traits. These categories are both objectively and subjectively defined. On the one hand, they have been created and shaped by capitalist society. Many were invented in the first instance to codify the oppression of a particular group of people. Often they have then been reinforced, or have even emerged, from below, as oppressed groups have sought to define their oppression in order to collectively resist it. The reality is that these social categories are both necessary and important for understanding the complexity of society but, at the same time, these categories *on their own* oversimplify the reality of social divisions and how they work in practice. However, through the lens of identity politics, these categories represent permanent communities that share immutable characteristics and interests. Women for example have a commonality not only because they all share experiences of sexism but also, because they are a fundamentally fixed social group with a shared path to social advancement. Identity categorisations are considered so powerful that they override the tensions and divisions between members of an identity group, in particular the political and economic divisions.

This outlook is manifest everywhere throughout political and cultural discussions. It is particularly useful for powerful people, who can use their identities to make their power or class position seem less relevant. For example Kamala Harris has staked out a political career by pursuing law and order campaigns, defending neoliberal economic policies and championing US imperialism. As the vice-president of the United States, she now occupies one of the most overtly political and powerful offices in the world, yet the liberal media frequently present her identities as Black, a woman and of immigrant parents as her most significant qualities and as reason to champion her regardless of her politics.[7]

While most proponents of identity politics refer to multiple identities, including class, in practice some are clearly considered more important than others. In all of the glowing tributes to Harris in the liberal media, her ruling-class position is mostly

---

7.   Purnell 2020.

ignored. It is typical for discussions of identity to brush over class. Where it is mentioned it is presented as a source of historic disadvantage or privilege, yet rarely incorporated as a dynamic or dominant influence over behaviour and attitudes. The one exception to this, proving the liberal nature of identity politics, is the "white working class" which has become a stand-in term for white racists.

The view that collective identity categorisation determines social behaviour goes alongside, and is reinforced by, the second concept: personal identity. Personal identity refers not simply to the personal experiences that people have as a result of the identity categorisations they fall under. Michael Kimmel, editor of *Privilege: a reader*, argues that these categories are the "foundations of individual identity", and that "our membership in dominant if invisible groups and our membership in visible yet marginalized groups – define us, providing the raw materials from which we fashion an identity".[8]

The idea that everybody has "an identity" is a relatively recent one. This is not to say that there were not previously notions of selfhood, nor that people in the past had a purely detached and external relationship to their identities. It is natural that people personally identify with and internalise aspects of their social categorisation. But this is different from the political view that everyone has "an identity", akin to their soul, which defines who they are at the deepest level. It is this concept that results in the essentialising of identity categories. Whether or not someone believes social identity categories to be "constructed" or "natural", this essentialist view elevates the characteristics that get ascribed to *personal* identity, making them the encryption codes for someone's inner essence. In this sense "personal identity" is an empty classifier, to which any social characteristic can be attached. Traits that get most commonly associated with personal identity are to do with race, gender and sexuality, as well as disability and mental illness.

Connected to this, is a political attitude that sees declarations and affirmations of personal identity as a positive phenomenon that

---

8.   Kimmel and Ferber 2017, p.12.

by their nature strike a blow against oppression. It's true that becoming more personally invested in identity can be a positive insofar as it raises political consciousness and leads to struggle. But insofar as it allows people to go on an inner journey of self-discovery, or as a means to advance individual careers, it has no role to play in the fight against oppression.

Personal experience

Identity politics combines identity essentialism with a strong focus on experience. It is the act of belonging to, or more accurately *being*, a certain identity that gives someone exclusive access to the "truth" of that identity and the oppression attached to it. As a result, "lived experience" is presented as the key to social insight and authenticity, and as a substitute for objective social analysis or engagement with political argument.

But the complexity and overarching structures of oppression cannot be understood from the vantage point of individual experience. For most people, the direct mistreatment and abuse that they encounter from family members, acquaintances and strangers, and particular agencies of the state, will be the most obvious and often the most emotionally hurtful manifestations of their oppression. But experiential accounts, while undoubtedly providing insights into the specificities of particular forms of oppression, do not necessarily help elucidate the structures that underpin them.

The idea that experiences of oppression are the key to political insight also leads to the valorisation of experiences of oppression, especially those that are traumatic. If experience confers knowledge, it follows that those who have experienced the most trauma will possess the most insight into the horrors of our society. According to this view, refugees who have been tortured physically and mentally for decades, denied contact and engagement with society, have been given the best social education available. While refugees are often politicised by their experiences, the torture many experience is so extreme, isolating and unrelenting that many are totally broken by the experience, or come to conclude that their oppressor can't be challenged. There is nothing inherently radicalising or educative about trauma.

It also means that those who have experienced oppression are seen as having unassailable moral authority that cannot be challenged or debated, regardless of their political perspective. In a piece entitled "an open letter to white 'allies' from a white friend" author Caitlin Deen Fair recounts an incident highlighting the absurd conclusions that are drawn from this standpoint:

> I was told by a fellow member of a group that I belonged to that the first step in the liberation of Black folks was to kill all the White women because they were tools of re-colonization... I knew I couldn't engage him on that; primarily because I don't know what his lived experience has been. He may very well have had legitimate experiences that tell him that this is the most reasonable and effective solution to the problems that we face... That being said, it is safe to say that it would be imprudent to challenge or engage in a "discussion" (read: argument) about it, particularly in movement spaces.[9]

According to this logic, it is impossible for those who have not experienced a particular oppression to disagree with those who have, or to take up debates over strategies and tactics. Those who don't fall into a given identity group can only be "allies" – the defining qualities of which are deference and passivity.

The idea that experience affords authority falls down, once again, due to the inevitable diversity within oppressed identity groups. There are as many experiences as there are members of any one oppressed group, and these can be vastly divergent. For example, the experiences of a poor Aboriginal person locked up in prison cannot be equated with those of a wealthy Aboriginal entrepreneur. Naturally these experiences lead to different political conclusions. The main way that this tension is resolved in practice is by someone setting themselves up as the arbiter of which experiences are most valid. Those who take on this role are mostly those who are relatively advantaged in comparison to the rest of the group, and who have an interest in becoming spokespeople in order

---

9. Fair in Kimmel and Ferber 2017, pp.290–291.

to push a particular agenda. As Olúfémi O Táiwò puts it in an essay critiquing this phenomenon:

> In my experience, when people say they need to "listen to the most affected", it isn't because they intend to set up Skype calls to refugee camps or to collaborate with houseless people. Instead, it has more often meant handing conversational authority and attentional goods to those who most snugly fit into the social categories associated with these ills – regardless of what they actually do or do not know, or what they have or have not personally experienced.[10]

This situation arises repeatedly in student unions, where the people elected to identity-based departments assume the authority to preside over all political activity that relates to their identity category. The Australian National University student union recently passed the following motion:

> Autonomous Department officers are elected members of the SRC that have the lived experiences and speak for the marginalised community they represent. Hence, it is imperative that anyone who is doing student advocacy that concerns a specific marginalised community properly consult with the department officers. This ensures that their campaigns and/or protest can truly reflect the needs of marginalised students on campus and avoid any kind of white knighting.[11]

Policies such as these are regularly used to censor solidarity and maintain control over politics on campus. In this case the policy was introduced after activists had been condemned for initiating a campaign against the privatisation of on-campus health services, and for moving a motion opposing the introduction of a Liberal think tank, the Menzies Institute, at another university. In both these cases, the activists had made the apparently grave error of failing to consult with relevant student union office bearers and clubs. In the

10.   Táiwò 2020.
11.   Australian National University Students Association 2021.

case of the healthcare campaign they were attacked as white knights because they had not consulted with the queer officer or the BIPOC officer, despite the fact that queer people need healthcare and racism is endemic in the medical system. It was also a failing to not consult the BIPOC officer in relation to the Menzies Institute motion because Liberal Prime Minister Robert Menzies was a racist.

Marginality

Another aspect of identity politics today is a focus on marginalisation. As we can see with the above student union motion, as well as the definition of oppressed groups provided by Kimmel, marginalisation is one of the most frequently referred to aspects of oppression, and is often used as a synonym for oppression. Marginality is also often equated with moral virtue.

Marginalised groups are those that are particularly small, peripheral and excluded in relation to other, comparable identity groups. This generally means being discounted and under-represented in culture and politics. Marginalisation is a factor in the oppression of several groups but, oppression cannot be reduced to this. Some oppressed groups, such as the working class and women, are too large to be consistently marginalised. On the other hand, there are plenty of marginalised groups who are not oppressed, such as people who live in the country or a range of small religious groups. And for oppressed groups who are small and marginalised, it is not necessarily the experience of marginalisation that is the most severe or relevant part of their oppression. For instance there are relatively few representations of trans people in politics and the media. While this reflects their ongoing oppression, it is clearly far less significant than the difficulty in accessing health services, lack of social acceptance and political attacks from the right.

The focus that identity politics places on marginalisation, which is also often interpreted in a highly subjective way, flows from the importance attributed to personal identity and identity expression. The lack of affirmation of particular identities in certain settings is not necessarily a clear indication of where oppression exists or how it operates. For instance, in response to the recent Australian census, some same-sex parents complained that their identity was being erased by questions about the biological fathers of their children. Mary from West Preston was apparently left "distressed" after filling out the census for her two children because, despite allowing for people to indicate whether they are same-sex parents, the census "forces you to say where the father is from".[12] This question was not aimed at erasing LGBTI people, but rather was used to generate statistical data about biological lineage.[13] Besides which, it is hard to believe that anybody of any marginalised identity or otherwise feels truly "seen" by the census, it is after all a giant bureaucratic survey involving millions of people answering a handful of formulaic questions in drop-down boxes.

At the same time that oppression is reduced to the experience of marginalisation, there is also a fetishisation of marginality that equates it to moral purity. The mere existence of minorities that defy mainstream norms and conventions is seen as an important political statement and act of resistance against the status quo. This often leads to a rejection of rights-based campaigns, aimed at giving oppressed groups access to more social inclusion and civil rights, as "assimilationist" and reflecting an aspiration to join the mainstream. An example of this was the hostility from some within the LGBTI community to the successful struggle for marriage equality.[14] This outlook puts the people who hold to it on the wrong side of many important struggles against oppression and rests on the defeatist conundrum that marginality is both the basis of oppression and the basis of resistance to it.

Another outcome of this approach is the argument that the most marginalised groups inherently represent the vanguard of struggle and must be centred at all times. An example of this is the insistence from some that trans women and sex workers lead International Women's Day marches.[15] While it is important to acknowledge the diversity inherent in any oppressed group, it is not the case that the smaller or more marginalised a particular group is the better they

---

12. Duke 2021.
13. Duke 2021.
14. See O'Shea 2011 for a discussion of these political attitudes and an overview of the equal marriage campaign.
15. See IWD Narm Melbourne [Facebook page].

will be able to lead struggle. This is a matter of political approach, not identity. But more often than not the preoccupation with elevating the most marginalised is not about strengthening struggle at all, but about demonstrating moral worthiness.

The political interest taken in sex workers also raises a number of other issues. Sex workers are a marginalised social group in terms of their size and insignificance to the economy or any major institutions in society. They are also stigmatised because the sex industry is only semi-legal, and is associated with low morals, and seen as a threat to family values and social order. But being involved in a stigmatised or semi-legal industry does not make people left-wing. In fact, the experience can draw people closer to their bosses. Many advocates for sex workers within activist milieus also advocate on behalf of the industry and deny that it is inherently sexist and exploitative. Instead it is purely the marginalisation and stigmatisation of both the workers and the industry that constitutes oppression. For these advocates the occupation of sex work is often talked about as a form of sexuality and as a personal identity trait, indicative of inner essence. The industry is the lifestyle and community that springs from this identity, and is often seen as part of the broader queer community. Therefore, the key struggle for sex workers is for a society in which this supposed identity and lifestyle can be embraced and allowed to flourish. Some even talk about this as a campaign for "self-determination" for sex workers.[16]

But sex workers are a qualitatively different kind of group from trans people, lesbians or gay people. Sex work is not a practice that represents the desired activity of an oppressed layer, and sex workers are not a group who share a gender or sexuality. Sex work is an occupation, not a personal identity, and the oppression that sex workers face is not based upon their (confected) identity expression being unvalidated or reviled. The disproportionate focus on marginality disguises these important differences and takes us further away from any serious understanding of oppression.

---

16. See for example https://feministsforsexworkers.com/.

Intersectionality

Intersectionality has become a core term in the identity politics lexicon. It is most often used to express political support for a range of oppressed groups simultaneously. Sometimes it is also held up as a method of social analysis. The overarching concept of intersectionality is that there are multiple forms of oppression in society and that they interact like "traffic in an intersection, coming and going in all... directions" as Kimberle Crenshaw put it in her 1989 essay that coined the term.[17]

Since it was coined, the term intersectionality has been tied retrospectively to Black feminism, and specifically to the critique that radical Black feminists made of mainstream second wave feminists, in arguing that both race and class were important to understanding women's oppression. For this reason, intersectionality is often presented as an alternative to conservative, single-issue variants of identity politics. But in reality intersectionality exists within the framework of identity politics, and it arose as a concept, not within radical movements but rather within the legal academy as a means to codify legal precedents. For Crenshaw, intersectionality was a way to overcome the lacuna in anti-discrimination law at the time, which could not account for the fact that Black women are affected not just by racism or by sexism but, experience a specific kind of discrimination because of their multiple oppressions. These legalistic origins demonstrate that intersectionality is neither theoretically nor politically based on the fight to overthrow oppression; it is limited to describing personal experience and finding resources for individuals within the system.

The application of an intersectional approach to personal identity is in close keeping with the prioritisation of personal inner essence and the focus on personal experience that we have already discussed. Kimmel, who is an advocate of this approach, describes how it is used:

> It's clear that the different statuses we occupy – by race, class, gender, sexuality, age, and so forth – all shape and modify one

---

17. Crenshaw 1989, p.149.

another. Sometimes one of these becomes a master status through which all others are filtered and in which all others become sort of adjectives to its noun. At other times, they shift and sort and collide in ways that can give you a headache. It's complex, and one always runs the risk of a slippery slope into an infinite regress, and by the time you're done enumerating all the different statuses you occupy, you are the only one of that specific combination, and therefore immune to any and all generalizations.[18]

A phenomenon connected to this chaotic quest for individual identification is the pejoratively named "oppression olympics", in which contestants compete over how many intersections they occupy and which ones represent greater moral value. Of course, some forms of oppression do affect people more harshly and some forms of oppression have been historically dismissed or ignored. Illuminating these nuances can have relevance for our struggles. But, more often than not, these games are about personal grandstanding. Take for example the petty territorial disputes surrounding which colours should appear, and in which order, on the pride flag attached to the new Pride Centre of Victoria.[19]

Another way that the language of intersectionality is used is to signal political support for a broad range of oppressed groups and social justice issues. This approach is encapsulated in the slogan: "My feminism will be intersectional or it will be bullshit". Today it is common for individuals and organisations to highlight these credentials by providing exhaustive lists of all forms of oppression they oppose or all the identity-based struggles they support. Though in some ways harmless, this tedious and arbitrary name-checking reflects an implicit theoretical position that rejects the term "capitalism" to describe the single social system in which all forms of oppression are rooted.

This brings us to intersectionality as a method of social analysis. Intersectional approaches to understanding oppression sometimes referred to as "intersectionality theory", have been popular in the academy for some time. Different theorists present different models

---

18.   Kimmel 2017 p.26,
19.   See Feltscheer 2017 and Amedi 2017 for some of the commentary on this.

of intersectionality, from Kimberle Crenshaw's traffic metaphor through to Patricia Hill Collins' "interlocking systems of oppression" that form a "matrix of domination".[20] All of these models take experience as their starting point and see the ways that different oppressions intersect as primarily experiential. So for example a Black woman will experience both racism and sexism, and it is on this basis that we can deduce that racism and sexism intersect, rather than any concept of how the two may be structurally connected. For models of intersectionality that include class, the same methodology applies; class is one of many potential sites of experiential oppression. Involved in this a rejection, mostly made explicit by intersectionality theorists, of the Marxist understanding of class, which is to see it not only as a source of oppression but also as the key determining social relationship of capitalism. Used in this way, class relations can make sense of the contradictory totality of capitalist society, which in turn provides an explanation for the root cause of every other form of oppression.

Instead of seeking to understand different forms of oppression as based in a totalising set of social relations, intersectionality models assume society to be fundamentally fragmentary. Its components may intersect, they may be interlaced, or even interlocked in a grid, or map or matrix, but they all have no necessary connection to one another. Marxist Delia Aguilar has argued the result of this is that:

> The identities that intersect are divested of their structuring material ground, resulting in a purely discursive analysis characteristic of postmodernism/poststructuralism... The existence of a multiplicity of modes of domination and oppression, the litany of which can be lengthy, is incomprehensible when dissociated from capitalism as a system.[21]

In the absence of a coherent materialist explanation of how different forms of oppression are tied together forming constituent parts of a coherent whole, categories of oppression and identity are static and discrete, and products primarily of cultural patterns. Hill Collins,

---

20. Hill Collins and Bilge 2020.
21. Aguilar 2015, p.211.

who is notable for the fact that she mentions structures throughout her work, ultimately falls back on cultural reductionism:

> The foundations of intersecting oppressions become grounded in interdependent concepts of binary thinking, oppositional difference, objectification, and social hierarchy. With domination based on difference forming an essential underpinning for this entire system of thought, these concepts invariably imply relationships of superiority and inferiority, hierarchical bonds that mesh with political economies of race, gender, and class oppression.[22]

This view of oppression accepts as a given the identity categories as they currently exist, as well as the ideological constructions that surround them. Each oppressed identity group is therefore oppressed by its culturally dominant inverse; Black people are oppressed by white people, women by men and so on, each operating on their own binary axis. Intersectionality is an attempt to transcend the single-issue approach that dominates the politics of various forms of oppression, but an incoherent one that cannot solve the underlying problems.

Privilege

Connected to this is privilege theory, which proposes that identity categories are not only the source of multiple forms of oppression, but also of multiple forms of privilege. According to this logic, non-oppressed identity groups enjoy unearned privileges as a result of their identities. These privileges are immovable, as Kimmel puts it: "one can no more renounce privilege than stop breathing".[23] This means that those with privilege have an ineradicable interest in maintaining the oppression of others.

One of the most influential texts informing this approach is Peggy McIntosh's "White Privilege: Unpacking the Invisible Knapsack".[24] Today this proverbial knapsack is unpacked well beyond activist

---

22. Hill Collins 2000, p.71.
23. Kimmel 2017, p.10.
24. McIntosh 1989, pp.10–12.

circles. It is a staple resource in the cultural diversity seminars and workshops. There are also many spin-off knapsacks, listing the invisible privileges enjoyed by men, by settlers, by non-disabled people and more.[25] The number of privileges that any one individual can have is limitless. At the same time, they need to be weighed against the oppressions someone suffers. This can result in some tricky calculations and is another way in which the "oppression olympics" comes into play; the weight given to specific privileges and oppressions is necessarily fraught and contested. One example of the tangles this produces can be found in a piece entitled "The peculiarity of Black trans male privilege" in which the author provides an account of all of the ways they are supposedly a beneficiary of male privilege, while also clearly being oppressed as a result of the combination of their identities.[26] The only insight to come out of this somewhat tortured discussion is that an individual can experience multiple things simultaneously and have no idea how to understand any of them. Privilege theory adds more fragments to the intersectional matrix, while still avoiding any form of analysis that can draw them together.

Notable in this regard is the kind of privileges that privilege theory tends to focus on and those that it tends to ignore. The day-to-day experiences people have when they go to the shops, apply for jobs or engage with culture are the main sites of privilege that are highlighted. Privilege here becomes associated with the absence of specific forms of discrimination or brutality meted out to others. It is a privilege to not be targeted by the police, a privilege to not be sexually molested, a privilege to be eligible for welfare, a privilege to not live behind bars. None of these are privileges in any meaningful sense of the word. Worse, defining privilege in this way mirrors the discourse of the right, who insist that welfare is a privilege rather than a right in order to more effectively withhold support for the oppressed.

At the same time, larger patterns of social inequalities that can be observed by looking at overall wealth distribution, how production is organised and who wields political power are rarely

---

25. See for example Gilio-Whitaker 2018 and Shea in Kimmel and Ferber 2017.
26. Ziegler in Kimmel and Ferber 2017 pp.209–211.

discussed. If anything, there is a class blindness that is manifest in privilege theory. Oftentimes the everyday supposed privileges that are pointed to are a result of class inequality as much as they are a product of racial or gender inequalities. For instance McIntosh's references to being able to afford housing and to being able to easily find a publisher are largely attributable to the advantages of being middle class, as opposed to white. And the idea that even these two examples can be put on the same plane seems like calculated political ignorance; one is a basic human right, the other is an irrelevance outside tiny circles of academics and writers. Its inclusion however is an indication that the people most invested in identity politics move in these circles. Another example is a 2019 *Overland* article entitled "Where are all the disabled academics?", in which author Amber Karanikolas discusses the traumatic experience of learning that she may one day have to disclose her mental illness, which is part of her identity, in order to be admitted as a lawyer. The upshot is that she successfully became a lawyer.[27]

Another aspect of this class blindness is the decontextualisation of the relative advantages and disadvantages afforded to different groups within the working class. Racism, sexism and other forms of oppression lead to inequality within the working class. This takes the form of wage discrepancies, unequal access to services, biased treatment at the hands of the state, cultural discrimination and myriad other forms. This means that workers who do not face oppression as a result of their (other) identities will have relative, situational advantages over others. One example that is often pointed to is job interviews, where one worker may receive a job because a specific form of discrimination works against another applicant. There are plenty of studies which show that this happens regularly throughout all of the stages of the job market. The most important factor in these occurrences however is the job market itself, which is controlled not by workers, but by bosses who benefit from its ruthless and dehumanising logic. To focus on the supposed privileges of individual workers in these scenarios is to ignore the key dynamic of social privilege at play. Worse still, this framing often results in drawing

---

27. Karanikolas 2019.

an equivalence between bosses and workers on the basis of their identity, which both trivialises the chasm of privilege between these two social layers and wrongly presents workers as co-conspirators in the oppression of other workers. Far from this being the case, the reality is that inequalities based on oppression within the working class, that supposedly constitute privileges, actually reinforce the oppression of the whole working class.

Following on from our discussion of cultural reductionism in relation to intersectionality, privileges are overwhelmingly thought of in a similar way. Members of non-oppressed identity groups have a shared interest in oppression because they are culturally dominant. This collapses vastly divergent layers of people into one group, and it confers onto other oppressed layers and individuals the full weight of the crimes and brutality of the capitalist state. For example Sarah Maddison has argued, as part of the growing field of settler-colonial studies, that all non-Indigenous people are settlers, including all migrants and anti-racists:

> Settlers are a diverse and multi-ethnic group, whose identities have been shaped by settler colonialism in a range of ways, but who in different ways are all complicit in sustaining colonial relationships… [S]ettler privilege means that some combination of our economic security, citizenship, relationship to land and place, mental and physical health, cultural integrity and spiritual life, family values and career aspirations are *literally not possible* were it not for the dispossession of Indigenous people.[28]

Throughout her book *The Colonial Fantasy*, she uses the terms "settlers" and "settler state" interchangeably, effectively arguing that there is no separation between the two. For Maddison, colonisation, and the ongoing racist treatment of Aboriginal people, is not primarily the result of the economic and political interests of the ruling class but is rather the result of the cultural domination of non-Indigenous people. Non-Indigenous people, simply by existing in Australia, have a settler mentality and are perpetrators of racism. The idea that

---

28. Maddison 2019, p.14.

colonisation is the imposition of a different set of values on another group greatly diminishes the real story of violence and genocide that marked the colonisation of Australia. Moreover, to claim that the current racism towards Aboriginal people is the result of an ongoing cultural clash is social evolutionism of the most patronising kind. In this reading Aboriginal people are an historic, unchanging race of people encoded with a set of unchanging cultural beliefs. It is the denial of this supposed essence that constitutes Aboriginal oppression, rather than the litany of crimes committed by the modern state: murders in custody, child removal, land dispossession, entrenched poverty and underfunding of Aboriginal communities resulting in, among other things, a life expectancy for Aboriginal people that is ten years lower than the average.[29]

Flowing from this is a focus, becoming increasingly dominant in identity politics discussions, on the psychological state of mind that supposedly comes along with privilege. Those from non-oppressed groups purportedly think in privileged ways, regardless of their overall social position or their politics. Privileged psychology manifests in a series of political beliefs and ideas, ranging from outright bigotry, irrational fear, ignorance, entitlement, and even staunchly anti-oppression politics. As an explanation for explicitly bigoted opinions, this erases all of the structural and ideological processes that produce these political ideas. It also ignores all of the social conditions that may lead people to personally adopt these distorted views. It instead proposes that bigoted ideas are not a distortion; they are a valid and natural way for those in non-oppressed groups to think about the oppressed. It is in fact those who take on anti-oppression values that are at odds with their true nature, and are destined to be in constant torment as a result. Robert Jensen elaborates on this in his piece "The Fears of White People", which is also a popular resource for cultural diversity training:

> Virtually every white person I know, including white people fighting for racial justice and including myself, carries some level

---

29. See Humphreys 2021 for a Marxist analysis of Aboriginal oppression, from colonial invasion to today.

of racism in our minds and hearts and bodies. In our heads, we can pretend to eliminate it, but most of us know it is there. And because we are all supposed to be appropriately anti-racist, we carry that lingering racism with a new kind of fear: What if non-white people look at us and can see it? What if they can see through us? What if they can look past our anti-racist vocabulary and sense that we still don't really know how to treat them as equals? What if they know about us what we don't dare know about ourselves? What if they can see what we can't even voice?[30]

The absurd assertion that everyone is a racist at heart sums up the fatalism and passivity at the heart of identity politics.

Political strategy

The overarching objective of identity politics is to maximise the recognition of and representation for particular identity groups. Given the assumption that people have a set of shared interests based on their identity, the idea is that individuals in powerful positions who are drawn from particular identity groups will effectively represent the interests of that group. Of course, there is the possibility of betrayal; some of those who make it into positions of power will cross the Rubicon, hence the criticism of #girlbosses or their Black, brown, gay, trans equivalents. But these individuals are seen as aberrant, and the solution is to find the "right kind" of representatives who will remain loyal. This is the key strategy of identity politics, uniting its right and left proponents.

At the same time, the inbuilt fatalism means that oppression can never really be overcome. Those who are not racially oppressed can never become genuinely anti-racist, and the same goes for all equivalent identity groups, who will inevitably seek to reproduce their own privileges. Where possible, however, material privileges should be renounced. This does not mean that the capitalist class should be expropriated. It means that highly paid and more comfortable sections of the working class should give up their advantages. In Australia, there is a long history of feminists calling for male

---

30. Jensen 2005, p.38.

workers to give up their "masculine dividend" in the form of wage cuts.[31] Another phenomenon that plays into this was the wave of individual donations to Black people in the US during the 2020 Black Lives Matter (BLM) protests. While many middle-class allies with means and white guilt cheer this on as a successful procurement of "reparations", the reality is that it misdirects blame away from the governments and companies responsible for racism. And rather than a focus on protest and joint struggle, it marketises and individualises solidarity in a way that is ineffective, patronising, and mired with petty scandals.[32]

The more prominent remedy for privilege is, however, personal salvation achieved by sustained introspection aimed at deprogramming our inner bigot. Hence the popular call for people to "decolonise your mind". Redemption can never be fully realised, but there is moral virtue in spending a lifetime doing penance, especially if it is highly publicised. This modern day "white man's burden" is particularly suited to the lifestyle of academics like Maddison. It is also the basis for a booming cultural diversity industry.

This pessimistic and fundamentally conservative outlook also leads to a focus on cultural, rather than structural, reform. This both fits with the view that structures arising from dominant identity group interests are unassailable, and with the narrow interests of the self-selecting minority of representatives from oppressed groups, who want to find a place for themselves in the system. The focus on cultural reform is twofold. One side to it is the proliferation of campaigns aimed at raising the cultural profile of certain groups by incorporating cultural iconography into the branding and practices of various institutions. The growing presence of rainbow insignia and other statements of LGBTI inclusivity is testament to this. As is the wave of pro-Indigenous cultural support, from Australia Post's brave decision to update their addressing guidelines to include traditional place names through to the tokenistic acknowledgement of Aboriginal elders before many events, including at congregations of the direct oppressors of Aboriginal people, such as government ministers and mining bosses.

---

31. Rosebourne 1988.
32. Dzotsi 2020.

The other side of cultural reform is the establishment of an identity politics "rules-based order". These rules include knowing where each identity group is situated on the moral hierarchy of oppression, observing strict guidelines of allyship, and using the latest language without questioning its ideological content, for example calling every non-Indigenous person a settler. Observing rules like this takes the place of political debate and education. Nigerian author Chimamanda Ngozi Adichie, who has recently been on the receiving end of such rules-based moral puritanism, has written an essay about this phenomenon titled "It's Obscene" in which she accurately describes the atmosphere that has developed around discussions of oppression as one of intolerance, intellectual poverty, and "angels jostling to out-angel one another".[33] It has also become fodder for the right wing, who are better able to crusade against so-called "political correctness" and "cancel culture", when they can point to this phenomenon to discredit the struggle as a whole.

By far the most important rules of identity politics are those concerning authenticity and legitimacy; who has the right to speak on questions of oppression, and in what ways. This frequently comes up in discussions about art and literature, as I foreshadowed in the introduction. Another example is the criticism directed at Craig Silvey's 2020 book, *Honeybee*. Silvey is a cis man; however, the central character in his book is a very sympathetically portrayed trans man. Most of the criticisms of Silvey reflected the competition for territory in the book industry, reflecting the extremely unrepresentative interests of trans novelists, who use their criticisms of Silvey to claim themselves as representatives of the whole trans community and promote their careers.[34] In one of several articles debating whether Silvey had the right to write and publish this book, *The Guardian* asked: "Even if it's written well, should it have been written at all?"[35] It has become commonplace for censorship to be suggested on the basis of the identities of authors, yet it jars with hundreds of years of literature in which authors have necessarily,

33. Adichie 2021.
34. See Ernest Price's comments in Hyde 2020.
35. Hyde 2020.

and largely uncontroversially, written characters based on imagination and social observation, rather than on biographical reporting. This aspect of literature should be defended as something that contributes to our collective understanding of and empathy towards a range of human experiences.

There is an even longer history of empathy and humanism in political and social struggle. On countless occasions, those who have not had direct experiences with oppression have fought alongside those directly oppressed, both because they are passionate about injustice and, often, because they recognise that their own struggles are intimately bound with the struggles of others. Yet the logic of identity politics is to eschew this.

In response to the murder of George Floyd in the US in 2020 there was an unprecedented wave of protests across the globe. In Australia, African immigrants, who are regularly victimised by the police and demonised in the media, felt moved to call solidarity protests. Their attempts were neutered when they came under heavy fire from Aboriginal activists and their army of white supporters. The young African activists were denounced as "settlers", were accused of not centring Aboriginal people, and failing to recognise that only Aboriginal people had the right to call Black Lives Matter protests. Meriki Onus, one of the leaders of activist group Warriors of Aboriginal Resistance (WAR) took to Twitter to attack the young Africans: "Imagine the audacity to organise a BLM protest on stolen Aboriginal land without the involvement of mob...most importantly families who have had loved ones taken by the racist Australian system".[36] The Africans promptly agreed to take down their event, explained that they were deeply sympathetic to the racism faced by Aboriginal people and had never intended to monopolise the rally. These explanations did nothing however to abate the barrage of attacks.

The effect of this was to prevent a group of people victimised by racism from protesting for their rights and expressing solidarity with other, similar struggles against racism. Denying oppressed people the right to protest has nothing to do with fighting oppression. This, and all of the other examples and problems I have gone through,

---

36. Onus 2020.

reflect the fact that identity politics is not just a set of misguided assumptions. It is a form of politics that systematically points us away from the system responsible for oppression, and from the forces that have an interest in fighting it. It is a block to solidarity and struggle. It focuses instead on individuals and the most superficial of cultural phenomena, and provides political cover for petty mindedness and self promotion.

The roots of identity politics

Originating in the US, identity politics as we know it today became established in the late 1980s across the Western world. It was a product of the defeats and distortions of the social movements of the previous decades. The decline of social struggle and rise of neoliberalism drove back the working class and the left. At the same time, a layer of middle-class professionals from various identity groups emerged and became entrenched. Within the academy, this layer developed ideological justifications for the social movements' retreat from the goal of liberation, and helped to develop a more progressive face for neoliberalism. Simultaneously, governments established identity-based bureaucracies, allowing a cohort of diverse professionals to advance their careers within the system while providing governments with cover for neoliberal reforms. This model continues to be used in government and the corporate world today. A substantial section of the capitalist class and the political establishment is wild for diversity.

This section is divided into three parts. We will begin by looking at the social movements and their decline. We will then look at the academisation and ideological degeneration of radical anti-oppression politics. The final section will discuss the institutionalisation of diversity and identity politics, and the implications that has for the struggles against oppression.

The social movements and their decline

The late 1960s and '70s saw impressive campaigns against oppression of various forms. These were part of a global radical upsurge in struggle. Students were revolting, and were turning to anti-capitalist politics. In Europe, a number of countries were brought to the brink of revolution. The anti-Vietnam War movement was highly significant, especially in Australia and the US. Various anti-racist movements, inspired by the anti-colonial struggles and the civil rights movement in the US the decade before, also sprang up. There was a women's liberation movement, and then a gay liberation movement. All these movements put forward radical demands and were tactically centred on protest and struggle, which helped to inspire and grow a new, radical, left which argued that these movements were interconnected parts of a greater struggle against capitalism.

The specific politics of the upsurge did, however, vary between countries. One of the most important variables was the participation and influence of the organised working class. Despite the revisionist narrative that only students were involved, in many countries workers played a major role. This was especially the case in Australia. Working-class militancy was on the rise at the time, and this made a big political impact on the student radicals and the emerging new left. It also meant that the movements, in particular the anti-war movement, were led not only by students but also by trade union, Labor left and Communist Party leaders. It was also these organisations that provided the main base for the demonstrations, especially in Melbourne where the workers' movement was strongest. The women's liberation movement, though quickly dominated by middle class women, was initially influenced by these factors. It was established by student radicals and had been preceded by an early victory for equal pay won by the left-wing and male-dominated unions.[37] The Aboriginal radicals fighting racism and for land rights were also deeply connected with the left-wing militant unions, which initiated strikes and black bans that were critical to the struggle.[38]

In the US the culture was different. Militant Black workers had played an important role in the anti-racism struggles of the period, and workers were disproportionately opposed to the war. But the trade union bureaucracy was more right wing and the broader workers' movement less radical. Connected to this, the socialist left

---

37. For an overview of the struggle see Wood 2015 and for an important case study see Fieldes 2005, pp.107–131.
38. Foley 2001.

was relatively weak. This meant that the social movements were more dominated by students, and were under greater influence from liberal politics. It is logical, therefore, that it was in the US that precursor currents of identity politics began to develop.

One of these was privilege theory. As Candace Cohn, a revolutionary socialist active at the time, explains: "The specific use of white-skin privilege concepts...to analyse oppression began in one tiny section of the Stalinist left".[39] It was far from mainstream during the radical phase of the movements, when people were looking for points of unity rather than division. Two Maoists, Noel Ignatin and Theodore Allen, coined the term "white privilege" in the 1967 pamphlet "White Blindspot". They argued that:

> The US ruling class has made a deal with the (mis)leaders of American labour and through them with the masses of white workers. The terms of the deal are these: you white workers help us conquer the world, and enslave the non-white majority of the earth's labouring force, and we will repay you.[40]

As Cohn argues, this position was informed by their sectarian politics. They viewed the primary struggle in the world as that "between the revolutionary Third World and US imperialism" and they "counterposed questions of Black and Third World oppression to the American class struggle". More than this, they were explicitly hostile to the struggle of American workers, rejecting the idea that they needed to organise around their own needs and their own oppression and presenting American workers as "little more than potential cheerleaders for Third World Liberation struggles, cheerleaders who must renounce their imperialist privileges – that is, their wages, benefits and possessions".[41]

A similar political approach began to emerge within sections of the women's movement that saw women's oppression as a product of a mutually beneficial alliance between ruling-class and working-class men. This idea coalesced as "patriarchy theory" and became

---

39. Cohn 2020.
40. Allen and Ignatin 1967.
41. Cohn 2020.

increasingly theorised throughout the 1970s.[42] Another precursor of identity politics that arose early on in the women's movement is embodied in the slogan "The personal is political", which emerged alongside the establishment of "consciousness raising" sessions. People often enter politics due to a personal awakening about their own oppression and these sessions, in part, were established to facilitate this. At the same time, many of them were set up with a specific political methodology in mind: women would come to these sessions to discuss their personal problems and then attempt to draw political conclusions from them.[43] These discussions of personal problems could lead people to take social action on the streets or to turn inwards, towards introspection and individualist lifestyle solutions. As the women's movement, along with the other social movements, began to go into decline, this latter strategy became more pronounced.

Another strand of identity politics developed out of a sub-section of the Black feminist movement in the US. As I have mentioned in relation to intersectionality, Black feminism saw itself somewhat in opposition to the mainstream feminist movement and was, throughout the 1960s and early '70s, a more radical variant of it, one that sought to bring questions of race and often class to the fore. However, by the mid to late '70s, Black feminism was becoming dominated by middle-class politics. The Combahee River Collective was one manifestation of this. One of the activities of the collective was to host retreats involving Black, lesbian women, most of whom were academics. A statement written by the collective that came out of one of these retreats in 1977 is widely credited with coining the term "identity politics". While the statement is filled with radical verbiage, and makes reference to the enemy of capitalism and the need for collective action on the road to liberation, it also argues for an isolationist and sectional approach immediately identifiable with modern day identity politics:

> Above all else, our politics initially sprang from the shared belief

---

42. See Bloodworth 1990 for a critique of patriarchy theory.
43. See Hanisch 1970 for an endorsement of "the personal is political" and an account of consciousness raising groups.

that Black women are inherently valuable, that our liberation is a necessity not as an adjunct to somebody else's may because of our need as human persons for autonomy... We realize that the only people who care enough about us to work consistently for our liberation are us. Our politics evolve from a healthy love for ourselves, our sisters and our community.[44]

It is no coincidence that the acute pessimism articulated here, in the argument that those outside of narrow identity categories can never sincerely fight against the oppression of others, surfaced at the time that the struggles of the previous years were in severe decline. It was emblematic of the direction in which many leading figures from the movements were turning.

The period of the late 1970s and early '80s was one of profound defeat for the social movements, for the working class, for the oppressed and for the left. However, this defeat did not play out evenly, and its impacts have been contradictory. The working class was singled out for special punishment. The most important attacks of the early neoliberal period were against working-class organisations, with the explicit aim of crushing rank-and-file industrial militancy. In some countries this was achieved with naked class warfare. In Australia unions were "brought to the table" and union leaders became some of the key peddlers of neoliberalism. But regardless of the method used, across the world the working class was subject to the most aggressive ruling-class attacks since the Great Depression.

The effect on other identity groups was more mixed. The social movements had a major impact on public opinion and succeeded in winning significant reforms for legal equality. These could not easily be wound back. Nor was it in the interests of large sections of the ruling class to do so, at least not openly. Many of the most important reforms, for example equal pay and land rights in Australia, were undermined throughout subsequent decades. On the other hand, some changes continued to take place, especially on secondary issues such as representation, symbolic inclusion, and so on. This

---

44. Combahee River Collective 1977.

was driven by a growing layer of middle-class professionals drawn from oppressed identity groups, who began to find homes in government bureaucracies and the academy. As this layer shifted upwards, they also shifted rightwards, working to deradicalise the politics of oppression and to facilitate the smooth incorporation of a diverse range of identity groups into the system.

Theorising identity politics

As the struggles were sent into retreat, discussions about oppression became more centred in the academy. Academics with a focus on oppression were no longer oriented by vibrant resistance from the oppressed, and they were given opportunities to climb further up the ranks of the academy. As Aguilar argues, this led to a

> pronounced change in the works that emerged expounding on the themes of gender, race and class. The view that a meaningful exposition of their interaction demands an understanding of capitalist operations was soon to be swept away by the collapse of social movements and the onset of conservatism. By the mid-to late 1980s, conservatism was becoming entrenched, necessitating adjustments in intellectual perspectives in order to remain *au courant* in an increasingly complicit academy.[45]

In keeping with the fragmented nature of the university, academics focused on "their own" issues of oppression and developing specialised theories to respond to them. Rather than aiming to understand society in its totality, this approach centred academics' preferred issues and built a partial picture of society around that arbitrary focal point. Core to this was a shift away from materialist methods of analysis and from seeing class divisions as fundamental. It involved a sharp turn towards subjectivism and a focus on ideology, culture and discourse. Framing questions of oppression around identity rather than structures of inequality was the result. As Moran puts it:

> By the 1980s and '90s, identity was completely embedded in the

---

45. Quoted in McLaren 2020.

popular, political and academic lexicon – the language of "identity politics" was *de rigueur* in activist and academic spaces; questions of cultural, racial, gender and sexual identity dominated the social sciences, arts and humanities.[46]

This shift was part of a broader assault on materialism and on Marxism that was underway in the academy and throughout activist milieus and the left, not only in the US but also across Europe and most of the rest of the world. Described by Ellen Meiksins Woods and others following her as the "retreat from class", this phenomenon was the perfect intellectual complement to neoliberalism.[47] Postmodernism and post-structuralism emerged as the main theories that both arose from and justified this shift. Postmodernists reject the existence of objective reality and deny the possibility of objective knowledge. They suggest instead that everything is culturally relative and created through discourse. Society is nothing but a discursive contest over different realities – or more accurately, narratives – none more valid than another.

French philosopher Michel Foucault, while providing some valuable insights into the nature of sexuality and sexual oppression as well as the history of prisons and state punishment, was one of the earliest forerunners of postmodernism.[48] His position on power is one of the most influential aspects of his work. He rejected the Marxist view that power is based on social control and argued, alternatively, that power is dispersed throughout society:

> Power should not be conceptualized as the property of someone who can be identified and confronted, nor should it be thought of (at least in the first instance) as embedded in particular agents or institutions. Power is not a possession of the Monarch or the Father or the State, and people cannot be divided into those who "have" it and those who don't. Instead, power is what characterizes the complex relations among the parts of a society – and the interactions among individuals in that society – as relations

---

46. Moran 2018.
47. Wood 1985.
48. See Humphreys 2017 for a Marxist discussion of Foucault's work on sexuality.

> of ongoing power... Power, then, is...a fluid, all-encompassing medium, immanent in every sort of social relation.[49]

If power is present everywhere and nowhere in particular, then the social layers who own capital and run the state are not especially powerful. This has immediate implications for how we understand oppression. Rather than seeing it as rooted in institutions and structures controlled by the ruling class for their benefit, it has no root source and is reproduced everywhere. By the same measure, the struggle against oppression should not be aimed at capital or the state, nor can it attempt to mobilise the latent power of the working class; such a defined source of power does not exist.

Society, for Foucault and his followers, must be understood, and interacted with, as a fragmented sphere of cultural relationships that are constituted and reconstituted through language and symbols. Therefore, the way to challenge oppression is to deconstruct dominant cultural paradigms, by creating alternative symbols and narratives that centre the oppressed. This is possible because individuals move "fluidly" through the world and, given there are no structural sources of power, all have equivalent social agency. Individuals can therefore discursively redefine themselves and their reality.

In many ways Foucault was the consummate neoliberal theorist. While formally critical of neoliberalism, he saw it as a potentially positive cultural process that allowed for greater fluidity and helped give rise to the "neoliberal self", an individual defined by their consumer choices and their individual choices of identity.[50] In this way he completely ignores the class dimension of neoliberalism, which consisted not primarily of elevating individuals to consumer status but of attacking the ability for the working class to collectively organise. There is also no attempt to deal with the fact that individuals do not all have equivalent "market power" and that neoliberal reforms were about weakening the economic position of the working class. Instead, Foucault accepts the ideology used to

---

49. Foucault 1980.
50. Quoted in Hardy 2021 (from Foucault's 1979 lecture series).

promote neoliberalism as an accurate portrayal of society As Jane Hardy argues in the *International Socialism* journal:

> Foucault uncritically borrowed terms from bourgeois economics that recast workers as "entrepreneurs" possessing "human capital", cutting against the Marxist understanding of the working class as possessing only its ability to labour. Such an understanding collapses the central conflict between workers and capital in the process of production.[51]

Another two theorists who heavily influenced the development of identity politics were self-described "post-Marxists" Ernesto Laclau and Chantal Mouffe. In their key 1985 text *Hegemony and Socialist Strategy* they take for granted Foucault's starting point and argue that society is just an "ensemble" of "discrete elements" not derived from, or even necessarily connected to, material reality. In this view social class has no structural meaning; the way people are organised in relation to production has no real impact on their social agency or the shape of society as a whole.

Despite this renunciation of materiality, Laclau and Mouffe did recognise identity categories as meaningful. This is not because identities are reflective of structural divisions and inequalities – which, of course, don't exist in their framework – but because they are culturally articulated through symbols and language. These identity categories are perpetually unstable because:

> A conception which denies any essentialist approach to social relations, must also state the precarious character of every identity and the impossibility of fixing the sense of the "elements" in any ultimate literality.[52]

This means that identity can be differently articulated at different points, new identity groups can emerge, and others can disappear. For Laclau and Mouffe, who wholeheartedly subscribed to neoliberal talking points, the working class in the 1980s was a disappearing

---

51. Hardy 2021.
52. Laclau and Mouffe 1985, pp.231–232.

identity. It was being politically and culturally marginalised and, therefore, was becoming obsolete. This vacuum would be filled by the cross-class identity groups that had come to the fore during the social movements. These groups would drive the discursive struggles through which the elements of the ensemble could be rearranged. In this sense they argued for something resembling a totality whilst simultaneously defying the very concept:

> This ensemble is not the expression of any underlying principle external to itself – it cannot, for instance, be apprehended either by a hermeneutic reading or by a structuralist combinatory – but it constitutes a configuration, which in certain contexts of exteriority can be *signified* as a totality...an articulated discursive totality, where every element occupies a differential position.[53]

Although elements share no common properties, they can be assembled via discourse, allowing for Laclau and Mouffe's political ambition, which is to build a "hegemonic social project". Within pluralistic democracies, identity groups can be brought together through the use of symbols, and can then win cultural hegemony throughout society. Here we have adherence not only to neoliberal ideology, but to one of the key liberal fantasies about Western capitalism: that it is a system based on pluralism and democracy.

Postmodernism, and its relatives, post-structuralism and post-Marxism, offer no way to overcome, or even challenge, oppression. The spread of these theories served to entrench the conservative drift of movement leaders and activists as they became further removed from significant struggle. At the base of these theories is a profound fatalism that accepts, and even embraces aspects of, the system as it is. By ignoring structural reality, and especially by ignoring structural inequality, these theories relegate struggles against oppression to minor disputations over language and culture, encouraging fragmentation, individualism and passivity. All of these are core elements to the ensemble that is identity politics.

Though Foucault, Laclau and Mouffe developed these theories

---

53. Laclau and Mouffe 1985, pp.254–255.

several decades ago, there has been no serious break with the logic they laid down within the academy. This is particularly the case for theoretical work related to identity and oppression. There have been several theories that have emerged within this field that are described by their proponents as new, and even as representative of a break from identity politics.

Queer theory and intersectionality theory are the two most obvious examples of this. However, there is nothing fundamentally new in these theories. Queer theory, despite its claims to be a radical rejection of identity essentialism, is based, as Marxist Sherry Wolf describes, on "the middle-class idea that we are all oppressed primarily as individuals by other individuals and therefore any resistance to oppression must be individual... In effect, queer is a/n (non)identity that is supposedly unique to every individual".[54] Intersectionality theory similarly claims to be an advance on postmodernism and traditional identity politics. But, as we have discussed, it relies on the same postmodern subjectivism that fails to account for the structural underpinnings of oppression and the fundamental class divisions in society.

Moreover, while some of the contemporary theorists operating within these theoretical frameworks can provide some useful insights through their focused research, there is today an overwhelming prioritisation of personal reflections and anecdotes over attempts to theorise the social basis of oppression.[55] To paraphrase Aguilar, outside of the work of small handfuls of Marxists, the majority of sociologists, feminists, race theorists and queer theorists make the *system* behind oppression disappear, and in so doing, render it, along with the identities and oppressions it creates, eternal and invariant.[56] This, more than anything, is the legacy of the "retreat from class" within the academy.

---

54. Wolf 2009, p.195.
55. See Hill Collins and Bilge 2020 and Kimmel and Ferber 2017 for examples of recent books, on intersectionality and privilege respectively, that reflect this trend.
56. Aguilar 2015, p.215.

Diversifying the system

While these intellectual developments lay the foundations for identity politics, it was the incorporation of the oppressed into the institutions that govern capitalist society that really entrenched and popularised the ideas. The contradictions are dramatic. On the one hand, oppression continues to ruin and damage the lives of millions, and structural inequality and discrimination are baked into capitalist society, along with ideologies of bigotry that back them up. At the same time, modern capitalist society, particularly in the West, has also shown itself able and willing to absorb suitably tamed representatives of oppressed populations into the highest positions in the state and the economy. Opportunities have increasingly opened up for oppressed faces to move into high places, whether it be within government bureaucracies, corporate management structures, or various cultural institutions.

This has led to a degree of diversification among those who rule and manage the system. Though there are growing numbers of CEOs and politicians from oppressed backgrounds, the biggest changes have been in the middle classes, where there are now multiple pathways for career advancement. This is both a generalised phenomenon across nearly all sectors and institutions, and a product of the proliferation of organisations and bureaucracies established specifically to promote the rights of the oppressed. These material shifts have led to increasing political and cultural acceptance of diversity, and the common sense idea that progress against oppression primarily consists of cultural reform and expanding representation. They have also given rise to a layer of professionals and bureaucrats who have an active interest in promoting identity politics.

The process of incorporating more diverse layers into the system began during the social movements themselves. This represented a concession forced on the ruling class by the strength of sentiment generated by the movements. Yet it was also an attempt to neuter them. At the height of the Black rights movement in the US, President Richard Nixon famously used the slogan of "Black Power" to make a case for the cultivation of the

Black bourgeoisie in order to quell the struggle.[57] In this and other ways, far-sighted sections of the ruling class hoped to stabilise their system.

Starting in the 1970s but particularly throughout the '80s and '90s, there was a period of organic experimentation with top-down diversification. Initially it was women who were afforded some opportunities to climb the ranks of state bureaucracies and the corporate ladder. Over time, to a lesser extent, the same began to happen for various racialised minorities and other oppressed groups. Out of this process it was comprehensively proven that the recognition and inclusion of oppressed identity groups posed no threat to the system. Not only did it present no challenge to class inequality, it also presented no fundamental challenge to the oppression of those groups themselves, merely giving it a new gloss.

This process was also readily incorporated into the neoliberal agenda of the time. As members of oppressed groups moved into prominent and powerful positions and whole industries were created around the celebration of particular identities, the individualism at the heart of identity politics came into its own. Identity diversity became a marketing ploy, connected to rampant consumer culture and cynical corporate branding. Much of this involved ghoulishly incorporating the slogans and symbols of the liberation movements that preceded it. No movement underwent this transformation as comprehensively as Gay Liberation. The rise of the pink dollar, and with it the rise of a gay bureaucracy spanning both the private and public sector, has partially redefined the fight for equal rights to one based around individual expression and consumerism.

Over subsequent decades, the capitalist system has only shown more enthusiasm for identity diversity and the corporate co-option of social justice issues and even protest movements. The most recent example is BLM, which was aggressively seized upon by corporate America. Along with advertising gimmicks, this has resulted in a new round of affirmative action within the upper echelons of society, as

---

57. Baradaran 2019.

this *Financial Times* report, written in the aftermath of the 2020 BLM protests reveals:

> As scrutiny of white, male corporate boardrooms intensified during the worldwide demonstrations following Floyd's murder, 148 S&P 500 companies appointed a Black director, up from just 52 appointments in the same period a year earlier. From July 1 2020 to May 19 2021, a third of newly appointed directors were Black, up from 11 per cent from the same period a year earlier... Nasdaq has proposed new listing rules that would require companies to have two diverse directors – including one who self-identifies as female and one who self-identifies as Black or another under-represented minority group.[58]

The value of identity diversity for the capitalist system goes further than "woke" corporate brand building. It is also key for the political branding of a particular section of the ruling class. It has allowed sections of the establishment to present themselves as progressive while presiding over obscene levels of inequality and injustice. Again, this was particularly useful during the neoliberal period which saw both inequality and injustice increase sharply. Nancy Fraser describes the role played by the new "progressive spirit" of identity politics in this period:

> Exuding an aura of emancipation, this new "spirit" charged neoliberal economic activity with a frisson of excitement. Now associated with the forward-thinking and the liberatory, the cosmopolitan and the morally advanced, the dismal suddenly became thrilling. Thanks in large part to this ethos, policies that fostered a vast upward redistribution of wealth and income acquired the patina of legitimacy.[59]

This progressive posturing continues to be favoured by a section of the political class, as well as the liberal media outlets that back it. This is not a minority current within the ruling class. Despite the

---

58. Temple-West 2021.
59. Fraser 2019, p.16.

fact that there continues to be a vocal and well resourced right wing that coheres itself on the basis of opposing social justice and identity politics, the tide of establishment opinion is flowing in the other direction. Joe Biden's performatively diverse cabinet appointments are an example of this. In Australia, the Victorian Labor government, led by Daniel Andrews, is ostentatiously "progressive", and takes every opportunity to demonstrate its identity politics credentials. For example the government's high profile infrastructure project of building level crossings on the train line is adorned with symbols of its supposed commitment to diversity and equality. The project has its own gender affirmation policy, a focus on engaging women in the project, is proudly "Steminist", has committed to incorporating Aboriginal culture into the design and construction of the crossing, has a program to recruit Indigenous, disabled and refugee young people to the workforce, has a trans Inclusion Capability Officer assigned to the project, and has a podcast dedicated to issues of identity inclusion run out of the project.[60] Even governments and political parties that are not concerned with presenting themselves as progressive are often willing to engage in harmless virtue signalling in relation to particular oppressed groups.

The benefits of diverse integration and representation for the ruling class go much further than public relations. Over the past 50 years it has proven very useful as a way to carry out with impunity policies that entrench oppression, to neutralise sections of the population that may otherwise be adversaries and to build political and electoral power bases. The process of state integration of various identity groups means that there is a permanent pool of existing and aspiring bureaucrats and professionals, drawn from these groups, who have similar interests to governments in generating superficially progressive demands for recognition and representation.

In Australia, the federal Whitlam Labor government began the incorporation of social identity groups into the state. This was both in response to the social movements and was part of Whitlam's broader agenda of shifting the ALP from its historical roots in the workers' movement to being a party oriented to and led by the

---

60. Level Crossings Removal Project 2020.

progressive middle class. One of the first groups to be integrated was women, beginning in the early 1970s. The Whitlam government appointed Elizabeth Reid as the world's first women's advisor to a head of state in 1973. Reid fitted the bill perfectly as a senior tutor of philosophy at the ANU and associated with the bourgeois Women's Electoral Lobby (WEL).[61] WEL represented the right wing of the women's movement and from the outset its activities had received positive encouragement from sections of the ruling class.[62] Reid's appointment marked not just the entrance of women into positions of authority that they had previously been excluded from but the emergence, more specifically, of the femocrats: a layer of feminist bureaucrats and academics who occupy positions that are specifically about representing women's interests from a feminist perspective. Feminist sociologist Anna Yeatman describes it in this way:

> It is a labour market which depends on the persisting legitimacy of the ideology of feminism. It is the political force of feminism which leads governments to create these advocacy positions and which demands of their female occupants a commitment to feminist ideology.[63]

This process was not isolated to women. A study into the proliferation of identity politics in the Australian state conducted by Elizabeth Fells describes that, from the 1970s onwards: "Australian governments began to be active in the area of social identity, introducing a number of social identity portfolios – Aboriginal Affairs, Islander Affairs, Ethnic Affairs, Youth, the Aged and Multicultural Affairs".[64] These portfolios were tied to budgets and, often, departments which existed ostensibly to "ensure that the concerns of the groups are considered and addressed. In addition, they implement policy and program responses to promote equity and provide support services to assist these groups".[65]

61. Arrow 2017.
62. Women's Electoral Lobby, n.d.
63. Yeatman 1990, p.61.
64. Fells 2003, p.104.
65. Fells 2003, p.105.

On the surface, the turn away from state spending on services and welfare that characterised the neoliberal period appears to conflict with the expansion of these bureaucracies. Throughout the 1980s and '90s various programs, services and bodies relating to social identity underwent severe funding cuts or were sometimes dissolved entirely. But despite money being taken out of programs that had some benefits for the oppressed, the facade of social inclusion was largely maintained. There was a growing recognition that having particular identity groups on board could be used to help to sell right-wing policies.

For example, the femocrats were useful supporters of the Hawke government's attacks on the working class in the mid 1980s. Hawke established a body called the Social Security Review, headed up by feminist sociologist Bettina Cass. The review led to a number of regressive welfare reforms, including a policy that required custodial single parents (mostly women) to pursue non-custodial parents (mostly men) for child support payments before becoming eligible for welfare assistance from the state. This measure resulted in redistributing the burden of welfare off the state and onto the working class. It also played to the right-wing anti-working class prejudices about "deadbeat dads" and it made it harder for working-class women to break ties with men, including those who had been abusive. For Cass and other middle class feminists it was celebrated as a means to redistribute wealth from men to women.[66]

Both sides of politics in Australia have recognised the value of this model. An interesting observation made by Fells based on the data she collected is that the funding and maintenance of portfolios and departments related to social identity do not necessarily correlate with the expected politics of the major parties: "social identity activity, innovation, emulation and commitment do not appear to have a partisan explanation".[67] Both the ALP and the Liberal party have repeatedly cut funding to services and programs related to social identity, and have consistently invested, both politically and financially, in identity-based

66. See Yeatman 1990 for a useful discussion of this.
67. Fells 2003, p.109.

communities according to their political interests. Although the ALP ties itself more to social identity groups who are perceived as being connected to progressive left campaigns, such as the LGBTI lobby, both parties have successfully used the banner of "multi-culturalism" to recruit bureaucrats from migrant constituencies. Both parties have also successfully cultivated their own layer of loyal Indigenous spokespeople and bureaucrats. In exchange, the members of oppressed groups who become staffers, committee members and heads of agencies can become the active oppressors of their own communities.

Bringing representatives of Aboriginal communities to the table has other benefits too, particularly around the issue of land rights. Negotiated outcomes with trusted leaders can give governments and corporations important access to land and resources by drawing a line around complicated processes and mapping out a mutually agreed pathway that avoids decades-long court cases. This simul-taneously provides certainty for investors and state officials while integrating the struggle for land rights into state structures, all under the guise of "community consultation".

The treaty process currently being conducted by the Victorian government is a good example of these dynamics. Negotiations are conducted between the state government and traditional owner groups/corporations. Officially the state government is working with a range of these groups, but in reality the organisation they have fostered and that heads up the process is the undemocratic and untransparent Federation of Victorian Traditional Owner Corpora-tions (FVTOC). This body receives major funding and a seat at the table to be part of a "nation building" project spanning five years, that consists of making decisions about the land that have to be constantly scrutinised and approved by the Department of Premier and Cabinet. The government refers to this as "self-determination", yet in reality it represents a way for a select group of Aboriginal-run corporate entities to advance and to become delivery partners for the state government, while also offering the ALP a way to build up a layer of loyal Black bureaucrats.[68]

---

68. *Self Determination Reform Strategy*, n.d.

Beneath this layer of higher level bureaucrats, there are several layers of "street level bureaucrats" working in social services, the community sector and identity-based NGOs. Though many of these organisations can administer useful services and roll out programs that can provide important support to oppressed groups, they are locked into the system in several ways. They are mostly dependent on the state for funding and are beholden to a moderate political outlook necessary to fulfill the requirements of contracts and grant applications. Within all of these organisations and the wider milieu they are part of, there are many opportunities for career advancement for those who play their cards right. This means promoting a set of politics about oppression and identity that are individualistic and conservative. Talking about the system responsible for oppression is anathema; instead the focus is on piecemeal and superficial cultural reforms. An example is the recent overhauling of the Safe Schools program, a government-funded intervention aimed at making schools more inclusive for LGBTI students. In the face of homophobic and transphobic attacks from the right-wing media, the contract of Marxist co-founder of the program Roz Ward was terminated and the content watered down so as to make it clear that there is no intention to make political arguments about oppression, only a focus on fostering respectful interpersonal behaviour.

Another example of the inbuilt conservatism that has come along with the institutionalisation of oppressed identity groups is the recent craze of cultural diversity and safety training. A whole industry has been developed around the idea that the only way to combat oppression is to educate people about cultural tolerance. The books, seminars and ongoing programs that aim to do this are generated by many of the identity-based organisations that I have described, both in the public and private sectors. Bosses everywhere are happily taking up these programs. The individualised and symbolic nature of their teachings means that bosses and managers can easily attain certification as an "anti-racist" or "LGBTI-inclusive" workplace, while at the same time acquiring another set of tools and language to intimidate and bully workers with. Robin DiAngelo's *White Fragility,* a book that has been widely used as part of corporate anti-racism workshops, provides a perfect example of this dynamic. Louise O'Shea describes:

> What to many might be an encouraging sign in the apartheid-like conditions of the US – that most workers forced by their boss to undertake diversity training frequently express a pre-existing opposition to racism and take umbrage at the corporate diversity trainer accusing them of it – is to DiAngelo simply evidence of ever more stubborn fragility and egregious prejudice. We're supposed to relish her tales of dragging workers over the coals for minor transgressions and delight in their transparent displays of fragility and "racial stress" when they object. But this is no win for anti-racism. It *is* a win for the parasitic diversity industry. It *is* a win for bosses who have bought themselves some protection against discrimination proceedings through hiring people like DiAngelo.[69]

The Marxist alternative

Identity politics is a dead end for the oppressed and anyone looking to seriously challenge injustice. Marxism offers an alternative. As a theory it is based upon understanding society as a unified, contradictory totality. This means that it can be used to explain the complexity and variability of different forms of oppression, while also recognising that each exist within and because of the domination of one social class by another. These social relations point to where power lies and how it might be challenged and the material basis of oppression done away with.

Oppression and capitalism

Oppression will continue to exist, in different forms, so long as the structures of capitalism remain. Even when certain effects of oppression are mitigated through reforms and cultural shifts, and even when some individuals or layers drawn from oppressed groups can alleviate their own oppression, the system will continue to generate

---

69. O'Shea 2020.

divisions in the population, backed up by both structural inequality and ideology. Examining the core dynamics of this system is an essential starting point for understanding oppression.

The fundamental social division in the capitalist system is between workers and capitalists, because this division is the basis for production, without which there would be no society. Production is controlled by the capitalist class and is based upon the frenzied and competitive accumulation of capital in order to make profits. The minority ruling class depends upon the exploitation of the labour of the majority, the working class, to make these profits. Given this precarious dynamic, oppression is an indispensable tool to maintaining the economic and political power of the ruling class. The working class itself is socially discriminated against and oppressed in multiple ways, for example the denial of access to decent healthcare and housing. In addition other groups are marked out for oppression in order to serve the interests of particular sections of the capitalist class. Some forms of oppression, for example against women, pre-dated capitalism and were incorporated because they proved useful.[70] Others arose with capitalism, such as the development of biological racism out of slavery.[71] Other forms have emerged as a result of imperialist campaigns, both historic and recent; think for example of Islamophobia. And still others have emerged as a result of existing structures of oppression, for example homophobia and transphobia developing from women's oppression.

It is this oppression, and the reactionary ideologies created to justify it, that generate identities in the first place. In order to justify the singling out of particular groups for specialised forms of discrimination, arbitrary characteristics are amplified and presented as justification for that treatment. For example, the use of Africans as slaves on the cotton plantations laid the basis for the idea of black skin inferiority. With the creation of such racism came the creation of race-based identity groups.

As well as being imposed from above in this way, group identification is also often reinforced and even cultivated from below. For

70. Bloodworth 1990.
71. See Williams 1944.

example, struggles against racism have been strengthened by, and in some ways necessitate that, those being racially discriminated against identify themselves as collective. Some identity groups have been very consciously forged by the oppressed group itself. Gay people, and more recently trans people, have had to fight to define themselves as an identity group, rather than as people medicalised for behavioural deviance. In all cases, social identities are more than cultural; they are categories that are rooted in the social relations of capitalism, and it is because of this that they take on a real material basis and become significant political categories. And, at the same time, these categories are inherently contradictory and imperma-nent, and will be abolished under a classless society that has no need for oppression.[72]

Class, while being the basis for identity groups itself, is also a major factor in the composition of all other identity groups. All identity groups, except for groups based on class, consist of people from different classes. The class divisions within identity groups have become more substantial, and more politically important, in correlation with the diversification of the system, and over the time that identity politics has become more entrenched. Because it is now more possible for members of oppressed groups to be part of the ruling class and the middle class, the wealth divisions within these groups are widening.[73] But more important and indicative of these wealth differentials are the differentials in social power between classes. Those who have substantial decision-making power over their own lives and the lives of others are bosses and leading politicians and, to a lesser extent, managers and high-rank-ing professionals and bureaucrats. The fact that more people from oppressed groups now occupy these positions is one of the clearest indications that the favoured strategy of identity politics, expanding representation, does not have a meaningful impact on the lives and

---

72. See Garnham 2018 for a more detailed discussion of identity categories and their contradictions.
73. See Peetz and Murray 2017 for a discussion of how the wealth gap between women in Australia has widened. See Kochhar and Cilluffo 2018 for data about the gaps between high earning and low earning sections of the Black, Asian, and Latino population in the US.

forms of structural oppression experienced by substantial layers of people within those same groups.

Moreover, those who have power and receive privileges as a result of their position in the system have an interest in preserving these positions and in preserving the system itself. In this sense it is precisely the success of identity politics, in winning more diverse representation, that undermines its core political premise: that non-class identity is the fundamental line of social division.

Solidarity and Revolution

Solidarity is the enduring catch-cry of all serious struggles against oppression. Solidarity is often misunderstood today as a term that refers to symbolic gestures of support or as interchangeable with the concept of allyship, which is about passive support and assumes a fundamental opposition of interests between identity groups. It is neither of these things. It is fundamentally about power not symbolism, and it is based on an understanding of the unity of interests between different layers of society, embodied most importantly in the working class.

Solidarity is firstly the process linking together struggles in order to make each more powerful. This is a necessity because of the system that we are up against, and it is especially important for groups that are the most marginalised. It is impossible for example for Aboriginal people, trans people, or refugees to win liberation without significant support from other social layers. They are simply too small and socially peripheral to confront the ruling class and its state. It is necessary for social movements that aim to achieve meaningful victories to win over significant minorities of the population, if not majorities, to their cause.

This is not to say that within particular movements the leadership and input of those directly affected by oppression is not crucial. In fact, precisely because of these experiences, they will often be the most motivated to initiate struggle and are uniquely placed to inspire others to join the movement. But it is not sufficient to then call on others to gather around like a cheer squad. Building solidarity is not based upon moral chastisement, nor on sympathetic paternalism. It is based fundamentally on the recognition of shared interests and a collective, democratic struggle.

One of the main ways that a common interest between oppressed groups is established is by recognising the common oppressor. Even without a thoroughgoing analysis of capitalism, this often becomes clear to people, especially in the course of struggle. Different groups are oppressed by the same governments, scapegoated by the same media outlets, attacked by the same police. As well as having a shared experience of oppression at the hands of these forces, when our side deals a blow to them on one front, it is a victory for all of us. For instance, forcing a government into backing down on one regressive policy can often have the effect of making them less willing to go after other groups, as well as giving the broad left more confidence. And because there is a tendency for struggle to break down the hold of bourgeois ideology, the more that people engage with struggles not just against their own oppression, but also against that directed at others, the more that the ideas that can divide us are undermined.

The movement that the term solidarity is most closely associated with is that of the working class. There are a few reasons for this. Firstly, it is the working class that, of all oppressed groups, has the most social power. In fact it has a social power that is unique across the entire span of human history, the power to stop the flow of profits at the point of production. This economic strength gives working-class demonstrations of solidarity serious muscle. On multiple occasions the deployment of this power has played a crucial role in struggles against oppression, for example winning equal pay and land rights in Australia. Today there is a lack of awareness of this important aspect of solidarity, both because identity politics has pushed people's conception of struggles against oppression into the realms of culture and symbols, and because the workers' movement is weak. This in turn makes all of our other struggles weaker. Workers still make up the majority of most demonstrations today, but usually as individuals, rather than as an organised force prepared to take strike action or initiate industrial bans on behalf of the movement. It is undoubtedly the case that such actions would have substantially strengthened the recent BLM protests, the climate strikes, and every other social movement.

The other reason that the working class generated the solidarity principle is because it is a collective class. Workers have no power as individuals; they can only threaten production collectively. This is true within workplaces, but the collectivity of the working class goes beyond this. Under capitalism, production is divided into millions of processes carried out across millions of workplaces. The more that workers can link up with struggles at other workplaces, the more power they wield.

A couple of important things flow from this. One is that workers have an interest in extending solidarity to other groups of workers, and in breaking down sectionalism and the appearance of competition between different sections of the working class. Another is that workers have an interest in overcoming all forms of oppression. The working class consists of all other oppressed groups, but also oppression sows ideological and political divisions which are a barrier to collective struggle.

For workers to get to a point where they have enough power to challenge the ruling class for power, thus overcoming their oppression, there needs to be a high level of democratic coordination across many sections of the class. For this to happen, workers need to be conscious of the oppressive and divisive tactics of the ruling class, and to have a strong sense of common purpose with groups of workers from many different identity backgrounds. In this sense, conscious political opposition to oppression is not distinct from or an optional add-on to class consciousness. High levels of class consciousness – meaning an ability for workers to understand their collective class interests and objectives – necessarily implies opposition to oppression. This is not to say that workers come to this consciousness automatically. Struggle, and even more so, revolution, play a big part in shifting views. Also crucial is political intervention and argument.

More than just challenging oppression throughout the course of struggle and revolution, workers represent the only force that can eradicate oppression altogether. A socialist society ruled by the working class will necessarily be run democratically and without arbitrary forms of discrimination. This comes back again to the nature of the working class in relation to production. It has no ability to exploit any other layer because it does all of the work. And it is a majority class that is only powerful as a collective. Therefore under workers' rule there is no material basis for arbitrary divisions or discrimination. Without these material underpinnings, there is no reason for cultural norms and backward ideas that spring from inequality to continue. After a period of development under socialism, oppression in all of its forms will be eradicated. Where capitalism cannot survive without oppression, socialism cannot survive with it. The working class is the only force capable of building such a society and in this way it represents the only universalising social agent, capable of delivering its own emancipation and, at the same time, liberation for all of humanity.

The Marxist tradition

Marxists have always taken seriously the task of eradicating oppression, and have been at the forefront of struggles against it. For Marx and Engels it was essential to understand as much as possible about oppression. They dedicated serious time to investigating the roots of women's oppression, understanding the struggles of various national minorities, coming to grips with the dynamics of colonialism in India, slavery in the US and the occupation of Ireland. All of this was important for building a picture of capitalist society and its historical development. However, more important than these specific areas of research were their theoretical breakthroughs about the core dynamics of capitalism.

It is this that has made Marxism the most enduring framework through which the specificities of oppression have come to be understood. Over the past 150 years, every serious attempt to theoretically understand any form of oppression has involved an engagement with Marxist ideas. And I would argue that the most useful insights have been those developed by Marxists. It would not be difficult to provide a lengthy list but I will limit myself to a few examples: Eric Williams' brilliant 1944 work tracking the dialectical entwinement of the roots of racism, the slave trade and the birth of industrial capitalism; Walter Rodney's study *How Europe Underdeveloped Africa* (1972); CLR James' work on the Haitian revolution and on the struggles for Black rights in the US; the contributions of British Marxists

Chris Harman and Lindsay German on the history of the nuclear family and its centrality to the oppression of women; the more recent work by a range of Marxists into the roots of trans oppression. The argument raised, often within academic circles, that Marxism cannot explain anything but the economy and that other theories must be used to understand oppression, is not based in fact. It instead comes from an anti-Marxist, liberal political perspective and is justified on the basis of identity politics moralism. It is a shame that some socialists have capitulated to this sentiment and themselves argue for a watering down of Marxism by calling for it to be merged with counterposed liberal theories like intersectionality.

Not only have Marxists always taken seriously the task of theorising oppression but also, and intimately connected to this, the real Marxist tradition is one of fierce resistance to every manifestation of oppression. Revolutionary Marxists can be found all throughout the history of capitalism on the frontlines of the struggles of the oppressed. From the revolutionary communards of Paris 1871 to the recent struggles for abortion and women's rights in Latin America, we have fought against women's oppression. From the Russian revolution through to the struggle for Palestinian liberation today, we have fought for the liberation of oppressed nations. From the anti-slavery revolts through to the ongoing fights for Black and Indigenous rights today, we have stood against racism. From opposing the bloodshed of World War I to opposing the crimes of the Western wars in the Middle East, we have stood against imperialism.

Some of the threads of this tradition have been contorted by Stalinism, but the real Marxist tradition has nothing to do with support for authoritarian regimes and the oppressive crimes that have been committed in their name. The real Marxist tradition is summed up by the often quoted statement from Lenin that the revolutionary party must become the "tribune of the people".[74] In some ways more important today is the rest of the quote from which this phrase is taken. It is Lenin's argument that the revolutionary party must become the "tribune of the people" and must "react to every manifestation of tyranny and oppression, no matter

---

74. Lenin 1902.

where it appears, no matter what stratum or class of the people it affects".

The second part of this quote is often left out however. It is not enough, as the first part in isolation suggests, for socialists to stand shoulder to shoulder with the oppressed. The task of revolutionaries is to use this position to argue for the oppressed and their supporters to take up the vantage point of the only force that can win true liberation. As Lenin goes onto say, revolutionaries must

> generalise all these manifestations and produce a single picture of police violence and capitalist exploitation; who is able to take advantage of every event, however small, in order to set forth *before all* his socialist convictions and his democratic demands, in order to clarify for *all* and everyone the world-historic significance of the struggle for the emancipation of the proletariat.[75]

In other words, in order to win liberation for each, we need liberation for all, and it is only the struggle of the working class that points the way. It is the role of organised socialists to fight for this perspective in practice, and to provide the theoretical and political arguments for it.

References

Adichie, Chimamanda Ngozi 2021, "It is obscene: a true reflection in three parts", *Chimamanda.com*, 15 June. https://www.chimamanda.com/news_items/it-is-obscene-a-true-reflection-in-three-parts/

Aguilar, Delia D 2012, "Tracing the roots of intersectionality", *Marxist Review Online*, 12 April. https://mronline.org/2012/04/12/aguilar120412-html/

Aguilar, Delia D 2015, "Intersectionality", *Marxism and Feminism*, edited by Mojab Shahrzad, Zed Books, pp.203–220.

Allen, Ted and Ignatin, Noel 1967, "White Blindspot", Marxists.org. https://www.marxists.org/history/erol/ncm-1/whiteblindspot.pdf

---

75. Lenin 1902.

Amedi, Roj 2017, "The Victorian Pride Centre's brown and black stripes are a bandaid solution", *SBS*, 26 August. https://www.sbs.com.au/topics/pride/agenda/article/2017/08/24/opinion-victorian-pride-centres-brown-and-black-stripes-are-bandaid-solution

Australian National University Students Association 2021, "Agenda – ANUSA Student Representative Council (SRC) 4", Motion 6.8: Department consultation, p.4, 11 August. https://anusa.com.au/pageassets/about/meetings/SRC-4-Agenda.pdf

Arrow, Michelle 2017, "Working inside the system: Elizabeth Reid, the Whitlam government, and the women's movement", Australian Women's History Movement, 5 March. http://www.auswhn.org.au/blog/elizabeth-reid/

Baradaran, Mehrsa 2019, "The real roots of 'Black Capitalism'", *New York Times*, 31 March. https://www.nytimes.com/2019/03/31/opinion/nixon-capitalism-blacks.html

Bloodworth, Sandra 1990, "The Poverty of Patriarchy Theory", *Socialist Review*, 2, Winter, https://marxistleftreview.org/articles/the-poverty-of-patriarchy-theory/

Cohn, Candace 2020, "A Marxist Critique of the theory of 'white privilege'", *Red Flag*, 4 July. https://redflag.org.au/node/7254

Combahee River Collective 1977, Combahee River Collective Statement. https://www.blackpast.org/african-american-history/combahee-river-collective-statement-1977/

Crenshaw, Kimberle 1989, "Demarginalizing the Intersection of Race and Sex: A Black Feminist Critique of Antidiscrimination Doctrine, Feminist Theory and Antiracist Politics", *University of Chicago Legal Forum*, 1, 1989.

Duke, Jennifer 2021, "Gay parents frustrated by 'biased' father and mother questions in census", *Sydney Morning Herald*, 12 August. https://www.smh.com.au/politics/federal/gay-parents-frustrated-by-biased-father-and-mother-question-in-census-20210811-p58hsj.html

Dzotsi, Emmanuel 2020, "The least you can do", *Reply-all*, 162 [Podcast], GIMLET, 18 June. https://gimletmedia.com/shows/reply-all/z3h94o

Fells, Elizabeth 2003, "The proliferation of identity politics in Australia", *Australian Journal of Political Science*, 38, 1.

Feltscheer, Mitch 2017, "VIC Pride centre adds Brown & Black stripes to LGBTIQ Flag for P.O.C", *Pedestrian*, 1 August. https://www.pedestrian.tv/news/vic-pride-centre-adds-brown-Black-stripes-lgbtiq-flag-p-o-c/

Fieldes, Diane 2005, "Equal pay: The insurance industry struggle, 1973–75", *Rebel Women in Australian Working Class History*, edited by Sandra Bloodworth and Tom O'Lincoln, Red Flag Publications.

Foley, Gary 2001, *Black Power in Redfern 1968–72*, PhD thesis, Victoria University. https://vuir.vu.edu.au/27009/1/Black%20power%20in%20Redfern%201968–1972.pdf

Foucault, Michel 1980, *Power/Knowledge: Selected Interviews and Other Writings*, edited by Colin Gordon, Pantheon Press.

Fraser, Nancy 2019, *The Old Is Dying and the New Cannot Be Born: From Progressive Neoliberalism to Trump and Beyond*, Verso.

Garnham, Sarah 2018 "Against Reductionism: Marxism and Oppression", *Marxist Left Review*, 16, Winter. https://marxistleftreview.org/articles/against-reductionism-marxism-and-oppression/

Gilio-Whitaker, Dina 2018 "Unpacking the Invisible Knapsack of Settler Privilege", *Beacon Broadside*, 8 November. https://www.beaconbroadside.com/broadside/2018/11/unpacking-the-invisible-knapsack-of-settler-privilege.html

Hanisch, Carol 1970, "The personal is political", *Notes from the Second Year: Women's Liberation,* edited by Shulamith Firestone and Anne Koedt. https://webhome.cs.uvic.ca/~mserra/AttachedFiles/PersonalPolitical.pdf

Hardy, Jane 2021, "The myth of the 'neoliberal self'", *International Socialism Journal*, 171, Summer. http://isj.org.uk/neoliberal-self/#footnote-10080–8-backlink

Hill Collins, Patricia H 2000, *Black Feminist Thought: Knowledge, Consciousness and the Politics of Empowerment* (2nd edition), Routledge.

Hill Collins, Patricia and Sirma Bilge 2020, *Intersectionality* (2nd edition), Polity Press.

Humphreys, Jordan 2017, "Foucault's 'History of Sexuality': A Marxist Engagement", *Marxist Left Review*, 14, Winter. https://marxistleftreview.org/articles/foucaults-history-of-sexuality-a-marxist-engagement/

Humphreys, Jordan 2021, "Capitalism, colonialism and class: A Marxist explanation of Indigenous oppression today", *Marxist Left Review*, 21, Summer. https://marxistleftreview.org/articles/indigenous_oppression/

Hyde, Justine 2020, "Interview: Craig Silvey on writing from a trans perspective: 'A novelist is required to listen, to learn'", *The Guardian*, 30 September. https://www.theguardian.com/books/2020/sep/30/craig-silvey-on-writing-from-a-trans-perspective-a-novelist-is-required-to-listen-to-learn

IWD Narm Melbourne [Facebook page]. https://m.facebook.com/IWDNarrmMelbourne/

Jefferson, Dee 2021, "Dark Mofo festival weathered the backlash against Union Flag and a First Nations boycott, but the impact will be lasting", ABC News, 6 July. https://www.abc.net.au/news/2021–07–06/dark-mofo-tasmania-arts-festival-impact-backlash/100252542

Jensen, Robert 2005, *The Heart of Whiteness: Confronting Race, Racism and White Privilege*, City Lights Publishers.

Karanikolas, Amber 2019, "Where are all the disabled academics?", *Overland Journal*, 15 July, https://overland.org.au/2019/07/where-are-all-the-disabled-academics/

Kimmel, Michael and Abby Ferber 2017, *Privilege: A Reader*, Routledge.

Kochhar, Rakesh and Cilluffo, Anthony 2018, "Income Inequality in the US Is Rising Most Rapidly Among Asians", Pew Research Center, 12 July. https://www.pewresearch.org/social-trends/2018/07/12/income-inequality-in-the-u-s-is-rising-most-rapidly-among-asians/

Laclau, Ernesto and Chantal Mouffe 1985, *Hegemony and Socialist Strategy*, Verso.

Lenin, Vladimir Ilych 1902, *What is to be done?*. https://www.marxists.org/archive/lenin/works/1901/witbd/iii.htm

Level Crossings Removal Project 2020, "Training for the Future online resources". https://levelcrossings.vic.gov.au/careers/training-for-the-future/podcasts

Lynch, Caz 2021, "Asking for our blood", *Overland*, 22 March. https://overland.org.au/2021/03/asking-for-our-blood/

Maddison, Sarah 2019, *The Colonial Fantasy: Why White Australia Can't Solve Black Problems*, Allen & Unwin.

McIntosh, Peggy 1989, "White Privilege: Unpacking the Invisible Knapsack", *Peace and Freedom Magazine*, July-August.

McLaren, Jesse 2020, "Marxism and Intersectionality", *Monthly Review*, Spring.

Moran, Marie 2018, "Identity and Identity politics: a cultural materialist history", *Historical Materialism*, 26 (2).

Onus, M [@Meriiki] 2020, [Tweet], *Twitter*, 31 May. https://mobile.twitter.com/MerikiKO/status/1267019594822070272

O'Shea, Louise 2011, "The campaign for equal marriage rights", *Marxist Left Review*, 2, Autumn. https://marxistleftreview.org/articles/the-campaign-for-equal-marriage-rights/

O'Shea, Louise 2020, "White Fragility is a Corporate Cult", *Red Flag*, 23 July. https://redflag.org.au/node/7283

Peetz, David and Georgina Murray 2017, *Women, Labor Segmentation and Regulation: Varieties of Gender Gaps*, Palgrave Macmillan.

Purnell, Derecka 2020, "Why Black progressive women feel torn about Kamala Harris", *The Guardian*, 12 August. https://www.theguardian.com/commentisfree/2020/aug/12/kamala-harris-joe-biden-vp-Black-progressive-women

Rosebourne, Stuart 1988, "Economic management, the Accord and Gender Inequality", *Journal of Australian Political Economy*, 23. https://www.ppesydney.net/content/uploads/2020/05/Economic-management-the-Accord-and-gender-inequality.-under-the-Hawke-government.pdf

Ross, Selina 2021, "MONA's David Walsh apologises for Dark Mofo flag controversy as calls grow for Carmichael to go", ABC News, 24 March. https://www.abc.net.au/news/2021-03-24/david-walsh-apology-over-mofo-blood-flag-controversy/100023988

Self Determination Reform Strategy n.d., Victorian State Government. https://www.delwp.vic.gov.au/aboriginalselfdetermination/self-determination-reform-strategy

Táiwò, Olúfémi O 2020, "Being in the room privilege: elite capture and epistemic deference", *The Philosopher*, 108, Autumn. https://www.thephilosopher1923.org/essay-taiwo

Temple-West, Patrick 2021, "US companies step up pace of hiring black directors in wake of George Floyd murder", *Financial Times*, 26 May. https://www.ft.com/content/79252e5b-1242-496b-9371-100bcc1327a3.

Williams, Eric 1944, *"Capitalism and Slavery"*, University of South Carolina Press.

Wolf, Sherry 2009, *Sexuality and Socialism: History, Politics, and Theory of LGBT Liberation*, Haymarket Books.

Women's Electoral Lobby, "WEL history: How it Began" n.d. https://www.wel.org.au/wel_history

Wood, Ellen Meiksins 1985, *The Retreat From Class: A New "True" Socialism*, Verso.

Wood, Katie 2015, "Australian unions and the fight for equal pay for women", *Marxist Left Review*, 10, Winter. https://marxistleftreview.org/articles/australian-unions-and-the-fight-for-equal-pay-for-women/

Yeatman, Anna 1990, *Bureaucrats, Technocrats, Femocrats: Essays on the Contemporary Australian State*, Taylor and Francis.

DARREN ROSO

Trotsky and the early years of the French Communist Party

Darren Roso has published in *Overland, Revueperiode, Contretemps* and *Vientosur*. His forthcoming books, *Daniel Bensaïd: From the Actuality of Revolution to the Melancholic Wager* and *Karl Korsch: Heretical Marxist of Weimar Germany*, are to be published by Brill Historical Materialism.

Lenin and Trotsky – from 1917 on these two names had always been mentioned in one breath. Moreover, whereas Lenin had remained distant, Russian, admirable but incomprehensible, Trotsky had caught the imagination of the French working-class movement. He had become theirs, and his involvement in the affairs of the PCF had made him the best-known Bolshevik leader in France.

– Robert Wohl, *French Communism in the Making, 1914–1924*

I N THE FIRST PLACE, why write about Trotsky and the early years of the French Communist Party?[1] Well, Trotsky's writings on France were simply excellent. Trotsky was one of the most important theorists of revolution in the West, and his intervention into the French section of the Comintern set revolutionary politics to work in real time during the post-war upsurge of class struggles. Trotsky's intervention into the early years of the French Communist Party (PCF) shows the pitfalls of centrism and entrenched reformism

---

1. I would like to thank Ian Birchall, Isabelle Garo, Omar Hassan and Tom Bramble for reading earlier versions of this article, a talk presented at Marxism 2021. Their comments were helpful.

within a party proclaiming itself revolutionary, the possibilities and new perspectives opened for working with revolutionary syndical- ists, and how to translate the experience of the Russian Revolution into the Western European social formations.

Trotsky's role in the early years of the PCF gave answers to key difficulties of revolutionary tactics and strategy in the West: the united front, struggle for working-class hegemony, relation of the working class to other social strata, combining the war of position – patient medium-term struggle, with the war of manoeuvre – insur- rection against the bourgeois regime, and revolutionary intervention.

This is qualitatively distinct from the idea, popularised by Stalin- ism, of mechanically applying "Leninism" to French conditions. Instead, Trotsky had an intimate knowledge of and acquaintance with the French labour movement, its leaders and many militants, and combined this with his decades of revolutionary work to make the case for how the early French Communist Party could act in the concrete situation to overthrow capitalism.

The reality was that the early French Communist Party was not a revolutionary party in a genuine sense; there was an absence of an actual revolutionary party even *after* the Tours Congress of Decem- ber 1920, a combination of factors hindering the development of the party in a revolutionary direction prior to the definitive victory of Stalinism in French conditions (1925–27). This is significant because it shows the differences between what a party says of itself, that it, a communist party affiliated to the Comintern taking itself to be revolutionary, and what it actually is in its material and practical reality. Trotsky's interventions were about dealing with this fact. The tragedy of the early years was that prior to Stalinism the party was not a cohered and revolutionary organ, while the Bolshevisation process that claimed to carry out that work eventually produced one of the most authoritarian Stalinist parties in the world and defini- tively buried the prospect of the party actually becoming a genuinely revolutionary party instead of an appendage to Moscow.

This tragedy is substantiated beyond reasonable doubt by the newest books like Julien Chuzeville's *A Brief Revolutionary Moment: The Creation of the Communist Party in France*, as well as the older, classic books like Alfred Rosmer's *Moscow under Lenin*. Trotsky intervened into this tragic situation in real time. In the interval between 1920 and 1924 Trotsky had to *politically convince* elements of the party how to act if it were to make gains and wage revolutionary struggle. There is a lot to learn from Trotsky's effort to convince the French party what actual Marxist and revolutionary politics consists in.

But I have to make a qualification: I'm writing about what one could call *the fallible Trotsky think-tank*. I am against imaginary historical counterfactuals and I am not suggesting that if only the PCF had followed every one of Trotsky's words to the letter, then everything would have been settled. In the relatively open horizon between the foundation of the PCF and Stalinisation, counting some short four years, there was a distance within the concrete situation itself between an ideal revolutionary party and the actual reality of its practice; a distance between a mass workers' party and revolutionary program in practice and much heterogeneity of political orientations from left to right within it. It is within the distance between the revolutionary ideal and the paltry reality, a distance very concrete and historically specific, that *politics can be thought.* That's what we look at here, Trotsky's political thought; the *fallible Trotsky think-tank* as he intervenes into the French section.

The war years

Trotsky was in Paris during the First World War, active among the Russian exiled socialists, the French syndicalists and the left-wing socialists, who wanted to draw a line of opposition to the war against the French Socialist Party's and trade union bureaucracy's support for it.

Trotsky recollected in his memoirs how Jules Guesde, head of the so-called Marxist wing of the French Socialist Party, "proved to be capable only of laying down his untarnished moral authority at the altar of 'national defence'", while the leader of official syndicalism, Jouhaux, "'denied' the state during peacetime, only to kneel before it during war".[2] The Socialist leaders joined the war cabinet and

---

2.   Trotsky 2012b, p.245.

viciously campaigned against its opponents; the syndicalist trade union bureaucracy put a lid on strikes.

Yet there was resistance. Alfonse Merrheim, leader of CGT metal workers, set up the Committee for the Resumption of International Relations (CRRI) in early 1916; it was a loose network. Before the war, Merrheim had written seriously on the economic underpinnings of the inter-imperialist rivalry. The CRRI was small, but committed to criticising the Socialist Party and the syndicalist leadership of the CGT and doing underground illegal work to propagandise against the war. These people were incredibly courageous, they faced jail time or being sent to the war front for their activities.

Trotsky was in close contact with the most advanced anti-war activists in France, Alfred Rosmer and Pierre Monatte, who came from the revolutionary syndicalist tradition. They held weekly meetings, which Trotsky attended. Though uneven, these people were undoubtedly influenced by Trotsky. Rosmer and Monatte, who were the editors of the paper *La Vie Ouvrière*, were revolutionaries, committed to working-class self-activity and self-emancipation. Trotsky also met the revolutionary poet Marcel Martinet. Of Monatte, Trotsky said, he "never for a moment inclined toward reconciliation with militarism or the bourgeois state".[3] Rosmer "stood closer to Marxism fundamentally than to the Guesdists".[4] And in Martinet, Trotsky wrote, "the artist lived side-by-side in him with the revolutionary, and both knew how to act in unison".[5] As a side note, Trotsky read Martinet's play, *La Nuit,* while aboard the military train during the civil war. He then wrote a preface to it, in which he said Martinet "is a communist trained in the school of the syndicalist group of *La Vie Ouvrière*, that is to say, in a good school".[6]

That says everything.

La Vie Ouvrière and other left-wing socialists had never yet encountered the kind of socialism Trotsky stood for. Trotsky

---

3.   Trotsky 2012b, p.247.
4.   Trotsky 2012b, p.247.
5.   Trotsky, quoted in Paizis 2007, p.39.
6.   See Trotsky's preface here: https://www.marxists.org/francais/trotsky/livres/litterature/nuit.htm. Translation by Darren Roso.

"represented a type of Socialism that Rosmer and Monatte had never seen...[he] talked of making a revolution as if [he] meant it".[7]

Ambiguities and political differences came through in the debates in the Committee for the Resumption of International Relations. The leading Zimmerwaldians – those who attended and prepared the September 1915 anti-war gathering in Zimmerwald – of the French left were committed to the existing unity of the CGT and the Socialist Party, and many were pacifists, well to the right of the Zimmerwald left. Lenin's revolutionary approach to the imperialist war was foreign to them, and Alfonse Merrheim, who went to Zimmerwald as a moderate pacifist, had already predicted the outbreak of war in his articles for *La Vie Ouvrière* and argued for working-class resistance to it, yet he later shifted to the right and become an opponent of the Bolsheviks. Lenin had no real contact with the French anti-war opposition either.

Trotsky's role in the Committee mattered; he took up the fight against the moderates in it. The moderates said that you couldn't criticise the Socialist Party too much, you couldn't criticise the vacillating leaders of the Centre too much, you couldn't reject the imperialist-patriotic socialists too much, because at the end of the day, once the war ends – many socialists thought the war would be over very quickly – there'd be the same old unity within the Socialist Party and the trade unions. The Internationalist Menshevik, Julius Martov, who was also in Paris at the time, initially close to Trotsky, encouraged these fantasies of unity. But Trotsky campaigned for a more intransigent line, one that would take the fight up to the imperialist socialists as well as the centrists, like Longuet – Marx's grandson who gave the war socialists political cover. Trotsky's campaign for a more active approach to the war won him the support of left-wing socialists, syndicalists and anarchists; one of the classics of the time, Fernand Loriot's *Zimmerwald Socialists and the War*, was clearly influenced by Trotsky. Before Trotsky's exile from Paris, he was able to win the most courageous of the French left towards a more clear-cut Marxist revolutionary orientation, but this was by no means complete.

---

7.   Souvarine, quoted in Wohl 1966, p.135.

Tours: the fruit of a missed encounter

As the war accumulated death, stinking corpses and broken souls, strikes began to mount, soldiers' revolts broke out, and the anti-war opposition within the Socialist Party, led now by Loriot and Souvarine, was gaining more support and in view of a majority. This posed a political problem: do you break with the Socialist Party, because of the presence of centrists like Longuet and the social-patriotism of Renaudel and Blum, or do you remain in the party, fight for a majority and try somehow to transform the party from within?

To briefly outline the sequence of events: the Second Congress of the Comintern was held in July 1920, where the Bolsheviks argued to settle accounts with reformism in the Socialist Party, and the Tours Congress, taking place in December of that year, voted as a majority to become the official section of the Comintern, shaping the French labour movement for decades to come. The pro-war, intransigent reformists like Léon Blum stormed out, split and formed their own smaller group, and in effect, the Communist Party was the largest party of the French working class. To its right, a smaller reformist current tenaciously tried to rebuild itself. The Communist Party was in a good position to deliver the reformists harder knockbacks to destabilise their influence in the working class.

Trotsky was for a split initially, but the Committee of the Third International, the official French section of the Comintern, made the case for staying in the Socialist Party until they won the majority. I think it was Rosmer who first convinced Lenin of this point. The Committee of the Third International, made up of Boris Souvarine, Loriot, Rosmer and Monatte, was already affiliated to the Comintern, with its members active as syndicalists and/or in the Socialist Party.

There was a regroupment going on between the left of the Socialist Party and the revolutionary syndicalists. Many, like Loriot and Marthe Bigot, were rank-and-file activists in the teachers' union. The revolutionary syndicalists were absolutely central to the founding and further dynamics of the Communist Party. There was much crossover between syndicalists and the Socialist Party activists: some syndicalists were inside the Socialist Party already while others were outside, but joined the party after Tours. For the syndicalists outside the Socialist Party, after Tours the PC had to prove the party was new, different and ready to fight to overthrow capitalism. Because of that, the Tours Congress was not just the outcome of an internal battle within the Socialist Party, but a combined effort of left-socialists and revolutionary syndicalists.

Importantly, however, the founding of the Communist Party at Tours involved leaders who knew which way the wind was blowing, but were not sincere revolutionaries. Many of them were freemasons, pacifists, careerists of all types. Two names stand out in the early Communist Party: Marcel Cachin, who was the editor of *L'Humanité* in the Socialist Party, and Ludovic-Oscar Frossard, its secretary. They went into the Communist Party after Tours, maintaining their posts, pretty much unchanged. Here's what Rosmer said of the two:

> Cachin was a man devoid of character, who had been an ultra-chauvinist at the beginning of the war, running errands to Mussolini on behalf of the French government. Then he had swum with the stream, and now professed to be a sympathiser with Bolshevism, although, in his articles, he had condemned the October rising and basically loathed the Bolsheviks. Of Frossard it is enough to say...[that] starting out with sympathies for Zimmerwald, he was to end up as a minister under...Pétain [the Vichy regime that welcomed the Nazi occupation].[8]

Faced with this difficulty, Trotsky and Lenin thought the best course ahead was for the fusion of revolutionary syndicalists and the left to gather their forces and drive out, defeat or neutralise the right and the centre of the new party. This was a precondition for revolutionary action. They had no illusions in these unreliable people. Lenin summed it up to Trotsky: "It would be good...to drive out all these weathercocks, and to draw into the party the revolutionary syndicalists, the militant workers, people who are really devoted to the cause of the working class".[9]

The centrists and entrenched reformists in the new party had to be fought. Time was already running out. Not only was France at the centre of the European counter-revolution intent on smashing the

8. Rosmer 2016, pp.33–4.
9. Trotsky 1971.

Bolsheviks and workers' power, internally, the class struggle *began to decline quickly after 1920*, especially after the May Day general strike was ruthlessly defeated: 22,000 rail workers were sacked and three-quarters of the CGT's union members left in the year that followed the defeat.

Trotsky pointed out, after the war, that social democracy could save capitalism, helped by the absence of a revolutionary party. The post-war radicalisation would never lead straight to working-class victory in Western Europe. Trotsky argued, "It is all too obvious today just what was lacking for victory in 1919 and 1920": *a revolutionary party*. "Not until the powerful post-war mass ferment had already begun to ebb did young Communist parties begin to take shape, and even then, only in rough outline".[10]

In a certain sense, the Tours Congress was symptomatic of a *missed encounter*: nothing at all in the world predestines elements to combine, for a revolution to take shape. Historical time has its share of plasticity and chance. Revolutionary politics thinks through how the elements of a conjuncture can come together, combine, and overthrow capitalism.

The Communist Party after Tours had to build with the *missed encounter already behind them*, with the class struggle on the downturn. This was the problem revolutionaries in the West failed to solve in time. It would be wrong to say all hope was lost, because political intervention could still shape events. From this vantage point, the time Trotsky put into the French section was very precious. Nothing preordained the subsequent failures of the French section to build and make good on the already missed encounter; even if the revolutionary chance was missed, more medium- and longer-term perspectives of building a revolutionary party in the West were on the table.

Given space limitations I can only outline four parts of the political debates: syndicalism, the centrist illusions in bourgeois democracy, the united front debates and cohering an interventionist party after the Le Havre strike.

---

10. Trotsky 2017, p.9.

Syndicalism

Despite the genuine convergence of syndicalists and socialists, Trotsky insisted on the need for political, ideological and theoretical clarity. After the October Revolution, the progress represented in the Charter of Amiens became an obstacle to further advance. The Charter of Amiens was proposed in 1906, agreed on the autonomy of the trade unions from political parties; it was the Erfurt Programme for the syndicalists, articulating direct class struggle against the bosses to the expropriation of capital. The syndicalists split, some travelled to the right, others to Bolshevism. Some, like Monatte, wavered about where to go. Monatte did not join the Communist Party until 1923, which was sectarian. Monatte was one of the best and most principled militants, but he didn't understand the importance of the party even after the October Revolution, when the question was settled.

Trotsky took responsibility for unity with the syndicalists. But he did not neglect political clarification. To remain a syndicalist after the October Revolution was to fail to incorporate the knowledge and experience, the genuine leap forward class struggle politics took, from that event.

Trotsky spelled out four mistakes the syndicalists made. First, they denied politics, ignoring the role of the state. This is a slight caricature. Fernand Pelloutier, the foremost organiser and theoretician of revolutionary syndicalism, made the case that the *Bourse du Travail* movement be nationally coordinated to overcome the economic and corporatist nature of local trade union struggles. Pelloutier may have denied politics but even his articulation of reform and revolution was political. The pre-war CGT had already featured debates between its reformist and revolutionary wings over the relation between trade union militancy and the state. The anti-war campaigns in the lead-up to the First World War, culminating in the joint campaign between the SFIO and the CGT against "the Three-Year Law" were about politics, not crude economics.

Second, they failed to draw the full implications of the "active minority". The active minority was essentially the vanguard of the class, the most militant section of workers who were waging struggle against the bosses, the best of the Amiens Charter, so to speak. If the new Communist Party were to be genuinely revolutionary, they would be its backbone.

Third, certain anarcho-syndicalists incorrectly separated the party and the trade unions, one of the impasses of the Charter of Amiens, which stipulated that politics should have no place in the trade unions. But this meant it was *impossible* to coordinate revolutionary politics at the rank and file level to defeat the trade union bureaucracy. A bourgeoisified trade union bureaucracy had emerged in the CGT before the outbreak of war; it effectively opposed the outcome of the Tours Congress and would split the trade unions to smash the revolutionary rank and file sympathetic to the SFIO. Yet even before Tours, a reductive conception of the party and class blinded many syndicalists to the need to defeat the ossified reformist bureaucracy in the Socialist Party, who as the unchallenged *political* representatives of the working class could play a decisive role. Not all syndicalists or former syndicalists had a reductive conception of the party and the trade unions; as Ian Birchall rightly points out, Rosmer had presented the CGT as a "hybrid" organisation functioning as a political party and a trade union at the same time.[11]

Lastly, the syndicalists prioritised the trade unions over the soviets when it came to the problem of *power*; there was a debate, therefore, about the organs of working-class rule, inevitably posed after the October Revolution.

The theory and practice of the revolutionary syndicalists, beyond a certain limit, remained subordinate to *bourgeois hegemony*. Trotsky's entire polemic against revolutionary syndicalism provides us with an example of how the *development* of a political doctrine takes place: throughout the course of history, a doctrine is tested, illuminated, reaches a threshold through its own contradictions that need resolution. This is what happened to syndicalism faced with the historical experience of the October Revolution. Trotsky's Marxism presented a *whole* project of revolution as an alternative; it was necessary to safeguard the best and most militant traditions of the syndicalists, while also settling accounts with their retrograde dogmas.

---

11. See Birchall 2020.

Centrist fudge

If Trotsky, through bonds of friendship and politics, was sympathetic to the syndicalists, he was utterly contemptuous of the centrists and the right.

Centrism in the Communist Party was *a politics of wasting time*, attached to the bourgeois republic, unable to set to work a politics based on revolutionary class struggle. Revolutionary opportunities are precious, yet vanishing moments. Then, and only then, does bourgeois political domination break down for a time. In such moments, decisiveness and timeliness are vital, lest the moments slip away and vanish. After the Tours Congress, class struggle was on the downturn, the revolutionary moment was slipping away. But in this context, the centrist leader of the party, Frossard, spent "two years giving [the Bolsheviks] a lesson in the art of evasion", an approach that, consciously or otherwise, gave the bourgeoisie of France time to regroup.[12]

The centrists weaselled their way through the "21 conditions", the measures designed to chase all forms of opportunism out of the ranks of the newly forming communist parties. The 21 conditions, which were not voted on at Tours, were supposed to settle admission to the Comintern: they called for a complete break with reformists and the expulsion of all those who were against the dictatorship of the proletariat. They were designed to ensure that those like Longuet and Blum were shut off from the Comintern. Yet it was an illusion to think that a set of regulations could stem such opportunism. Rosmer later explained: "But what [the Bolsheviks] didn't and couldn't know, was the lengths to which these men would go with their skilful manoeuvres, for they had received their training in the practices of parliamentary democracy. They could pull more tricks out of the bag than the suspicious Russians could ever imagine".[13] Frossard would agree to a principle in Russia, then in France turn his back on it.

The centre and right wing reject the united front

The debate over the united front was a concrete example of the severe limitations of the centre and the right. Opposition to the united front

---

12. Rosmer 2016, p.82.
13. Rosmer 2016, p.82.

policy within the ranks of the Communist Party came most forcefully from the right and the centre, the then majority. Rejection of the united front came at a time when the imperialist-socialists, like Léon Blum and Renaudel, had minority support within the working-class. This was different from Germany, for instance, where the Berlin left was against the united front. In France, it was the former revolutionary syndicalists who were for the united front because they were for mobilising mass class struggles. In a certain sense, the right wing of the Communist Party rejected the united front policy because, if they were to enter into a pact of common struggle with the outright reformists, it might have just shown how similar they were to each other. The right wing of the Communist Party refused to do this.

If the united front policy was about *exposing* the imperialist-reformist-socialists before the masses, the right wing and the centrists of the Communist Party refused to do this. That meant in practice that an important section of the Communist Party refused to show how the imperialist-reformist-socialists were opposed to revolution; the centrists had no answer to this, as they tailed the right. They sidestepped the fact that the working class must be shown the difference between the imperialist-reformist-socialists and Communists in practice and its own experience in struggle. That the right wing opposed the united front is telling: they knew the policy wasn't about the polite cohabitation of different organisations, but a struggle over hegemony within the workers' movement. The wearisome idea that the united front as a broad collaboration of the left for unity's sake is as naive as it is devoid of concrete political thought.

One of the fundamental arguments Trotsky made was against the so-called Left Bloc: a bloc between bourgeois radicals and social democrats with a view to forming government. The Left Bloc continued the principle of Republican unity going back to the French Revolution and was also a precursor to the Popular Front of the 1930s, and like that, a capitulation to bourgeois hegemony. To seriously continue republican unity meant to graft working-class politics onto the bourgeois revolution and therefore miss its specificity. The Left Bloc was a bloc between workers and a certain section of the bourgeoisie against another section of the bourgeoisie. Against this, Trotsky argued for a bloc of *all workers* against the bourgeoisie;

Trotsky's alternative was to build a bloc between all sections of the working class against the united power of capital. Central to Trotsky's orientation was working-class unity in opposition to the logic of class collaboration. This logic animated the Paris Commune, and I want to quote Trotsky to give a vivid idea of the united front in this context:

> The most glorious page in the history of the French proletariat – the Paris Commune – was nothing else but a bloc of all the organisations and shadings within the French working class, united against the bourgeoisie. If, despite the establishment of the united front, the Commune was quickly crushed, then the explanation for this is above all to be found in the fact that the united front did not have at its left flank a genuine revolutionary, disciplined and resolute organisation, capable of quickly gaining leadership in the fire of events.[14]

A thoroughgoing, consistent and bold revolutionary independence of the working class is at stake in this debate, able to combat the different forms of reformism in practice. In reality, Trotsky, on behalf of the Comintern, was waging a polemic against the majority of the French Party; it was a case where Comintern intervention was absolutely essential to getting politics right.

Party fatalism

Earlier I said that centrism is a politics of wasting time. Centrists can be very active in their wasting of time, with endless meetings and motions and debates, but they waste time from the point of view of taking workers' struggle forwards to victory. Towards the end of 1922, this became very clear when the party was tested in the face of the Le Havre strike.

Le Havre is a port city in the north of France. Metal and shipyard workers came out to fight wage cuts in June, when management announced a ten percent reduction of pay.

The Le Havre strike grew in intensity between July and August,

---

14. Trotsky 2019, p.200.

drew in not only the metal workers and shipyard workers, but port workers and sailors. It grew to 40,000 workers before turning into a general strike across the Le Havre region, called by the local unions. After the downturn of class struggle from May Day defeats from 1920 onwards, the Le Havre events were very, very significant. The strike was pivotal, and on 26 August, four workers were killed, the police and the military were called in, and 15 more were injured. The CGTU, the PCF-aligned trade union, called a general strike on the 29th in response, which fell flat.

The Communist Party failed the Le Havre strike. They did nothing for weeks, months even, but then called a general strike which they completely failed to prepare for and was a fiasco.

In the months leading up to the Le Havre general strike and the murder of workers, the Communist Party did nothing. Again, it was a 110-day strike. The syndicalist prejudices went hand in hand with centrist passivity. The centrists said, "The Party cannot undertake anything in this arena", and the syndicalists in the party also said the Party could not intervene into a trade union, economic matter; in the end, the murder of workers was "economics".[15] The Party didn't build authority among the strikers. The local mayor, a bourgeois radical, intervened, and others did too. Trotsky said: "Only one party did not intervene as such in this strike", the Communist Party![16] Then when the police murdered workers, the CGTU and the Party issued a slogan: the general strike! To reiterate: The Party that remained "a totally irrelevant entity", in the major battle between the Le Havre workers and "bourgeois society as a whole", supported an unprepared slogan for a general strike.[17] Newspaper clippings from *L'Humanité* were supposed to carry off a general strike. The result was a total farce, a total debacle. In this example, passivity and empty slogans went together.

These opponents of socialist revolution, the Blum socialists and trade union bureaucrats, were saved by newspaper clippings calling for a general strike. Of course, when the general strike was called with absolutely no preparation, with only 24 hours' notice, the reformists

---

15. Trotsky 2012a, p.971.
16. Trotsky 2012a, p.971.
17. Trotsky 2012a, p.976.

had a pretext: it is too risky to strike now. The failure of the French Party's orientation caused demoralisation, sent a section of workers into passivity, and strengthened the hands of the reformists and trade union bureaucratic syndicalism. The party would never regain this time.

Now, I'm interested in the political alternative, what the French Party should have done, in Trotsky's words. His proposals were entirely realistic. They show what interventionism means, in the distance between the ideal and the reality. I quote Trotsky at length; his political logic has universal relevance:

> In France, such slogans [like the call for a general strike] are formulated much more readily than in any other country. They are experts at it. What was necessary was to explain to every single working man and woman, the agricultural workers, the peasant men and women, what had happened in Le Havre. In Le Havre, they killed four workers, after having killed a million and a half in the War. It was necessary to display, where possible, photographs of the dead workers, and photographs of their daughters and sons.
>
> Correspondents had to be sent there who understand such questions and the lives of the workers, comrades capable of going to the families of the dead workers, sharing their anguish, and explaining the entire appalling story to the working class. It was necessary to mobilise thousands of the best Communists and revolutionary syndicalists, in Paris and across the country – to do this together with the CGTU, and send them everywhere, not just in every corner of Paris but across the entire country, in the cities and countryside, in order to carry out intensive propaganda. At the same time, leaflets and appeals had to be printed up with three or four million copies, in order to report on the events to the working class, explaining that we cannot let this crime pass without protest.[18]

Trotsky put forward a revolutionary realpolitik that could set the working class into motion through consistent political struggle:

---

18. Trotsky 2012a, p.977.

explain patiently, meticulously organise, trust that the working class may be receptive to this and would want to fight. The course of action would have also set the united front into operation; building on the outrage could have put the reformist socialists and trade union bureaucrats onto the back foot, putting the questions to them: What will you do? What do you propose to do against the bosses who just killed workers? Are you going to fight? The "slaughter in Le Havre [would have] represented for our opponents an almost fatal blow", Trotsky argued, if questions like this were built on.[19] If these questions had "been repeated day after day, by the party and trade union propagandists and agitators at every street corner, in every corner of the country, in every village where a working man or woman is to be found, during the course of one or two weeks. That would really have been a great experience for the workers' movement".[20]

Trotsky drew the conclusion that "the French Party has not yet achieved the absolute independence and freedom in action and organisation from capitalist society that it needs in order to utilise the crisis of this society freely and fully".[21] Of course, this was a problem, the party was not free to act, not able to intervene in the course of events; it was running on the spot as the world continued to move around it, where the bourgeois crisis passed quickly over to stability. Trotsky's standard of judgment for a genuine revolutionary party was that "the entire life of the Party must express a series of actions that form a chain, and this chain must lead to the greatest action of all, the conquest of power by the proletariat".[22] This was the ideal, but the reality of the Party, with Frossard at its head and centrists and reformists within the Party apparatus, was entirely different; remaining syndicalist prejudices contributed to the malaise too. The Party needed moulding, experience and time to rise to the revolutionary level; in the end, time ran out.

---

19.   Trotsky 2012a, p.978.
20.   Trotsky 2012a, p.978.
21.   Trotsky 2012a, p.963.
22.   Trotsky 2012a, p.965.

Final thoughts

It has only been possible to scratch the surface of Trotsky's contribution to the early years of the French Communist Party in this article. There were many things that could not be covered, but are valuable: Trotsky's attitude towards the anti-colonial struggle, winning over the peasantry, debates over the trade union movement, dealing with contradictory consciousness among workers and the struggle against the rise of Bolshevisation and Stalinism. I have left aside certain salient moments of the PCF's history, like the left leadership of 1923 when the Party campaigned against the occupation of the Ruhr, which needs its own balance sheet. The above is a glimpse of Trotsky's political and revolutionary thought when in a practical state, pertaining to the advanced capitalist countries. The French social formation, no doubt, was unique and changed substantially over the course of the twentieth century; in many ways, it was also unlike other advanced capitalist countries of the time, owing to its combination of revolutionary history, a particular agrarian context and the development of its modern state apparatus. Bourgeois political domination was fortified and strong – the early PCF had to counter the strategies deployed by a bourgeoisie experienced in the revolutionary overthrow of the feudal regime, the French Revolution, as well as the violent consolidation of modern capitalism through the repression of the 1848 revolutions and the 1871 Paris Commune. Yet the fallible Trotsky think-tank shows how class struggle politics can be thought. It laid some pointers as to how revolutionary struggle in the advanced capitalist countries can be waged and the pitfalls it faces. Without providing all the answers, the most important question Trotsky asked nevertheless remains with us: how to politically unify the working class's capacity to deliver a mortal blow to the bourgeois class and cast its rule into the annals of bygone history?

References

Birchall, Ian 2020, "The Comintern's encounter with syndicalism", *Marxist Left Review*, 20, Winter. https://marxistleftreview.org/articles/the-cominterns-encounter-with-syndicalism/

Chuzeville, Julien 2017, *Un court moment révolutionnaire. La création du Parti communiste en France (1915–1924)*, Éditions Libertalia.

Paizis, George 2007, *Marcel Martinet: Poet of the Revolution*, Francis Boutle Publishers.

Rosmer, Alfred 2016, *Lenin's Moscow*, translated by Ian Birchall, Haymarket Books.

Trotsky, Leon 1971, "The Errors in Principle of Syndicalism" in *Communism and Syndicalism (1923–1931)*, Labour Press Pamphlet. https://www.marxists.org/archive/trotsky/1931/unions/4-errors.htm

Trotsky, Leon 2012a "France Session 28 Comintern, 1 December 1922", from Riddell, John 2012, *Toward the United Front: Proceedings of the Fourth Congress of the Communist International*, Brill Historical Materialism Book Series.

Trotsky, Leon 2012b, *My Life*, Dover Publications.

Trotsky, Leon 2017, *First Five Years of the Communist International: Volume One*, Pathfinder Press.

Trotsky, Leon 2019, *First Five Years of the Communist International: Volume Two*, Pathfinder Press.

Wohl, Robert 1966, *French Communism in the Making: 1914–1924*, Stanford University Press.

LUCA TAVAN

The Italian left and the factory councils, 1919–1920

Luca Tavan has been an active socialist for eight years. He has been involved in campaigns against education cuts, for refugee rights, and in solidarity with Palestine. He is a regular contributor to *Red Flag*, and has produced a series of articles on the *Biennio Rosso*.

THE *BIENNIO ROSSO*, or "Two Red Years" in Italy from 1919–1920, were a key link in the chain of revolutions that swept the world after World War I. A mass workers' movement in the northern industrial centres attempted to launch a decisive struggle against the capitalist class. In the rural south, land occupations by peasants upended centuries-old social relations. The war and social upheaval it generated pointed to the burning need for a new regime capable of overcoming capitalist exploitation, as the revolutionary Antonio Gramsci recognised in August 1920:

> The war has plunged society into such a state of barbarity and demoralisation, heaped so many ruins upon ruins and let loose such a flood of meanness and cowardice, that only a youthful and energetic class, a class that is rich in the spirit of discipline and sacrifice, like the working class, will be able to restore order. Only through its example and through its ability to command, by holding State power firmly in its own hands, will it be able to give back to the apparatus of production and exchange the capacity to feed, clothe and house our people.[1]

---

1. Gramsci 1977, p.232.

In this period of crisis and hope, the October revolution in Russia appeared like a lightning flash. October clarified what political form this new power would take: a form of council democracy based on the mass organisations of the workplace, known in Russia as the soviet. The workers' councils in Russia showed that it was possible to smash the alienated and bureaucratic state apparatus and engage the majority of the exploited population directly in the administration of society.

Trotsky's founding *Manifesto of the Communist International* made it clear that the Bolsheviks considered this innovative political form to have universal relevance:

> To strengthen the Soviets, to raise their authority, to counterpose them to the state apparatus of the bourgeoisie – this is today the most important task of the class-conscious and honest workers of all countries... Through the medium of the Soviets, the working class will be able to come to power most surely and easily.[2]

But moving beyond these pronouncements to assimilate the lessons of the Russian Revolution was a difficult task, one which put all sections of the revolutionary left in Italy to the test. Harder still was applying the insights from this high point of class struggle to the different conditions they found themselves in. How can workers' councils emerge in countries dominated by large, legal trade unions? Was industrial organisation alone enough, or did the working class need to forge an alliance with other social strata? Perhaps most importantly, what relationship should the councils establish with the workers' existing political organisations? The Italian Socialist Party (PSI), as the largest and most prestigious organisation on the left, cast a shadow over every strategic debate.

This article represents an attempt to rescue the memory of the *Biennio Rosso* from a series of distortions. The factory council movement and occupations of 1919–1920 were eventually transformed by the Stalinised Communist Party (PCI) into its foundational myth. Antonio Gramsci, one of the period's most important

---

thinkers, had his political thought edited and warped posthumously to give intellectual ballast to the reformist project of the post-war PCI. In more recent decades, Gramsci has been recast in a number of new roles – as the intellectual antecedent of postcolonial theory, as an anthropologist, and philosopher of linguistics. These interpretations, informed by a generation-long period of political defeat, see Gramsci as a tool for contemplation, rather than a source of revolutionary insight.

Since the 1970s, an alternative current has emerged attempting to rediscover Gramsci's militant political activity in the *Biennio Rosso* in order to reclaim him from the parliamentary socialists and armchair academics. This has done much to connect Gramsci's later work to the lessons he learned during the factory council movement, and set the experiment in workers' democracy which shook Italian society where it belongs, in the context of the revolutionary wave of 1917–1923.

But in rightfully reclaiming Gramsci as part of the revolutionary Marxist tradition, the complexities and inadequacies of his early politics have often been overlooked. A revolutionary theorist and organiser of such magnitude deserves sincere and ruthless criticism. I will attempt to establish Gramsci's real relationship with the factory council movement, and challenge the myth that the councils were a product of Gramsci's unique genius. The factory councils emerged out of a dialectical interaction between radical intellectuals looking for the basis to build a proletarian state, and workers organically driving towards the creation of new institutions in their struggle to defend their living standards and class independence in the struggle against a war which threatened to consume everything.

Gramsci's role in the council movement was contradictory. On the one hand, it illustrated the need for revolutionaries to intervene into the day-to-day battles of the class, as Gramsci's small *L'Ordine Nuovo* group played an important role in catalysing and giving coherence to workers' struggle. On the other hand, it revealed serious limitations in Gramsci's understanding of "dual power". Gramsci took to heart the radical democratic impulse of the Russian Revolution and its focus on the emancipatory role of the working class. But his conception of the councils failed to fully grasp the primacy of *politics* in the revolutionary process. Under his leadership, they failed to develop beyond workplace organisations to form the embryo of a socialist state.

Another objective of this piece is to engage more seriously with the politics of Amadeo Bordiga, a central leader of a rival tendency that developed simultaneously alongside Gramsci's "council communism". Much of the revolutionary Marxist tradition has failed to engage seriously with Bordiga's conception of social change and his theory of the party. In most histories of the heroic period of the Communist movement, Bordiga has been restricted to a walk-on role as one of Lenin's foils during the debate on parliamentary participation at the Second Comintern Congress. But he was a hugely consequential figure within Italian Communism, who attempted to carve out an anti-reformist political tradition from as early as 1912. After 1917 Bordiga saw himself as the most strict applicant of "Leninism" to Italian conditions. But his role during the *Biennio Rosso* would reveal differences with the Bolsheviks which ran deeper than the tactical question of parliamentary participation.

I will also look at the relationship between radicals in the Socialist Party and the revolutionary syndicalists who were organised outside of it. Too often attempts to understand the development of revolutionary politics in the *Biennio Rosso* have focused solely on the factional divisions that emerged in the PSI during the radical upsurge. But the syndicalists, organised through the USI union federation and numerous local working-class institutions, represented a mass force which argued forcefully against the Socialist Party's reformism and more than once put their words into action. Radicals in the Socialist Party attempted to establish a political relationship with them, but largely failed to influence syndicalist militants positively in the direction of Marxism. This failure represents one of the great missed opportunities of the period.

The working class and the war

The First World War shook Italy's unstable political structure and produced a profound radicalisation. At the front, 615,000 Italians were killed, half a million disabled and a million wounded. Peasant conscript soldiers, forced to risk their lives for scraps of territory they'd never heard of, returned to Italy radicalised. Demonstrations emerged frequently against military conscription and domestic political repression, and spontaneous protests against food shortages quickly took on a political dimension. Before the war had even broken out, working-class resistance to militarism posed a serious challenge to the Italian state and its imperialist objectives. In June 1914, the shooting of anti-militarist demonstrators in Ancona sparked a general strike. The movement spread rapidly, with barricades going up in all the major cities. In the Emilia region, a workers' republic was declared as state power effectively collapsed. It took brutal force for the authorities to restore order.[3]

Alongside these brave but doomed uprisings, deeper shifts were taking place in Italian society which would lay the foundations for the *Biennio Rosso*. The productive demand generated by the war led to a massive expansion of the working class in the northern "industrial triangle" of Turin, Milan and Genoa. In Turin alone, the number of factory workers doubled during the war years, to reach 150,000.[4] Automobile production rose from 9,200 in 1914 to 20,000 in 1920. The value of FIAT's capital rose from 17 million lire to 200 million, while the industrial colossus Ansaldo employed 111,000 workers with a capital of 500 million.[5] A labour shortage gave workers in core industries enormous leverage, which translated into increased confidence and willingness to struggle.

At the same time, war production massively intensified the oppression of workers at the point of production. "Committees for industrial mobilisation" were created to institute martial law in the factories. Workers were tied to their jobs under threat of imprisonment, or deployment to the trenches. Strikes were outlawed, and all disputes were forcibly arbitrated through the committees.

Rather than fighting this shackling of the workers' movement, the leaders of the FIOM, the metalworkers' union which represented the vast majority of those working in war industries, chose to collaborate. This allowed the union leaders to have more of a say in the management of the plants – at the cost of sacrificing the living

---

3.   Behan 2003, p.16.
4.   Gluckstein 1985, p.163.
5.   Spriano 1975, p.44.

standards and organising rights of their members. A breach opened up between the FIOM officials and their rank and file.

To create a pressure valve for discontent, the union leaders encouraged the spreading of "internal commissions", bodies similar to shop stewards' committees in Britain or Australia. The commissions were bodies made up of leading unionists who had responsibility for representing the grievances of the workforce to management.

Initially, the internal commissions were highly constrained by the trade union leaders. They would present an official union "list" of five trusted workers to mass meetings, which would simply be ratified. Their vision for the commissions didn't go beyond helping to enforce negotiated agreements. But the commissions also had a formally independent existence, which created space for workers who wanted to use them to promote class struggle. Increasingly, radicals began looking toward the commissions as one of the few spaces for intervention in the repressive climate of the war. By early 1916, workers were organising to exert rank-and-file control over their representatives, as one young FIAT engineer recounts:

> In the course of their agitation the workers would nominate a commission to put demands to management. At the end of the negotiations the commissions reported back and workers would examine the part each representative had played... Thus there grew a process of creating a recognised workplace leadership.[6]

The war thus heightened the tensions between militants and moderates, revolutionaries and reformists in the union movement. It also sharply exacerbated the divisions in the political organisations of the workers' movement – the most important of which was the Italian Socialist Party.

The Italian Socialist Party

Formed in 1892, the Italian Socialist Party (PSI) was the first attempt to build a socialist workers' party throughout Italy. In line with the model of the Second International parties, the PSI was a broad

---

6. Quoted in Gluckstein 1985, p.171.

organisation. But unlike the German Social Democratic Party (SPD), it was highly ideologically heterogenous. Arfé has summarised its worldview as a combination of

> souped-up republicanism, adjusted corporatism, diluted anarchism, and a lively but rather woolly faith in the socialist destiny of humanity... [S]uch faith was the moral and ideological bond capable of holding together the new team and forging it into a single body.[7]

The party's ideological wooliness was combined with a loose-knit structure allowing the utmost autonomy for local groups.

The first tendency to take clear form on a national basis was the reformist wing of the party. Italy's Rome Congress in 1900 took place at the height of the SPD's Bernstein debate. Turati, the intellectual leader of the reformists, refused to join Bernstein's project of revising the fundamentals of Marx's theory of history. But the political strategy he advocated was strikingly similar: the workers' movement would achieve the transition to socialism peacefully and gradually, through the framework of parliament.

Numerically, the reformists always remained a minority in the party, but their strength came from implantation in important bureaucratic institutions. The reformists dominated the PSI's intervention into the town councils, the trade unions and its parliamentary grouping, which by 1913 had 52 elected deputies. The development of an openly reformist tendency within the workers' movement was intentionally fostered by a wing of the Italian state. Giovanni Giolitti, the prime minister for an almost uninterrupted period between 1900 and 1914, ruled Italy on behalf of a small cast of liberals, who played Socialists, Catholics and Nationalists off each other through endless coalitions, attempting to integrate and incorporate all.

The culmination of the reformist socialists' collaboration with Giolitti came in 1911. When the Italian state intervened aggressively into what is now Libya to snatch territories from the decaying

---

7.   Arfé 1977, p.15.

Ottoman empire, the Socialist parliamentary group gave support to Giolitti's government in exchange for an expansion of the vote. Giolitti gloated that the PSI had "sent Karl Marx up into the attic".[8] The brutality of the war – this was the first time that aerial bombardment was ever used on an occupied population – split the party. One group of MPs supported the war, while the party leadership and the General Confederation of Labour declared a general strike against it. While the strike was unsuccessful in its aims, the Libyan crisis polarised the socialist movement and gave spur to development of an open revolutionary tendency within the PSI. In 1912, at the Congress of Reggio Emilia of the Socialist Party, the left organised itself as the Intransigent Revolutionary Fraction.

Amidst these mounting battles between revolutionaries and reformists, Amadeo Bordiga, a young engineer, came to prominence in his native town of Naples. His first crusade was against the electoral opportunism of the PSI, which he later said "has an infamous history everywhere and always, but which reached a peak of pathological infection in Naples in the early twentieth century".[9] The Naples branch of the PSI was organised on the basis of permanently shifting alliances with different designated "progressive" forces completely alien to the workers' movement: from anti-clerical agitators to bourgeois republicans. Bordiga and his close comrades denounced the branch leadership in April of 1912, forming the "Karl Marx revolutionary socialist circle", with the aim of giving the Socialist Party's practice a solid Marxist foundation. At the party's youth conference that year Bordiga and his followers emerged as the clear leaders of the extreme left. By 1914 they had articulated an alternative program based on class independence and clearly revolutionary objectives, and re-entered the Naples branch to reorient the party. While Bordiga energetically challenged the reformist leadership of the PSI, his conception of a revolutionary alternative left much to be desired. His opposition to the gradualism of the reformists engendered a dismissive attitude to the day-to-day struggles which are an essential transmission belt for workers developing revolutionary ideas. His opposition to their parliamentary cretinism led him to

---

8.   Behan 2003, p.11.
9.   Quoted in Bordiga 2020, p.15.

wrongly conclude that socialism and democracy existed in diametric opposition. This engendered a dangerously dismissive attitude toward the limited democratic rights that existed for workers in Italy, which would ultimately culminate in his indifference and passivity in the face of the fascist threat in the early 1920s.

Between the revolutionaries and reformists were the "Maximalists", led by Giacinto Menotti Serrati, which dominated the party leadership. Serrati's group criticised the reformists from an apparently radical Marxist position. Their politics were characterised by extreme revolutionary rhetoric, and a workerism which ignored the needs and demands of other oppressed classes in Italian society. Beyond their radical verbiage, however, they usually failed to practically distinguish themselves from the reformists, focusing on agitation for democratic reforms and pouring endless energy into election campaigns. This faction would later be identified as "centrist" by Communists in the PSI, for Serrati's unwavering commitment to unity with reformist forces.

The syndicalist opposition

In this maelstrom of debate in the PSI, another current would emerge, eventually breaking with the established traditions of the socialist movement: syndicalism. The first syndicalist leaders were Socialist Party intellectuals who revolted against the increasing reformist integration of the PSI leadership.

Their politics took shape as part of an international current in the workers' movement. Syndicalism found expression in a variety of organisational forms, from the CGT in France to the IWW in America. The main themes that they emphasised were opposition to parliamentarism, direct action and revolutionary trade unionism.

Ralph Darlington argues that syndicalism was in part "a reaction to the deterministic conception of Marxism that dominated most of the labour parties of the Second International which saw history as governed by iron economic laws and excluded any genuine role for human consciousness and activity in shaping society".[10] But if syndicalism grew out of a rejection of the passivity and parliamentary

---

10. Darlington 2008, p.19.

fixation of the Second International parties, it generally failed to provide an alternative framework and strategy for social change. As the French syndicalist Pouget emphasised: "What sets syndicalism apart from the various schools of socialism – and makes it superior – is its doctrinal sobriety. Inside the unions, there is little philosophising. They do better than that: they act!"[11] The hostility of the reformist leaders to their arguments meant that the Italian syndicalists soon had to find a new home. In 1906 they were driven out of the mainstream union federation, the CGL. By 1908 they had been expelled from the PSI.

After their expulsion, the first generation of syndicalist organisers set about attempting to root themselves in Italian working-class life. With their emphasis on wildcat strikes and insurrectionary struggle they had the greatest success in places where the aggressiveness of employers and the state made explicitly reformist trade unionism unviable. The first wave of successful syndicalist organising took place in the rural Po Valley, where the reformist agricultural union, the Federterra, was unable to gain employer recognition. The country's railway networks and the arsenal at La Spezia, where strikes were expressly forbidden by law, also became syndicalist strongholds.

The syndicalists primarily organised their activities through the Chambers of Labour (*Camere del Lavoro*), local workers' centres which served as the focal point for the activities of different unions, co-operatives and workers' associations. Because of the often localised nature of workers' struggle, the *Camere* regularly acted more effectively than the official union bodies. Participation in the *Camere* reinforced the syndicalists' emphasis on local autonomy, as opposed to centralised organisation. In 1912 the syndicalists formed the USI, a rival union federation, and by 1913 it had half the membership of the reformist CGL. The syndicalists represented a healthy reaction to the PSI's growing parliamentary cretinism and the class collaborationism of the union leaders. But they were severely limited by their single-minded focus on direct action and neglect of both political organisation and serious strategising. Localised militant

---

11. Quoted in Darlington 2008, p.18.

struggle alone would never be enough to confront the intransigence of united employers, obstinate reformist trade union bureaucrats and a repressive state apparatus.

Italy's first national general strike in 1904 was led by the syndicalists, and put their leadership to the test. A mass strike emerged spontaneously after a police massacre of miners in Sardinia. The hesitancy of the Socialist Party allowed the syndicalists to take the lead and generalise the strike through the *Camere*. In Milan, a city virtually under workers' control, mass debates took place in a sports stadium about the future of the strike movement. The Socialists proposed a three-day demonstrative strike, while the syndicalists called for an indefinite struggle until the fall of the government. In such a polarised climate, this amounted to a call for a revolution. While the syndicalists' approach was admirable and superior to that of the PSI, no preparations had been made for such a struggle. With key sections of the workforce still working and no sign of mutinies in the army, the government simply had to wait for the strike to collapse.[12]

Another unsuccessful strike in 1912 cost the syndicalists their foothold in Turin. Against the moderation of the CGL union leaders, they again crudely counterposed their demand for an unlimited general strike. Again, the workers who followed their lead were isolated, and after a long struggle returned to work on humiliating terms.[13]

These and other similar experiences discredited the syndicalist leaders and bolstered the authority of the reformist union bureaucrats for years to come. The syndicalists presented a bold and principled opposition to the reformists, but had not developed a realistic strategy for winning the majority of workers to revolutionary politics.

The Socialist Party in crisis

The outbreak of World War I created a crisis for the European left. The Italian Socialist Party refused to join other parties of the Second International in openly supporting the war. All factions agreed unanimously to send delegates to the Zimmerwald conference,

---

12. Behan 2003, p.14.
13. Levy 1999, p.49.

and Serrati defied the Italian censors by publishing the grouping's anti-war manifesto in the pages of *Avanti!*[14] But when it came to moving beyond proclamations, the leadership took a fundamentally passive approach, summed up by their formulation "neither support nor sabotage". As one *Avanti!* article on the tasks facing the left put it: "Study, yes, for today we can collect the materials necessary for action tomorrow. But action today, on concrete and immediate questions? No, no, no!"[15]

This position of calculated ambiguity was shattered by the war and its aftermath. In 1915 the Italians abandoned their neutral posture and invaded Austria, creating new and unavoidable tensions within the socialist movement. These divisions were exacerbated by news of a revolution in Russia. The Russian Revolution was greeted with more enthusiasm in Italy than perhaps anywhere else in the world. "Let's follow Russia" was a popular song amongst radicalised soldiers returning from the front. In August 1917, an official delegation of Russian Mensheviks had been sent to Italy to secure international support for the ruling Provisional Government and a continuation of the war. To their dismay, they were greeted in Turin by enthusiastic cries of "Viva Lenin!"[16] Serrati rushed to affiliate the PSI to the Communist International, the new centre of world revolution established by the Russian Bolsheviks. The PSI was the first mass party to join.

Meanwhile the reformist wing of the PSI hailed US President Woodrow Wilson's diplomatic efforts. As nationalist fervour raised its head, the reformist Turati inched toward open support for the war effort. Turati ardently warned against any attempt to replicate the Russian experience: "Any attempt at violent revolution...can have only two possible results: either *the bloody suppression of the revolt*, or in the most favourable case – *a purely superficial transformation of the political structure*. Reforms are the only great and sure path".[17]

The Socialist Party was paralysed by these divisions, which arose

---

14. Cammett 1967, p.40.
15. Quoted in Gluckstein 1985, p.168.
16. Cammett 1967, p.40.
17. Quoted in Gluckstein, 1975 p.175.

in the context of rising struggle. The monumental riots of August 1917 provided a glimpse of what was to come. Workers walked out on strike when bakeries failed to open due to supply shortages. Mario Montagnana, a worker in the Dietro-Fréjus plant described the scene: "Instead of entering the factory, we began a demonstration outside the gates, shouting 'We haven't eaten. We can't work. We want bread!'" When the factory owner assured them a delivery of bread was on its way and urged them to return to work,

> [t]he workers were quiet for a moment. They looked at each other as though they were tacitly conferring. Then all together shouted: 'To hell with the bread! We want peace! Down with the profiteers! Down with the war!' And they left the factory en masse.[18]

The August events were a consciously anti-war insurrectionary movement. According to one historian, "The strikes…were reminiscent in many ways of those in Petrograd in February. Women and youth had a vital part in them, trying to fraternise with the carabinieri and shouting, 'Don't fire at your brothers'".[19]

The PSI showed itself incapable of leading this monumental rebellion. On the 23rd an assembly of PSI and union leaders met, ostensibly to provide some leadership to the movement. After a day of furious discussion, both reformist and "revolutionary" PSI leaders concluded that they had little to offer. They issued a vaguely worded flyer praising workers for their resistance to the "stupidity and provocations of the authorities", assured them that the movement was "in good hands" and asked workers to avoid acts of "useless violence".[20] Without any direction, the revolt was easily contained in Turin, and suppressed with brute force. Participants estimated the number of dead at 400, with a further 2,000 wounded. Eight hundred and eleven socialist and anarchist leaders were arrested, and hundreds conscripted to fight at the front.[21]

By 1919 Italy was caught in a "strike frenzy". That year saw 1,663

---

18. Quoted in Cammett, 1967, p.52.
19. Ferro 1989, p.201.
20. Cammett 1967, p.54.
21. Cammett 1967, p.54.

industrial strikes, involving more than a million industrial workers, three times the 1913 figures. Strikes continued to increase in 1920. Peasant strikes and land occupations also exploded, from 97 in 1913 to 189 by 1920.[22] The dramatic increase in struggle prompted workers to join the existing organisations of the left en masse. The PSI increased its membership almost tenfold – from 23,000 in 1918 to 200,000 in 1920. The CGL union grew from a quarter of a million members to two million.[23]

For all their differences, every wing of the PSI took a passive approach to spontaneous workers' struggles. The reformist Turati justified incorporation into the state and collaboration with employers. Every new electoral gain, every new contract signed with employers heralded another step toward socialism. The ostensibly more radical Serrati asserted "We, Marxists, interpret History, we do not make it, we move in time according to the logic of facts and things"[24]: revolutionary rhetoric could be combined with passivity in practice.

Bordiga tended to recreate the same logic. He argued that the most important task was for revolutionaries to maintain a "pure" political line, avoid involvement in day-to-day struggles, and hold faith that the future revolution would sweep revolutionaries like himself into the leadership of the workers' movement. While Bordiga modelled himself as a "Leninist", he failed to understand one of Lenin's key insights – that struggles for reforms under capitalism played a crucial role in the development of revolutionary consciousness.

In a country marked by periods of intense militancy, there was no organised revolutionary tendency that could grasp the link between existing struggles and the objective of working-class revolution.

Gramsci's Marxism

Antonio Gramsci was to become the most consequential Marxist thinker of the Biennio Rosso. Gramsci was able to pursue a genuinely creative, flexible and novel project of building workers' power in Italy

---

22. Neufeld 1961, p.57.
23. Dunnage 2002, p.48, p.50.
24. Coutinho 2012, p.6.

in large part due to his independence from the stifling and dogmatic traditions of Italian socialism. Gramsci developed his ideas quite independently of the main tendencies of Second International Marxism in Italy.

Antonio Gramsci was born on the southern Italian island of Sardinia, one of the most economically underdeveloped areas in the country. His early politics were a combination of class hatred and southern nationalism. He later recalled:

> What spared me from becoming a completely lifeless rag? The rebellious instinct I felt against the rich as a young boy... This instinct extended to all the rich who oppressed Sardinian peasants, and so then I thought it was necessary to fight for the national independence of the region: "Throw the continentals to the sea!" How many times I repeated those words.[25]

Gramsci joined the PSI's youth federation in 1914. His activity in the party was overwhelmingly in the field of cultural discussion and criticism, a common preoccupation for more moderate members of the youth organisation. Gramsci saw cultural struggle as a key means for breaking workers from individualism and raising the horizons of their activity:

> [E]very revolution has been preceded by an intense labour of criticism, by the diffusion of culture and the spread of ideas amongst masses of men who are at first resistant and think only of solving, day by day, hour by hour, their own immediate economic and political problems for themselves, without ties of solidarity with the others who find themselves in the same conditions.[26]

In 1917 he founded, outside of the official structures of the party, the "Club of Moral Life", in an attempt to create a practical alternative to the passivity and empty rhetoric of the Maximalists. But his conception of socialist education was abstract and moralistic. According to Coutinho, one of the main texts discussed by the

25. Santucci 2010, p.47.
26. Quoted in Coutinho 2012, p.9.

Club were the moral maxims of Roman emperor-philosopher Marcus Aurelius![27]

A dramatic turn in the class struggle would soon rip Gramsci from the lofty heights of "proletarian culture", and force him to confront the burning questions faced by the workers' movement. Gramsci was suddenly thrust into prominence in the Turinese labour movement in traumatic circumstances. The repression of the August 1917 bread riots saw virtually the entire local leadership of the PSI jailed, and Gramsci was made editor and sole journalist of the party's local paper. His first piece, written in August 1917, hailed the still-unfolding Russian revolution as a proletarian act that opened up the historical possibility of socialism. Gramsci's politics in this period contained a streak of voluntarism, the belief that revolution could be made as an act of will. In his article "The Revolution Against Capital" he wrote:

> The Bolshevik revolution is based more on ideology than actual events... The Bolsheviks renounce Karl Marx and they assert, through their clear statement of action, through what they have achieved, that the laws of historical materialism are not as set in stone, as one may think, or one may have thought previously.[28]

While somewhat crude, Gramsci's formulation was a reaction against the stifling determinism that infected so much of the PSI. Gramsci's burning imperative was to find a means to translate the revolutionary energy of Russia into a roadmap for international revolution through proletarian self-activity.

In May 1919, Gramsci and his small group of collaborators formed a new journal, *L'Ordine Nuovo*. Its initial content reflected the grouping's old culturalist inclinations. Gramsci later acerbically described it as a "journal of abstract culture, abstract information, with a strong leaning towards horror stories and well-meaning woodcuts...a mess, the product of a mediocre intellectualism".[29] But Gramsci already had one eye turned away from the horror stories and theatre reviews.

---

27. Coutinho 2012, p.10.
28. Gramsci, "The Revolution Against Capital", *Avanti!*, 24 December 1917.
29. Gramsci 1977, p.293.

He was busy enmeshing himself in new literature circulating through Europe: accounts of the practical experience of the British shop stewards' movement and the Hungarian and German Revolutions, and Lenin's *State and Revolution*, recently translated. Soon, Gramsci would perform an "editorial coup d'état" and convert *L'Ordine Nuovo* into a publication dedicated to the creation of soviets in Italy.

The origins of the councils

Calls to respond to the crisis in Italian capitalism by "doing as they did in Russia" echoed across the revolutionary left in Italy. For most, this meant founding soviets as new organs of workers' democracy. In March of 1919, Alfonso Leonetti wrote for the paper of the youth wing of the party that the creation of soviets was the "surest guarantee of the movement toward socialism". He chose to call this article "At the Dawn of a New Order".[30]

But how to move from rhetoric into a program of practical realisation? The question begs a comparison with Trotsky's classic account of how the soviet emerged in Russia:

> The Soviet came into being as a response to an objective need – a need born of the course of events. It was an organisation which was authoritative and yet had no traditions; which could immediately involve the scattered mass of hundreds of thousands of people while having virtually no organisational machinery; which united the revolutionary currents within the proletariat; which was capable of initiative and spontaneous self-control – and most important of all, which could be brought out from underground within twenty-four hours.[31]

In Russia factory organisation and trade unions were constantly suppressed. Workers were only able to construct mass organisations in the context of revolution. In Western Europe, by contrast, there were strong traditions of trade unionism and mass legal workers' parties. The process of the councils' emergence was far more painstaking, as radicalising workers attempted to find a way

---

30. Williams 1975, p.90.
31. Trotsky 2016, p.90.

to break out of the shackles imposed by their own trade union officials and reformist leaders, who favoured containment and class collaboration.

The internal commissions became the focal point of the attempt to build soviets in Italy – it is from their structures that the factory council movement would spring. By the beginning of 1919, the entire organised working class in Turin were debating the role of the commissions.

The reformist wing of the PSI and the trade union officials wanted the commissions to be bodies for pursuing class collaboration. They viewed the commissions as one vehicle for their program of a pluralist democracy, where workers would be accepted into the institutions of the liberal state alongside parliament, the police and other bourgeois institutions. At the FIOM's Rome Congress in November 1918, the union spokesman Colombino proposed that the commissions "become permanent organs of 'workers' control', dealing with all problems of wages, discipline, etc. under the guidance and leadership of the Unions".[32] The reformist strategy for the internal commissions scored an apparent victory in early 1919. The Turin metalworkers' contract granted the eight-hour day and large pay increases, but also institutionalised the commissions and radically circumscribed their role. Members of the commissions would be forced to meet outside of work hours, and unions were forced to undertake a three-stage arbitration process before they were allowed to strike.[33]

This corporatist and "institutionalised" vision of industrial relations united various oppositional currents in outrage. The *Sindicato Metallurgico*, the syndicalist rival to the FIOM, denounced the 1919 Turin agreement as "little more than a penal code".[34] Two leading Turinese radical Socialists, Parodi and Boero, began drawing closer to Garino and Ferrero, the city's most prominent syndicalist leaders. They formed a "provisional committee" to combat the reformist leaders of the FIOM. They pledged to defend the right to strike, refuse collaboration with the war industry committees, and

---

32. Quoted in Levy 1999, p.131.
33. Levy 1999, p.133.
34. Levy 1999, p.134.

strengthen the internal commissions.[35] A wide variety of schemes were developed for the commissions on the radical left. The Russo-Polish technician Aaron Wizner, a Luxemburgist employed at FIAT, had pointed Gramsci to the internal commissions as an "Italian equivalent of Soviet style self-government" at the beginning of 1919.[36] It was this climate of ferment and ideological discussion around the role of workers' industrial organisations in general and the internal commissions in particular that generated the movement for workers' councils. Contrary to the Stalinist narrative, this drive was not the personal genius of Antonio Gramsci, but was made possible by an organic attempt by workers – inspired by patchy but exciting news filtering through from Russia – to break out of the bureaucratic straightjacket imposed by the FIOM bureaucracy.

Nevertheless, it was undoubtedly Gramsci's intervention through his journal *L'Ordine Nuovo* which was key in shaping the creation of the councils and giving them a systematic worldview and strategy. In a series of articles published from June 1919 onward, Gramsci attempted to answer the burning question, as he saw it:

> How can the immense social forces unleashed by the war be harnessed? How can they be disciplined and given a political form that has the potential to develop smoothly into the skeleton of the socialist state in which the dictatorship of the proletariat will be embodied?[37]

Gramsci argued, breaking with dominant thinking on the PSI's left, that the party alone was incapable of leading the working class to power. The PSI was incapable of organising the whole of the working class, because to do so would mean throwing its doors open to "the invasion of new supporters, not yet accustomed to responsibility and discipline",[38] thereby liquidating its politics and abandoning its historic task of leadership. In an article written in October 1919, Gramsci went further, arguing that the traditional

---

35. Gluckstein 1985, pp.173–4.
36. Levy 1999, p.135.
37. Gramsci 1994, p.96.
38. Gramsci 1994, p.98.

trade union structures were also limited, as a "type of proletarian organisation specific to the period of history dominated by capital".[39] The purpose of the unions was to bargain over the value of labour power, a function that "only makes sense within a regime of private property".[40]

While the power of the ruling class lay in its control overcapital, the centre of working class power was in the factory, which Gramsci described as their "national territory". Organising the factory was a precondition for working-class political power: "The factory council is the model of the proletarian state. All the problems inherent in the organisation of the proletarian state are inherent in the organisation of the council".[41] A new institution was necessary, modelled on the Russian soviets, which could educate the working class and prepare them to take power. The internal commissions had the potential to become this institution, but only if they were transformed:

> The workshop commissions are organs of democracy which must be freed from the constraints imposed on them by the bosses, and infused with new life and energy. At the moment these commissions have the task of curbing the power the capitalist exerts within the factory, and they perform an arbitration and disciplinary function. In the future, developed and improved, they should be the organs of proletarian power, replacing the capitalist in all his useful managerial and administrative functions.[42]

Gramsci's proposals had an electrifying impact. In August, the workers' representatives at FIAT-Centro, the largest factory in the country, dissolved the internal commission and called for the election of a council. Workers at FIAT-Brevetti developed the model that would be followed: only union members could stand for election, but all workers were given a vote. The councils were independent of official union structures, and aspired to embrace the entirety of the working class. By October 26, more than 50,000 were organised in

---

39. Gramsci 1994, p.116.
40. Gramsci 1994, p.117.
41. Quoted in Cammett 1967, p.82.
42. Gramsci 1994, p.98.

councils across Turin, by the end of the year more than 150,000. Again, it is important to emphasise that while Gramsci's political leadership catalysed the development of workers' councils, his proposals only had resonance because they related to the experience and needs of the workers' movement at a moment of extraordinary class struggle. In an open letter to council delegates on the role of his paper's program, Gramsci acknowledged this, stating that *L'Ordine Nuovo*

> only had value because it helped to give concrete expression to an aspiration that was latent in the consciousness of the working masses. This is why we were so rapidly understood; this is why the transition from discussion to realisation was effected so rapidly.[43]

The development of councils

The first several months of the council experiment were character-ised by seemingly unimpeded advance. At the end of October 1919, the first general assembly of the factory council deputies drew up a program for the councils. The program declared itself "an exposition of the concepts which underpin the rise of a new form of proletarian power... Its purpose...is to set in train in Italy a practical experi-ment in the achievement of communist society".[44] The tasks of the deputies outlined in the document fell broadly into three categories: the defence of the rights of workers, education, and the preparation for seizure of power in the factories.

On 1 November this grouping of deputies succeeded in taking over the leadership of the local FIOM branch in a stormy meeting. Next, they won the leadership of the Turin PSI and the local *Camere* to the project.[45] *L'Ordine Nuovo* reached its maximum circulation in the following edition. An article by Pietro Mosso on 22 November urged: "Make your council active, make it yours!"[46]

However, while the councils quickly drew into action the vanguard of the working class in the north, and their program of the

---

43. Gramsci 1977 p.94.
44. Quoted in Williams 1975, p.124.
45. Williams 1975, pp.138, 141.
46. Williams 1975, p.140.

councils expressed the highest aspirations, they never reached the level of asserting an alternative political authority to the capitalist state. They suffered from two critical limitations.

Firstly, they remained largely restricted to the task of asserting control over production on the factory floor. But while private property prevailed and political power remained in the hands of the capitalist state, it was impossible for workers to liberate themselves completely. The councils therefore had to be extended, like the soviets in Russia, to encompass political as well as industrial organisation. Attempting to assert control of production could exert contradictory pressures on the workers involved. One the one hand, it could advance the struggle by impressing upon them the need to take control of the broader administration of society and fight for political power. On the other hand, it could lead workers down the dead-end of advising management on how to improve production.

This danger was evident when the bosses at FIAT demanded productivity be increased to compete with American output levels. The rank and file reflexively rejected this proposal and a series of mass meetings angrily denounced them. But they were calmed by Boero and Garino, two leaders of the council movement, who argued that the power of the working class grew from their mastery of production and so they couldn't refuse attempts to increase output.[47] But, even with councils running the factory floor, these increases in productivity would still flow to the bosses in the form of profits. As things stood, the council leaders were unwittingly holding back an incipient strike movement against capitalist profiteering.

The intervention of the *L'Ordine Nuovo* group acted to reinforce the illusion, which motivated Boero and Garino, that controlling production was enough to challenge the capitalist class for power. They wrote:

> The working masses must take adequate steps to acquire complete self-government, and the first step along this road consists in disciplining themselves, inside the workshop... Nor can it be denied that the discipline which will be established along with

---

47. Gluckstein 1985, p.189.

the new system will lead to an improvement in production... So to those who object that by this method we are collaborating with our opponents, with the owners of the factories, we reply that on the contrary this is the only means of letting them know in concrete terms that the end of their domination is at hand.[48]

The other major limitation of the council movement is that with few exceptions it never became generalised outside of the big metalworks in Turin. Only Turin had both the large-scale production and traditions of independent rank-and-file organisations that encouraged the council process. To generalise the councils across the country and lay the genuine foundations of a proletarian state required an ability to transcend Turin's particular social conditions and evolve a strategy that could link its vanguard to the rest of the working class and the oppressed.

To rally the social forces necessary to challenge the old order; workers in Italy needed institutions capable of taking up the demands of other oppressed classes and social groups. The ability of the soviets in Russia to act as a political tribune of the oppressed, not just as economic institutions to control factories, was key to the success of the revolution. This political approach allowed workers' councils to win the loyalty of mutinying soldiers, rebellious peasants and religious and national minorities – building a coalition under the leadership of revolutionary workers that destroyed the capitalist state.

In Italy, there was a huge gap between the struggle in the northern factories and the social turmoil sweeping the rest of the country. Peasant land occupations were sweeping southern and central Italy on a massive scale. Fascist gangs began roaming the countryside and making their first attacks on Socialist Party headquarters. But these struggles were isolated from the council movement.

Overall then, the Italian councils marked a step forward in the construction of workers' power, but as institutions were marked by the weaknesses of the class that generated them. The Italian councils were hobbled by their economism – the fact that they were limited

---

48. Quoted in Gluckstein 1985, p.188.

to the supervision of production; and their sectionalism – their inability to extend their reach beyond the big battalions of the industrial working class and influence the rest of society. The councils nevertheless maintained an impressive authority and mobilising power among Turinese workers, as evidenced by their role in the 3 December general strike. In response to a reactionary nationalist attack on the Italian parliament, the council leaders could claim: "Without any preparation whatsoever, the factory councils were about to mobilise 120,000 workers, called out factory by factory, in the course of just one hour".[49] But by the end of 1919, even the anarchist Garino, one of the most fervent advocates of the council movement, was forced to admit that with the exception of organising demonstrations, the councils were failing to go beyond the tasks of the old internal commissions.

The PSI and the councils

The impasse of the council movement brought the question of political organisation to the fore.

Only a nationally organised revolutionary party could generalise the councils across the country, and in the process fight to overcome their limitations.

At their Bologna conference in October 1919 the PSI had shown superficially promising signs, pledging itself to the replacement of the capitalist state by workers' councils, and officially adhering to the program of the Third International.[50] But Serrati, the undisputed leader of the PSI's directorate, refused to move beyond verbal attacks on the reformists. Turati and his followers were allowed to remain in the party, pledging to act as a counterweight to the "foreign influence" of Bolshevism. Serrati paid lip service to the centrality of the council system: "The regime of the Soviets, of the councils of workers, is already a fact, not only in Russia, but everywhere".[51]

But the test of politics is practice, not rhetoric or lofty resolutions passed at conferences. When confronted with the reality of an emergent council movement, all major tendencies in the PSI

---

49. Quoted in Gluckstein 1985, p.194.
50. Cammett 1967, p.69.
51. Quoted in Davidson 1975, p.41.

recoiled in horror. Turati's reformists saw the potential for the councils to pose a direct challenge to the trade union bureaucracy and parliamentarians. Serrati's Maximalists were outraged at the idea that non-union workers could vote for representatives: he derided this as "anarchism". As an alternative to relating to the real movement of workers struggling to figure out the political form of their emancipation, the PSI leaders held a national council meeting in January 1920, in which the left-maximalist Bombacci was tasked with presenting legalistic plans for soviets, to be established by a future Socialist government.

Bordiga was by this point the undisputed leader of the different Communist groupings in the PSI, cohered through his newspaper *Il Soviet*. This meant he had an enormous amount of responsibility to give a lead to the council movement. Instead, he disavowed them. He based his hostility to the movement on the idea that workers' control of production was a reformist illusion so long as the capitalist state prevailed. Bordiga correctly identified the limitations of the current movement: if the councils did not fight for and win political power, they would also be unable to exercise true economic power in the workplace.

But Bordiga made no argument as to how revolutionaries could help lead the powerful movement already built by militant workers, in order to develop it into a revolutionary challenge to the state. Bordiga failed to understand that workers' power is something that emerges organically through the class struggle. Instead he thought the institutions of working-class government would be decreed from above after the Communist Party's seizure of power. "Tomorrow's soviets will have their genesis in the local sections of the Communist Party", Bordiga wrote. "These sections should make ready the elements that, immediately after revolutionary victory, will be offered to the vote of the proletarian electoral mass, in order to create the local delegates' councils."[52]

Bordiga therefore shared with Serrati, Turati and Bombacci a fundamental assumption of Second International Marxism: that the rule of the working class meant the rule of the party. His attempt to

---

52. Quoted in Coutinho 2012, p.19.

apply "Leninism" to Italian conditions relied almost exclusively on campaigning inside the PSI to rectify its reformist errors and build a genuinely "Communist" Party.

Bordiga failed to grasp the role that workers' self-activity played in developing the consciousness of the class, increasing its organisation and cohesion, and impressing upon them the ultimate need to seize state power. For Bordiga, partial struggles only wasted the energy of the working class. The most important thing was to wait for the "final push" which would result in the overthrow of capitalism:

> The working class will conquer the factories – it would be too slight and uncommunist for each workshop to do it – only after the working class as a whole has taken political power... All these constant vain efforts that are daily exhausting the workers must be channelled and fused together, organised into one big comprehensive effort that strikes directly at the heart of the bourgeois enemy. Only a communist party can and must exercise this function.[53]

This reflected the difference in Bordiga's and Gramsci's conceptions of the revolutionary process. Togliatti, one of Gramsci's close collaborators in the period, later summarised the debate in this way: Bordiga believed the party would base itself on "foreseeing a future moment when it will be called upon to lead the working class in the final assault for the conquest of power" whereas in Gramsci's view it should accompany the class in "all the intermediate positions it goes through".[54]

Gramsci's great strength was his drive to relate the goal of working class political power to the real movement of workers in struggle. But his attempt to learn the lessons of the Russian Revolution was the mirror image of Bordiga's. Heavily influenced by the French syndicalists he read, Gramsci saw the development of a "conciliar" theory of workers' revolution, as expressed in Lenin's *State and Revolution*, as the main contribution of the Bolsheviks. He neglected the other key lesson: the need to build a mass interventionist revolutionary workers' party to advance the process of self-organisation in the

53. Bordiga 2020, p.133.
54. Quoted in Gramsci 2014, p.30.

councils and lead them to victory.

In his first articles on the factory councils, Gramsci posed the workers' councils as the force that would shake the PSI out of its bureaucratic inertia and transform it into a genuine revolutionary party. In August 1919 he declared that the only change necessary to the party's 1892 program was a clause on the councils.[55] This was a fatal error. The appearance of workers' councils on the scene does not resolve the strategic political questions for the socialist movement – it only poses them more starkly. The task of combating reformist political forces – in particular the trade union bureaucracy over rank-and-file workers – remains urgent.

Gramsci grappled with the question of the party from a defensive position. The councils had already come under attack from all sides of the PSI and reached a point of crisis. Gramsci later recalled this as his greatest failure in a letter to a comrade:

> During 1919–20, we committed very serious errors which we are now paying for in full. For fear of being called *arrivistes* and careerists, we did not form a faction and try to organise it throughout Italy. We did not want to make the Turin factory councils into a directive centre which could have exercised an immense influence on the whole country, for fear of splitting the trade unions and being prematurely expelled from the Socialist Party.[56]

In January 1920 Gramsci was calling for a renewal of the Socialist Party. But to build a revolutionary tendency which could have led the councils to victory would have meant actively looking beyond the horizons of the Socialist Party, rather than seeking to renovate it. The most active and ardent proponents of the council movement were all either outside the Socialist Party, or fundamentally hostile to its political perspectives.

In Turin many of the most enthusiastic supporters of the councils were syndicalist activists influenced by anarchist and libertarian ideas. They were hostile to the notion of party organisation

---

55. Williams 1975, p.147.
56. Quoted in Williams 1975, p.145.

but enthused by the prospect of laying the foundations for a new industrial democracy. Gramsci worked closely with many of these individuals, including the influential worker leaders Garino and Ferrero, who played an instrumental role in the early assemblies of council commissars.[57]

Important ideological differences existed between the syndicalists and Marxists in the council movement. The anarchist Garino emphasised his disagreement with the notion of a collective "dictatorship of the proletariat". He recalled a conversation in Gramsci's office on the topic, in which he declared:

> [A]ll the rest I can agree with you, dear Gramsci, but on this point no. Even collective dictatorships little by little can transform themselves into dictatorships of groups of men and therefore restrict freedom... If tomorrow in Italy a dictatorship is established, call it what you want, the first to be shot will be us because we are against the Political state. [58]

This anarchist rejection of the necessity of working-class political power as a complement to control over the productive process was utopian. They had no viable strategy to defend the council movement from the sabotage of employers and the violence of the capitalist state. But while Gramsci could offer perfectly orthodox Marxist doctrinal criticism of anarchism's limitations, he had no alternative strategy for the councils. To convince the syndicalist leaders of a Marxist project and worldview, it would have been necessary to demonstrate in practice the importance of the councils moving from the terrain of *economics* to *politics*: taking up questions and organising social forces outside of the factories.

The Bolsheviks proved in 1917 that it was possible to rally activists from other political traditions to your strategy in a period of revolutionary upheaval. They were able to forge a revolutionary alliance with leftward moving Social Revolutionaries and Mensheviks because they had built an organisation which emphasised its differences with more moderate currents and argued for a strategy

---

57. Levy 1999, p.147.
58. Quoted in Levy 1999, p.208.

which could take the situation forward, summarised by their slogan: "All Power to the Soviets". The Petrograd Military Revolutionary Committee, which organised the insurrection in October, was even headed by a Left Social Revolutionary, Lazimir, who later joined the Bolshevik party.[59]

But Gramsci had no strategy capable of transcending the current practice of the councils, and moving toward a seizure of power. Rather than emphasising the fact that the revolution still had many tasks to complete, *L'Ordine Nuovo* tended instead to reinforce the syndicalist illusion that workers' control of production, isolated from a struggle for state power, could bring about a socialist society.

Perhaps the greatest impediment to relating to the syndicalists was Gramsci's unwillingness to break decisively with the political framework of the Socialist Party. As he came increasingly under attack from the reformist leadership, Gramsci attempted to defend his position in the party and prove his Marxist bona fides by ramping up his criticisms of the syndicalists. His major intellectual overture to them, the "Address to the Anarchists", written on the eve of the April 1920 general strike, struck an appalling tone. The article began by saying: "The Italian anarchists are very touchy because they are very presumptuous: they have always been convinced that they are the guardians of the revealed revolutionary truth".[60] It went on to defend the PSI as the only genuine embodiment of the proletariat: "The Socialist Party has always been the party of the Italian working people: its errors and shortcomings are those of the Italian working people itself".[61]

Recruiting key syndicalist militants to the construction of a new revolutionary Marxist party which could challenge the reformist leaders of PSI would have taken a protracted struggle. Practical collaboration and honest, intense ideological discussion would have been necessary. But Gramsci failed to adequately appreciate that these well-intentioned but muddled militants were already far closer to a revolutionary socialist position than the waverers, blow-hard centrist rhetoricians and seasoned cynical bureaucrats

59. Trotsky 2008, p.685.
60. Gramsci 1977, p.185.
61. Gramsci 1977, p.185.

who dominated the leadership of the PSI. This is the orientation that Trotsky urged at the Second Congress of the Comintern, when he emphasised that the syndicalists "not only wish to fight against the bourgeoisie", but unlike the reformists "really wish to tear its head off".[62] Trotsky's approach allowed him to win important leaders of the French syndicalist movement like Alfred Rosmer to communist politics. In Italy, conversely, virtually no significant syndicalist worker-leaders were convinced of the project of forming a revolutionary Communist Party.

Increasingly isolated within the reformist prison of the Socialist Party, Gramsci drew closer in March to the local supporters of Bordiga in Turin, and together they drafted an "Action Program" – which outlined two key tasks: "1) solving the problem of arming the proletariat; 2) arousing through the province a powerful class movement of poor peasants and small-holders in solidarity with the industrial movement".[63] This program represented a genuine grappling with the limitations of the councils, but without an organisation to carry out this perspective, it remained an abstract aspiration.

Tragically, Gramsci and his collaborators were grasping toward a solution to the problems of the councils just as the ruling class was gearing up for a series of major confrontations. There would be little time to put his new perspective to the test.

The April strike and the factory occupations

In April, Turinese workers were locked out by their employers in what came to be remembered as the "clock hands strike". What began as a trivial dispute about the implementation of daylight savings time spiralled into a confrontation in which the metalworks bosses demanded the complete dissolution of the councils. Their ambition was nothing less than ending the situation of "dual power" that prevailed in the factories. The intransigence of the employers meant that workers had no choice but to generalise the struggle. The resulting strike brought out 500,000, and drew in millions behind it. Riccardo Bachi stated:

---

62. Trotsky 2007, p.134.
63. Quoted in Gluckstein 1985, p.202.

In its extension it was certainly the most notable movement of solidarity one can recall in Italy. All the factories were closed. Only the most important public services continued to function, in a reduced measure. The municipal guards and customs officers struck, as well as the tram workers, the railroad workers, the post and telegraph workers.[64]

While the strikers fought bitterly to defend the councils, the PSI newspaper *Avanti!* refused to print their appeals for assistance. Turin was surrounded by machine guns, cannons and 50,000 troops – but in the end, the ruling class had no need to resort to open warfare. Isolated and demoralised, the strikers returned to work after a month. The last bulletin of the strike committee admitted defeat: "In view of the failure to extend the movement for workers' control throughout Italy, the divisional commissars recognise that the industrialists, supported by the armed force of the bourgeoisie, have once again imposed their will".[65]

At the height of the general strike, April 19–21, the PSI met in Milan. The conference had been abruptly moved from Turin because, as Gramsci bitterly observed, "a city in a general strike was not adapted to Socialist discussions".[66] When the delegates refused to authorise the extension of the strike beyond the Piedmont region, Gramsci denounced the leadership for its bureaucratism and passivity:

> The Socialist Party watches the course of events like a spectator; it never has an opinion of its own to express...it never launches slogans that can be adopted by the masses, lay down a general line, and unify or concentrate revolutionary action.[67]

Disgracefully, Bordiga joined the Maximalist leadership he despised in disavowing the strike, affirming his suspicion of spontaneous workers' struggles.

---

64. Quoted in Cammett, 1967, p.100.
65. Quoted in Cammett 1967, p.101.
66. Quoted in Cammett 1967, p.101.
67. Gramsci 1977, p.191.

While Gramsci's *L'Ordine Nuovo* group threw themselves into the strike, and furiously denounced the betrayal of the PSI leadership, they made a crucial mistake. For the duration of the strike, they suspended their publication, so as to put all their energy into the struggle. This deprived the movement of a space in which to discuss and promote revolutionary perspectives precisely at the moment when they were most needed.

On the other hand, the syndicalists of the USI played an instrumental role in organising the April struggle. They led successful strikes which shut down railways and ports to halt the transport of troops sent to crush the movement. They also issued clear national appeals for solidarity, urging: "Workers, help! Help! Proletarians of Italy, railwaymen, seamen, peasants, don't be sparing with your solidarity for the Turin comrades. Don't let the army converge on Turin. Don't be accomplices to a massacre".[68] The syndicalists struggled tenaciously, but militant action by a minority was not enough to win.

The defeat of the April struggle struck a decisive blow to the relationship between the syndicalists and Gramsci's *L'Ordine Nuovo*. A debate between the CGL and the *L'Ordine Nuovo* group dragged the syndicalists into the mix. The reformist Bianchi likened *L'Ordine Nuovo's* claim of Socialist Party betrayal to a syndicalist mentality. In response Gramsci's group responded with an explosive attack, not on Bianchi, but on the syndicalists! Pastore, writing in *L'Ordine Nuovo,* claimed disingenuously that the supposed syndicalist support for the April struggle was a mirage, and that their appeals for solidarity through the anarchist paper *Umanità Nova* had not added a single striker to the movement.[69]

The April strike was the decisive test for the factory councils, a test which they failed. After the return to work, the CGL leader D'Aragona negotiated terms which capitulated to virtually all the employers' demands.[70] The councils were severely limited in their functioning, and the council commissars were discredited for their inability to successfully lead the struggle to its conclusion.

---

68. Quoted in Gluckstein 1985, p.206.
69. *Avanti!*, Piedmontese edition, 6 May 1920, p.1.
70. Gluckstein 1985, p.208.

Severely injured, but hobbling on with their spirits not completely diminished, the Turin workers would shortly stumble into the final climactic strike of the *Biennio Rosso*: the September occupation of the factories. The occupations began when a months-long contract negotiation between the major employers in the north and the metalworkers' unions exploded in September 1920 amidst an atmosphere of extreme social tension.

Working-class living standards were being savaged by wartime inflation. Metalworkers were frustrated with conciliatory union leaders. The capitalist class were united in their desire for action against workers. The industrialist Rotigliano, later a supporter of Mussolini, said to the metalworkers' representatives: "There will be no concessions. Since the end of the war, we've done nothing but drop our pants. Now it's our turn. Now we're going to start on you".[71]

At the very end of August, bosses at the Romeo plant in Milan shut the gates on their 2,000 employees. In response workers occupied 300 factories across the city. Metalworks bosses ordered a national lock-out, and a tidal wave of factory occupations occurred. Half a million workers raised red and black flags over their factories, armed themselves, and prepared for a decisive struggle for control of production.

Like the April strike, the factory occupations were initiated on defensive terrain. The FIOM leaders utilised the occupation strategy in order to pre-empt a lock-out by employers, and attempt to escape an all-out strike. Angelo Tasca noted:

> [That] which is often represented as a culminating point of a revolutionary fever, was in its origin a simple substitute for the strike weapon, which had become too difficult to use; it was a low-cost method to enforce a new collective labour contract. The leaders of the FIOM had chosen the line of minimum force.[72]

Nevertheless workers weary from years of war, economic instability

---

71. Williams 1975, p.238.
72. Spriano 1975, p.58.

and struggle were determined to settle scores with the bourgeoisie and hold the factories for as long as possible. Paolo Spriano wrote: "these hundreds of thousands of workers, with arms or without, who worked and slept and kept watch in the factories, thought the extraordinary days they were living through 'the revolution in action'".[73]

The meaning of workers' control varied across the major industrial centres. In Turin, with more than a year of experience in self-organisation, the factory councils progressively took on more elements of control. At FIAT-Centro, the council met permanently and established commissions to take stock of inventory and raw materials, to organise transport and create an armed red guard. Virtually every metalworks was involved in producing weaponry for the movement's self-defence. Much to the consternation of polite society, the soviet emblem was raised over the Tabanelli auto factory in Rome, and the movement spread as far as Naples.[74]

The explosion of workers' self-organisation scared the bourgeoisie. Some factory councils found they were able to secure loans from commercial banks to purchase raw material and fuel. Bankers were hoping to curry favour with workers in case they successfully seized power!

Many councils demonstrated workers' self-discipline and vigilance. Alcohol was strictly forbidden and theft of equipment was punished severely by the factory councils. This was driven both by a desire to win popular support for their occupations, but also a profound sense that they were attempting to model a new, moral society inside the factory walls.

On the other side, there was festivity and enthusiasm, a genuine atmosphere of euphoria. Gramsci underlined the historic nature of the event: "The social hierarchies are broken, historic values overthrown".[75]

However, he warned, the occupation of factories was not the same thing as a political seizure of power. "It indicates the extent

---

73. Spriano 1975, p.21–2.
74. Spriano 1975, pp.61–2.
75. Spriano 1975, p.66.

of the proletariat's power", he said, but "it does not in or of itself produce any new, definite position. Power remains in the hands of capital; armed force remains the property of the bourgeois state".[76] How this political seizure of power would be carried out, however, was never clarified by the Turin revolutionaries. Gramsci did not yet have a conception of how to move from council organisation to an overthrow of existing society. His theory of revolution was missing an understanding of the process of insurrection – the organised dismantling of the institutions of capitalist repression and administration.

When a delegation of industrialists demanded the state intervene to wrest the factories back, Prime Minister Giolitti asked ironically: "And will you permit me to begin by bombarding your factories?"[77] Giolitti's alternative strategy allowed the ruling class to gain the upper hand. Rather than confront the occupations head-on, Giolitti decided to wait them out, and put his hopes in the desire of the Socialist leaders for compromise.

From September 9, representatives of the CGL union federation and PSI met in Milan to attempt to find a way out of the conflict. The reformist union leaders called the bluff of the PSI directorate, offering their resignations and pledging loyalty to the course of revolution, if the PSI were willing to lead it. Faced with a situation which marked a decisive break from normality, a working class under arms and half a million in control of their factories, the PSI leaders retreated. They decided to put the question of revolution to a vote.

Two motions were put to the national membership of the CGL. One, moved by the union bureaucrats, called for recognition of union participation in management, the most right-wing form of "workers' control", in which union leaders are given some of the privileges of capitalist bosses. The other motion, moved by representatives of the Socialist Party, called for the immediate socialisation of the means of production. The socialisation proposal lost narrowly by 591,245 votes to 409,569.[78]

---

76. Gramsci 1977, p.192.
77. Cammett 1967, 116.
78. Cammett 1967, p.119.

This process was a farce. The PSI leaders had no intention of leading an insurrection, and breathed a heavy sigh of relief when their motion failed. They had done nothing to win support for the occupations outside of the northern industrial centres, and made no preparations to see the struggle through.

While sections of the ruling class were disconcerted by union claims for participation in management, Giolitti convinced them that it was the best way to regain control and restart production. CGL representatives, politicians and factory owners boarded the same train to a summit to negotiate terms. On the train the prefect of Milan, seated next to an industrialist who had shot dead two workers two nights earlier, pointed to the union leader D'Aragona and declared "You see him? He's the saviour of Italy".[79]

By November, it was clear that the workers' movement had suffered a fatal blow. A wave of fascist terror began to sweep the country, while the capitalist class went on an offensive against the unions, and it became clear that the revolutionary period had come to an end. As Quintin Hoare writes:

> It was in the autumn of 1920 that fascist squads began to carry out raids on behalf of the landowners of North and Central Italy against both the socialist and Catholic peasant associations, and against socialistcontrolled municipalities such as that of Bologna or socialist papers such as the Trieste daily *Il Lavoratore*. And it was also during this period that a number of industrialists began to pour funds into Mussolini's organisation.[80]

The capitalist class had weathered the "Two Red Years", and were waiting for the moment in which they could exact their revenge.

The lessons of defeat

The council experiment was exhilarating proof of one of the essential claims of Marxism: the organic capacity of workers to find new ways of organising that point towards a liberated society. The *Biennio Rosso* was a period in which workers struggled to transform their

---

79. Williams 1975, p.265.
80. Gramsci 1971, Introduction, p.xlv.

social conditions and overcome exploitation, at the same time transforming themselves. As Gramsci reflected, years after the defeat of the councils:

> It was really necessary to see with one's own eyes old workers, who seemed broken down by decades upon decades of oppression and exploitation, stand upright even in a physical sense during the period of the occupation – see them develop fantastic activities; suggesting, helping, always active day and night. It was necessary to see these and other sights, in order to be convinced how limitless the latent powers of the masses are, and how they are revealed and develop swiftly as soon as the conviction takes root among the masses that they are arbiters and masters of their own destinies.[81]

But the councils, no matter how dynamic and libertarian, proved incapable of sidestepping the reality of organised reformism in the workers' movement. At every stage of their development, the Socialist Party and CGL served to contain, rather than encourage, the council experiment. From the earliest debates within the internal commissions, the reformist union bureaucrats had viewed any move toward workers' self-activity and class independence as a threat to their project of a pluralist democracy in which their organisations were engaged in permanent collaboration with the employers. The Maximalist leadership of the PSI, despite their verbal revolutionism, were unwilling to break with the traditions of unity which tied them to the party's reformist bureaucracy. When a real revolutionary crisis challenged them to move beyond rhetoric and organise a struggle for power, they stepped back from the abyss.

Though there was no shortage of confident revolutionary agitators, organisers and intellectuals in Italy during the *Biennio Rosso*, none offered a clear path forward for confronting the dominance of the PSI and seizing the potential of the movement.

The anti-party syndicalists, while bravely rejecting the collaborationist attitudes of the reformists, were unable to develop a strategy

---

81. Gramsci 1978, pp.419–20.

for advancing the councils. Their utopian belief that democratic factory organisation alone was capable of defeating the capitalist state reinforced the limitations of the council movement.

While Gramsci was eventually able to develop a more rounded appreciation of the limitations of the councils, and a program for their deepening, he had no political organisation through which to pursue this project. As an individual relying on a small grouping of intellectuals and a publication to influence events, Gramsci was powerless, caught between the twin poles of syndicalism and reformism. If Gramsci had combined his agitation for councils with a political battle against anti-revolutionary currents in the workers' movement, there was a chance they could have broken out of their isolation and developed a more serious challenge to the capitalist class. At the very least, more workers could have drawn clarifying lessons from the experience of defeat.

The abandonment of the workers' councils and factory occupations by the PSI directorate finally sealed the divorce between the revolutionaries and reformists in the party. Gramsci, who had been so hesitant to open up a breach during the *Biennio Rosso*, was finished with the Socialist Party after September. His invective against the PSI, which littered the pages of *L'Ordine Nuovo* in late 1920, has been described by Gwynn Williams as one of the "great hates" of all time.[82]

But it was Bordiga, who had argued insistently on the need to split from the reformists from as early as 1912, who dominated the process of cohering a revolutionary opposition. In 1920, he wrote: "nothing does so much as a good split... One will know in this way exactly who is a communist and who is not: there will be no confusion on this score".[83] When revolutionaries finally walked out of the PSI at the Livorno Congress in January 1921, they paid a heavy price, taking only a minority of the party's members with them. The Communists received 58,783 votes at Livorno, as against 14,695 for the reformists and 90,028 for Serrati's centrists.[84]

Gramsci's failure to translate his political ideas into an organised current meant that Bordiga's sectarian and destructive politics

---

82. Williams 1985, p.279.
83. Quoted in Davidson 1975, p.146.
84. Bordiga 2020, p.47.

dominated the new revolutionary left. The formation of the Communist Party of Italy (PCI) was a victory for Bordiga's vision of the revolutionary party as an isolated "army of the pure". While thousands flocked to the new PCI, with its claim to the heritage of the Russian Revolution, the party's early history was dismal. Throughout the early 1920s it was characterised by an implacable hostility toward those workers who had remained in the Socialist Party, and a classically Bordigan passivity in the face of the rising fascist threat.

While he initially acceded to Bordiga's sectarian leadership, Gramsci also began to articulate an alternative conception of a revolutionary communist party. Through a period of reflection on the failure of the councils, and the assimilation of the experience in the Communist International, Gramsci was able to make important contributions to the revolutionary tradition. Gramsci broke with Bordiga's conception of the party in 1924, and articulated his disagreements:

> We have not thought of the party as the result of a dialectical process in which the spontaneous movement of the revolutionary masses and the organisational and directive will of the centre converge, but only as something floating in the air which develops in itself and for itself, and which the masses will reach when the situation is favourable and the revolutionary wave has reached its height, or when the party centre thinks that it must start an offensive and lowers itself to the masses to stimulate them and carry them into action.[85]

Upon taking leadership of the party in 1924, Gramsci imbued the organisation with the most undeniably positive attribute of his early political career: his understanding of the need to be guided by an activist spirit. The conquest of a majority of the working class wasn't something to be passively awaited, but actively won through struggle.

At the same time, Gramsci was forced to come to terms with his

---

85. Davidson 2016, p.225.

earlier economism. In 1919, Gramsci had invoked revolutionaries to "study the capitalist factory as a necessary form of the working class, as a political organ, as the 'national territory' of workers' self-government".[86]

By the mid-1920s, he had come to the realisation that in order to rule, the working class must extend its leadership beyond the walls of Turin's factories, to embrace all oppressed and exploited social strata. Gramsci's 1926 essay, *Some Aspects of the Southern Question*, urging the working class to forge an alliance with impoverished peasants, was the culmination of this development.

"For the proletariat to become the ruling, the dominant class, it must succeed in creating a system of class alliances which allow it to mobilise the majority of the working population against capitalism and the bourgeois state". This means the working class championing the interests of other oppressed layers by "incorporating these needs into its revolutionary transitional program; and incorporating them among the objectives for which it is struggling".[87] But in order to rule, the proletariat "must throw off all traces of corporatism and all syndicalist prejudices and incrustations".[88] This line in particular reads not just as a diagnosis of the limitations of the Italian workers' movement, but a self-criticism. Gramsci's essay on the southern question marked a coming to terms with the "corporatism" and "syndicalist prejudices" of his own past political practice.

The revolutionary currents in the process of formation during the *Biennio Rosso* were tragically crushed between the twin pillars of fascism and Stalinism. Many of the greatest factory council militants were destroyed in the orgy of counter-revolutionary violence unleashed by Mussolini's *squadristi* in the early 1920s. Pietro Ferrero, the syndicalist leader, was hounded by fascist gangs and forced into a local Chamber of Labour which had been converted into a makeshift prison, where he was beaten and killed. Such was the climate of fear and repression that only five men and eleven women attended the funeral of a revolutionary militant who had influenced thousands.[89]

---

86. Gramsci 1971, p.292.
87. Gramsci 1994, p.316.
88. Gramsci 1994, p.320.
89. Levy 1999, p.226.

The newly-formed Communist Party was decapitated by the fascist regime. Its leadership was arrested, assassinated or driven into exile, while its activists were forced underground. The fascist prosecutor who sentenced Gramsci to imprisonment declared: "We must stop this brain from functioning for twenty years".[90]

While the fascists dedicated themselves to destroying those activists who were the living embodiment of the *Biennio Rosso*, the Stalinist bureaucracy in Russia was committed to preventing the revival of their legacy. After Mussolini's defeat, the Stalinised leadership of the PCI canonised Gramsci as the patron saint of its new strategy of "progressive democracy". Though it arrived draped in Marxist verbiage, this was nothing more than a reheated version of the old Socialist Party's parliamentary cretinism and class collaboration. Gramsci's words were mobilised in service of a bureaucratic reformism that would have repulsed him. The experience of the *Biennio Rosso* came full circle with the reimposition of reformist hegemony in the workers' movement.

The defeat of the council movement was total. But with only a few dazzling exceptions, the history of the communist movement has been defined by its defeats. If we can glean crucial lessons from this inspirational, yet ultimately tragic period about the nature of workers' power and the necessity of revolutionary organisation, then the sacrifice of those brave fighters won't have been in vain.

References

Arfé, Gaetano 1977, *Storia del Socialismo Italiano*, Oscar Studio Mondadori.

Behan, Tom 2003, *The Resistible Rise of Benito Mussolini*, Bookmarks.

Bordiga, Amadeo 2020, *The Science and Passion of Communism. Selected Writings of Amadeo Bordiga (1912–1965)*, ed. Pietro Basso, Brill.

Cammett, John, 1967, *Antonio Gramsci & the Origins of Italian Communism*, Stanford University Press.

Coutinho, Carlos 2012, *Gramsci's Political Thought*, Historical Materialism.

Darlington, Ralph 2008, *Syndicalism and the Transition to Communism*, Ashgate Publishing.

---

90. Quoted in Fiori 1990, p.231.

Davidson, Alastair 1975, "Gramsci and the Factory Councils", *Australian Left Review*, 1, 46. https://ro.uow.edu.au/cgi/viewcontent.cgi?article=1556&context=alr

Davidson, Alastair 2016, *Antonio Gramsci: Toward an Intellectual Biography*, Brill.

Dunnage, Jonathan 2002, *Twentieth Century Italy: a Social History*, Routledge.

Ferro, Marc 1989, *The Great War 1914–1918*, Military Heritage Press.

Fiori, Giuseppe 1990, *Antonio Gramsci: Life of a Revolutionary*, Verso.

Gluckstein, Donny 1985, *The Western Soviets. Workers' Councils Versus Parliament, 1915–1920*, Bookmarks.

Gramsci, Antonio 1971, *Selections from the Prison Notebooks*, ed. Quintin Hoare and Geoffrey Nowell-Smith, International Publishers.

Gramsci, Antonio 1977, *Selections from Political Writings 1910–1920*, Lawrence and Wishart.

Gramsci, Antonio 1978, *Selections from Political Writings 1921–1926*, Lawrence and Wishart.

Gramsci, Antonio 1994, *Gramsci: Pre-Prison Writings*, Cambridge University Press.

Gramsci, Antonio 2014, *A Great and Terrible World: The Pre-Prison Letters, 1908–1926*, Haymarket Books.

Levy, Carl 1999, *Gramsci and the Anarchists*, Berg Publishers.

Neufeld, Maurice 1961, *Italy, School for Awakening Countries: the Italian Labour Movement in its Political, Social, and Economic Setting from 1800 to 1960*, Cornell International Industrial and Labor Reports.

Santucci, Antonio 2010, *Antonio Gramsci*, Monthly Review Press.

Spriano, Paolo 1975, *The Occupation of the Factories*, Amsterdam University Press.

Trotsky, Leon 2007, *The First Five Years of the Communist International*, Volume 1, Pathfinder Press. https://www.marxists.org/archive/trotsky/1924/ffyci-1/index.htm

Trotsky, Leon 2008, *History of the Russian Revolution*, Haymarket Books. https://www.marxists.org/archive/trotsky/1930/hrr/

Trotsky, Leon 2016, *1905*, Haymarket Books. https://www.marxists.org/archive/trotsky/1907/1905/

Williams, Gwynn 1975, *Proletarian order: Antonio Gramsci, Factory Councils and the Origins of Italian Communism, 1911–1921*, Pluto Press.

JORDAN HUMPHREYS

Aboriginal unionists in the 1890s shearers' strikes: a forgotten history

Jordan Humphreys is a socialist activist in Sydney and a regular contributor to the *Marxist Left Review*.

The aboriginal natives do all kinds of station work, such as dipping, shepherding, yarning, wool rolling, and wool pressing for their tucker, with sometimes a shirt or pair of pants thrown in. It's a wonder they don't spear more whites than they do, as they are treated worse than dogs by a jugful.

> – a shearer's letter from Western Australia
> published in *The Hummer*, 1891.[1]

O N 13 AUGUST 1894, 90 "free labourers", the misleading euphemism given to workers willing to scab on strikers, arrived via a special train at Cobar. The shearing season in western New South Wales was about to begin, but this time the station owners were hell-bent on crushing the shearing unions

---

1. *The Hummer*, 19 October 1891, p.5. It should be noted that some of the language quoted from primary sources in this period includes terms which would be rejected by Aboriginal people today, such as "aboriginals", "darkies", "black fellas", etc. Contemporary readers should bear in mind that such language was widespread at the time and it is unsurprising that workers, some of whom had poor literacy at any rate, didn't use more progressive terms. I would urge readers to look at the substance of the arguments that shearers made rather than the outdated terms.

that had called out shearers across the colonies to strike from the beginning of August. Upon arrival the scabs broke up into three groups to travel to sheep stations at Gidgee, Tindarey and Coronga Downs with police escorts. They would have to be taken directly to the stations, as unionists had already convinced all the local hotels not to give them accommodation. Those bound for Tindarey were 10 miles up the Bourke road before they ran into trouble.[2]

A hundred unionists on horseback surrounded the scabs and the police, hooting at Inspector Armstrong, Sergeant Niles and his 17 officers. At the head of the unionists was one of the leaders of the strike camp, Andrew Stuart Stepney, known as "Black Andy". The police and "free labourers" pushed on ahead only to find that the gate on the road had been tied shut with wire and covered in branches. While the police went to work breaking open the gate, the unionists pushed against the crowd. Some rode their horses aggressively around the vehicles carrying the scabs, shouting at them, while others leaned over to argue with the men to abandon the scabbing operation and join the union. Every couple of miles the crowd paused as another gate had to be opened up and the scene repeated itself. During the delays a few "free men" would jump ship and join the unionists to be "received with cheers". At one gate a lynch pin of one of the trolleys used by the scabs was removed and the wheels fell off when it started up again. Somewhat humorously, Stepney spent half an hour arguing with a repentant young man – only to discover he was a plain clothes policeman.

The crowd swelled as it got closer to Tindarey. The miners from Villagoe, mostly Cornish, had left work to join the shouting and arguing with the scabbing operation. The union crowd trampled over the fences marking the station as private property, ignoring the warnings of police. It was only at 100 yards from the station sheds that the police formed a line strong enough to stop the unionists from advancing any further.

Despite being a veteran of the 1891 shearers' strike, the 15-mile

---

2. The following is drawn from the account in *Barrier Miner* (Broken Hill), 14 August 1894, p.2.

battle had clearly shaken Sergeant Niles, who postponed plans to escort more workers to the other stations. Fourteen of the scab crew had already thrown up their hands and joined the union, and Niles could only watch on as several hundred unionists, headed by Stepney, marched back up the road cheering. A week later Stepney and another striker, William Quinlan, were summoned to appear before the Cobar court on charges of "wilfully trespassing on the grounds of Tindarey station".[3]

The battle between the unionists and the squatters had only just begun. But in the press the fight between the claims of both was joined by a new concern – just who was this "Black Andy"?

The *Evening News* claimed that he was an "American negro". A letter sent to *The Worker* (Wagga) painted a picture of dangerous racial miscegenation at the Billagoe strike camp:

> "Black Andy" (Andrew Stuart Stepney) is representative of the union camp at Billagoe, 26 miles from Cobar, on the Bourke Road. A man named Russell, who is a half-caste Maori, is chairman of the camp committee, and for some time a New Zealand shearer, born in Germany, acted as secretary, with an assistant hailing from old Erin. One of the roustabouts on strike has a German father, a French mother, and was born in (Dam) Chicago. How's that for the brotherhood of Labour, Mr. Editor?[4]

To which the editor replied "That's all right".

Andy also appeared a few weeks later, and over 1,000 kilometres away, at Bowen Downs, leading striking shearers against one of the biggest stations in Queensland.[5] His appearance at Bowen Downs sent the conservative press into a frenzy.

3. *Barrier Miner*, 21 August 1894, p.2.
4. *The Worker* (Wagga), 8 September 1894, p.2.
5. As reported in *The Week*, 12 October 1894, p.5 and alluded to in *The Western Champion and General Advertiser for the Central-Western Districts*, 4 September 1894, p.7. The second article also claims that Andy was involved in a previous strike, although it is unclear if this means the strike in Cobar or a previous strike at Bowen Downs.

As a racist poem published in over a dozen papers across the country went:

> *Feller-toilers, wot's the matter ? Is the worker goin' buck,*
> *That we've got to find a leader in a pure-bred Yankee black?*[6]

The 8 September issue of *The Worker* (Wagga) reported Andy's reply to his new found celebrity. He was "very much hurt at the *Evening News* describing him as an 'American negro'"; Andy explained that his grandmother was Aboriginal, and claimed his father was a "Zulu chief". *The Worker* added that he had been a unionist since 1886.[7]

Stepney had been born in Adelaide around 1850,[8] and spent his early teenage years working on ships but came to hate the sea. He then worked at a pastoral station owned by the famous Chirnside brothers, who were some of the first to employ Aboriginal station hands,[9] but he left after six months because they refused to pay him wages. His mother died from alcohol and Stepney then found himself destitute in Melbourne. He is reported as saying that "whenever he got any little jobs the other boys persecuted his life", with one other boy cutting his knuckles with a knife for getting a job. At age 15 he appealed to a judge to send him to an industrial school in order for him to learn how to be a tailor. It's unknown if his request was accepted, but by around 1874 he was back in the country working on paddle ships and is said to have become a "well-known character on the Darling".[10] Decades later there were several letters in rural newspapers about the "Legend of Black Andy" in which people recalled him performing several amazing physical feats (he was often described as a "giant"). By 1887 he lived in Wilcannia, which one of his friends called his "home", and as noted joined the shearers' union. Stepney also participated in a shearers' strike in Hay, NSW during 1890[11] and amused a shearers' union meeting with tales about

---

6. *The Week*, 12 October 1894, p.2.
7. *The Worker* (Wagga), 8 September 1894, p.2.
8. Much of the following biographical detail comes from *The Age*, 24 July 1865, p.6.
9. Hone 1969.
10. *The Albury Banner and Wodonga Express*, 2 August 1912, p.23.
11. *The Hay Standard and Advertiser for Balranald, Wentworth, Maude*, 4 October 1890, p.2.

the conditions in the shearing sheds. He appears to have spent some time in Queensland after the 1894 strike, being a regular attendee and personality at the Mutti cricket games in 1898.[12] He died sometime in the late 1910s or early 1920s at Broken Hill.[13]

There are no books that acknowledge Stepney, in fact not a single currently published article even references his existence, and as we shall see he wasn't the only Aboriginal man caught up in the great shearing wars of the 1890s. In fact some hundreds of Aboriginal workers participated in the shearers' unions during the last two decades of the nineteenth century. This is a challenge to the stereotypical ideal of the Australian bush worker ingrained in our national culture. For much of the twentieth century the shearer was the epitome of the rugged proletarian White Australian. "The Bushman was not merely a white man of the standardised frontier type", wrote Vance Palmer who invoked the emotional imagery of a whole tradition of Australian intellectuals, "He belonged to the country he had made his own and no other; he had linked himself to it through his feelings and imagination".[14]

The participation of Aboriginal workers in the shearing strikes is also a challenge to left historians who have noted the racism of the shearers' unions and then mistakenly believed that Aboriginal workers played no role within the shearers' unions. Mark Wisely's thesis argues that white unionist shearers displayed only "paternal contempt" for Aboriginal workers.[15] This accords with much contemporary writing on the Australian working class and its relationship to Indigenous people. Sai Englert for instance has asserted that in countries with a history of settler colonialism such as Australia, "settler labour movements fought for the intensification of settler expansion and racial segregation...through colour bars, boycott campaigns and demands for expulsion". Furthermore Englert argues that in periods of heightened class conflict, settler colonial societies can resolve these conflicts by "intensifying the dispossession of

---

12. *The Western Champion and General Advertiser for the Central-Western Districts*, 6 December 1898, p.5.
13. *The World's News*, 26 September 1925, p.8.
14. Palmer 1954, p.155.
15. Wisely 2011, p.58.

Indigenous populations in order to improve the material conditions of settler workers".[16]

In regard to the unionised shearers and Indigenous people in Australia, all of this is a ridiculous exaggeration that is not backed up by the formal policy of the unions or their actual practice. It is rebutted by looking at the views presented in newspapers published by shearers' unions or those close to them at the time, such as *The Worker*, published by the Amalgamated Shearers' Union of Australasia (ASU) and then the Australian Workers' Union (AWU) in Wagga, NSW, and *Worker*, edited by the early trade union leader William Lane, who helped found the shearers' union in Queensland, and which was strongly associated with the shearers' union.

Englert's argument that settler societies can resolve periods of class conflict through passing on the benefits of colonisation to non-Indigenous workers doesn't fit with the actual history of class conflict in 1890s Australia. This was a period of intense class struggle in which tens of thousands of workers challenged the authority of the capitalist class and the state. There was a genuine fear in ruling-class circles that it could lead to a revolutionary situation, particularly following the flying of the Eureka flag at the Barcaldine strike camp in 1891 – which was interpreted as a declaration of insurrection by the Queensland colonial government. One thousand military personnel were mobilised to defeat the strike, and 13 of the strike leaders were arrested and charged with sedition and conspiracy.[17] These fears revived during the 1894 strike, which was even more violent than in 1891, epitomised by the burning of the riverboat, the *Rodney*, which was transporting scabs up the Darling River.[18] Yet the relationship between those workers and the Aboriginal population was very different from Englert's argument.

There is plenty of evidence of involvement of Aboriginal workers

---

16. Englert 2020, p.12. For a more detailed critique of the pitfalls of settler colonial theory, see Humphreys 2021.
17. See Svensen 1989. Some socialists at the time also shared the view that the 1890s was a revolutionary period in Australia, see for instance Lane 1993 [1939], pp.35–46.
18. Armstrong 2007.

in rural union battles throughout the 1890s. During the 1891 shearers' strike in Queensland, an Aboriginal man named Moffat was involved in fighting scabs, another Aboriginal man named Mickey was arrested for shooting at a sentry at the Delta station[19] and Aboriginal workers were a part of the strike camp at Charleville.[20] In NSW there were around 30 Aboriginal workers at the Warri Moffatt strike camp.[21] In 1892 a mass meeting of 50 Aboriginal workers at the Wallaroo Eucalyptus Works in Queensland voted to go on strike against low wages after asking the advice of a white unionist. The strike ended a week later in defeat, but with the workers burning an effigy of the boss.[22] Near Mungindi in the same year an Aboriginal shed worker asked the shearers' union representative if "it would do his mates any harm for the blackfellows to kick a bit to improve things". When the union rep assured him it "was all right", the Aboriginal workers went on strike. The Aboriginal agitator who had started the strike told the union rep that "Blackfeller better sit on bank of a creek for nothing than work for blanky squatters at the same price".[23]

To understand how these Aboriginal men found themselves in the turbulent union battles at the end of the century we have to put aside some established academic "truths" and try to reconstruct the actual relationship between shearers, their unions and Aboriginal workers in the last years of the nineteenth century.

It is often assumed that the shearers' unions universally excluded Aboriginal workers from membership.[24] Judith Elton recalls attending a meeting of trade unionists in South Australia in 1997 at which she was shocked to find that most people believed that the AWU "uniformly excluded Aboriginal workers from membership until the 1960s".[25] The author of a Sydney University PhD thesis from 2009 goes so far as to believe that there were no

---

19. *The Capricornian*, 16 May 1891, p.20.
20. *The Capricornian*, 30 May 1891, p.22.
21. *Worker* (Brisbane), 27 June 1891, p.3.
22. *Worker* (Brisbane), 13 August 1892, p.3 and 27 August 1892, p.2.
23. *Worker* (Brisbane), 19 November 1892, p.3.
24. See the historians quoted in Markus 1978.
25. Elton 2007, p.2.

Aboriginal shearers.[26] The reality is almost the exact opposite. While the early shearers' unions had racist rules that excluded various so called "foreign aliens" such as the Chinese, South Sea Islanders and "Afghans", these rules did not apply to Aboriginal workers (and some others like Maori workers and African Americans) in the shearers' unions of New South Wales, South Australia, Victoria and Queensland. This was later explicitly clarified when these shearers' unions amalgamated to form the AWU in 1894, whose rules stated:

> The union shall be open to all *bona fide* wage-earners, male or female, except Chinese, Japanese, Kanakas, Afghans, and other coloured aliens. (This shall not apply to Aborigines, Maoris, American negroes, or to the children of mixed marriages born in Australasia.)[27]

The Australian Shearers' Union was formed in 1886 in Ballarat, with similar unions being established across New South Wales and South Australia during the same year. Aboriginal workers were involved from the very beginning. As already noted, Andy Stepney had union tickets from 1886. In a series of articles in the *Worker*, early union leader AJ Sullivan remembers being asked to speak at a massive meeting of shearers in Wagga during 1885 which was run by an Aboriginal shearer named "Tommy", who had been commissioned to organise the union meeting by mostly white shearers at the Binya station in Merool. The meeting ended in a brawl between Tommy and some others, but laid the basis for the future Wagga branch of the shearers' union.[28]

An early experience that must have shaped the leaders of the shearers' unions was an organising tour of New Zealand at the end of 1886. The goal of this trip was to win shearers in New Zealand to unionism so they couldn't be used as scabs in the Australian colonies. While they initially focused on recruiting white shearers on the South Island, David Temple got into contact with Maori workers, who did the majority of shearing on the North Island, and found

---

26. O'Malley 2009, p.13, footnote 24.
27. Printed in the *Worker* (Brisbane), 20 April 1895, p.3.
28. Sullivan 2005 [1916].

them enthusiastic about the idea of unionism. Temple proposed that they would be open to joining en masse once the union's rules were translated into their own language.[29]

The Australian Shearers' Union joined with several other unions in NSW and SA to form the ASU in 1887. Throughout the late 1880s the union fought a running battle with the pastoralists, rapidly gaining thousands of members. The issue of Aboriginal workers was discussed in some detail at the 1891 ASU conference.

At this conference there was discussion about a motion moved by the Creswick, Victoria, branch of the ASU that would allow all Aboriginal workers to be admitted as life members of the union without paying any union fees, as long as they refused to work in non-union sheds like other ASU members. Temple supported this motion, arguing that "It is a graceful act to those from whom the country has been taken. No liberal minded man could surely object to this concession to the original owners of the soil". Cook, a delegate from South Australia, concurred, making the point that it would be a graceful act to allow Aboriginal workers to join without having to pay union fees considering "their circumstances were not the same as white men, and their earnings were not the same".

Some delegates objected to the motion on the basis that Aboriginal workers were less committed to unionism and so shouldn't get special treatment for their lack of interest, that "they were not altogether to be depended upon", and that if "poverty was a justification for free membership, there were numbers of white men who deserved similar consideration". These arguments were rebutted by delegates who drew upon their experiences organising Aboriginal shearers. Cook stated "there were 60 or 70 in South Australia, all good unionists". McInerney, from Young, NSW, said "he wished all the white men were as good as the Australian darkies – they were fine fellows as far as he saw. He knew a number who had cleared out of the shed when it was found 'non-union'". Percy, from Cobar, NSW, was "in favour of enrolling all the Aboriginals". He explained that "[in] one shed in Cobar an aboriginal was the only one of twenty who walked away for unionism".[30]

---

29. Merritt 1986, p.96.
30. All quotes from the record of the conference published in *Shearers' & General*

In the end a compromise motion was reached which waived the entrance fee for "pure bred aborigines" only. Whatever one thinks about this debate, the significant thing is that it was over whether special measures were needed to recruit more Aboriginal workers, not over whether they should be members or not. As well, at least some of the unionists in the debate articulated an awareness of the dispossession of Indigenous people and its consequences.

These attitudes weren't limited just to shearers in Victoria, New South Wales and South Australia. The Queensland Shearers' Union (QSU), despite complaining that the ASU was too soft on the "coloured question", also refused to exclude Aboriginal workers in the union rules. Even the short-lived right-wing split from the QSU, the National Union of Labour based at the Wolfang station, supported employment for Aboriginal workers.[31]

It was more difficult in the more recently colonised sections of the continent such as Western Australia and the Northern Territory. In far-flung places like the Kimberley frontier the pastoral industry was much more dependent upon Aboriginal labour. Unionisation was also much slower to develop, with a stable shearers' union not being formed until 1900 in Western Australia. Here slavery-like conditions for Aboriginal workers were rampant; many station owners were also involved in the "black-birding" trade that would see Aboriginal workers used as forced labour for the pearling industry. They would also "trade" the Aboriginal people who lived on their land with other station owners when they needed them, and were constantly pushing for the police to do more to crush any sign of Aboriginal resistance.[32]

The issue of Aboriginal workers wasn't confined just to the official rules of these unions or the 1891 ASU conference. A number of articles in the newspapers of the shearers' unions reveal both the strengths and limitations of the union members' attitudes to Aboriginal workers.

At the end of the nineteenth century the genocidal wars of conquest that had torn control over the land out of Indigenous

---

Labourers' Record, 15 June 1891, p.2.

31. Merritt 1986, p.189.

32. See Owen 2016.

hands was still within living memory, and in fact continued in some parts of the colonies. The British colonists had taken control over the whole continent through the use of force. You could try to justify this, ignore it, glamourise, condemn or feel guilty about it, but few at the time, as compared to later generations, really tried to deny the basic fact of what had happened.

While they aren't free of various racist ideas about Aboriginal people, the general attitude of the vast majority of articles, letters and editorials within the newspapers of the early shearers' unions that discussed these issues was acknowledgement that the colonisation was based on theft without any moral justification, sympathy for the situation this put Aboriginal people in, and condemnation of the continuation of violent attacks upon Aboriginal communities by the police and pastoralists.

So an 1892 article printed in the *Worker* (Brisbane) argues:

> I've yet to learn, don't you know, that the immortal British Empire or any other speck of country owns by sheer right divine all the land it can get its clutches on. There's no more natural sense in a bleary-eyed officer with gold lace and a taste for rum, sticking a few feet of stick, with a few square inches of painted calico attached, into the ground and saying "I annex this 'ere country", than there is in you or me taking a trip across to Europe and going through the same pantomime at Brighton or Monte Carlo. You or I've got exactly the same "right" as the gold laced gentleman who appreciates rum. The only thing is that he has a title deed in the shape of a few thousand tons of men of war, with guns enough to blow the unfortunate natives to little small bits if they object. Wonderful justice, isn't it?... The aboriginals had more right to be in Australia than we had, looking at things justly.[33]

Other articles repeat the same point: "In the long ago a Christian nation crossed the seas and took from a happy race who had never wronged them, their country, out of which they afterwards made many millions of pounds".[34] "A great deal of nonsense is talked about

---

33. *Worker* (Brisbane), 16 July 1892, p.4.
34. *Worker* (Brisbane), 26 January 1895, p.1.

the benefits white men confer on native races when they conquer them and annex their country. In many cases the whites make the blacks, to all intents and purposes, their slaves."[35] Another states that the squatters "pushed their civilisation...by the crack of the rifle and flour mixed with arsenic".[36] A long article about a recent inquiry into the mass killings of Aborigines in Queensland prompted the writer to

> remember, in bygone years, men having the mission to 'disperse' myalls for the convenience of white settlers, or in plain English, a license to shoot, kill, or frighten away from the path of the white man the lawful owner of the soil.

The writer recommended that the inquiry use as evidence a white settler's rifle that he claimed had notches in it for each Aborigine he had killed.[37]

Some articles acknowledged not just the initial theft but also the ongoing injustice this created, as in this 1895 article that quoted a recently published pamphlet:

> It seems well to consider here our "debtor" account with the aboriginals. Queensland has, so far, alienated about 10,000,000 acres of freehold land, and leased about 300,000,000 acres for pastoral occupation. For the first we have received about £6,250,000 in cash, and for the leased land we receive £332,800 annual rental. Since the year of separation, 1869, or ever since 1842, we have not expended £50,000 for the benefit of the aboriginals, and have never since then, or before, paid them a single shilling of cash, clothes, or food, for even one acre of land.

The article added: "Why? Because they are too weak to compel justice, and we are too unjust to accord it without compulsion".[38]

There are also constant articles in the shearers' press about the ongoing massacres of Aboriginal people across the continent.

---

35. *The Worker* (Wagga), 22 April 1899, p.2.
36. *Worker* (Brisbane), 28 May 1892, p.4.
37. *Worker* (Brisbane), 9 May 1896, p.10.
38. *Worker* (Brisbane), 27 April 1895, p.3.

"The natives of Queensland", one article states, "are treated as veritable outcasts, and their lives are freely taken in certain districts on the smallest provocation, and no questions are asked".[39] Another explains:

> The accusations made in the house of commons re outrages on blacks in Queensland are very lightly treated in the dailies, who know very well the solid truth of the charges... The Australian aboriginal has been cruelly shot down in many parts and treated like a beast almost everywhere.

The article ended: "This is the truth which no ignorance or lying can hide".[40]

While there are many sensationalist articles about the trials of Aborigines for murder and other crimes, the spread of diseases in Aboriginal communities[41] and the impact of alcohol, there are also more sympathetic articles. An article entitled "White and Blackfellow law" protested against the charging of one Aboriginal man for killing another Aboriginal man according to conditions laid out in tribal law. The writer was particularly horrified at the thought that this might end with the Aboriginal man being sent to a "lunatic asylum...where he will be practically caged like a wild animal", instead arguing: "let us recognise there is Blackfellow law and customs that we need not impinge upon".[42] The killings of Aborigines by police were regularly reported[43], as were reports which detailed how the police and the local bosses worked together to exploit Aborigines. One describes how the local judge and the police would let Aborigines out of jail early in order to go back to work for the squatters, but if they left of their own accord they would be "handcuffed and leg-ironed" when brought back.[44] Another article reports that an Aboriginal man was kept in jail for six days before seeing a judge, charged with some

---

39. *Worker* (Brisbane), 28 May 1892, p.4.
40. *Worker* (Brisbane), 4 June 1892, p.1.
41. *Worker* (Brisbane), 9 December 1893, p.1.
42. *Worker* (Brisbane), 11 March 1893, p.1.
43. For instance *Worker* (Brisbane), 29 August 1896, p.12 & 19 June 1897, p.11.
44. *Worker* (Brisbane), 15 April 1893, p.3.

minor crime.[45] When a unionist was brought before the courts on the charge of "indecent assault" towards an Aboriginal woman the *Worker* argued it was right that the judge should find him guilty, and urged the shearers not to act like "brutes and beasts" towards Aboriginal people.[46]

The shearers' papers also had many articles about the exploitative conditions faced by Aboriginal workers, including the reprinting of exploitative contracts Aboriginal workers were forced to sign,[47] the kidnapping of Aboriginal girls by station masters to be used as forced domestic labour,[48] the non-payment of wages to Aboriginal roustabouts,[49] and so on. There is however some ambiguity about the status of the Aboriginal worker.

For instance one article argues that:

> [N]o one grudges the aboriginal his minimum wage of half-a-crown a week. His services are probably worth very little more. The gap between his civilisation and ours is a great deal too wide for him to leap across. His old free and easy life of independence was a bad training for the new conditions of wage slavery with which he is expected to grapple, or be wiped out. His great sin against civilisation is that he is not industrious and thrifty, and that he will not work. He has no economic value in a capitalistic state of society. The kanaka is ahead of him in this respect, as also are the other coloured races. The blackfellow is the wild human animal that cannot be economically tamed. He won't cut cane, he won't dig in mines, he won't become a navvy.[50]

While this article expresses the idea that Aboriginal workers were poorly able to participate in the capitalist economy, it also recognises the free and independent life for Indigenous people that existed before their dispossession and the inhumanity of the capitalist

---

45. *Worker* (Brisbane), 9 December 1893, p.1.
46. *Worker* (Brisbane), 11 July 1891, p.1.
47. *The Hummer*, 19 October 1891, p.5.
48. *Worker* (Brisbane), 25 June 1892, p.2.
49. *Worker* (Brisbane), 17 September 1892, p.3.
50. *Worker* (Brisbane), 7 October 1899, p.5.

work process. It is also in contrast to other images of Aboriginal workers in the shearers' union press. One article reports that on a station an "aboriginal took the job and did the work well", but after he finished his work he was paid a lowly 33s. The article commented "so much for the "fair and reasonable" squatter".[51] There are multiple positive accounts of Aboriginal workers standing up to bosses and demanding better pay or conditions, such as in the strikes already described. As well there are accounts of white unionists interceding in disputes between Aboriginal workers and bosses to demand that the Aboriginal workers get paid the correct amount.[52] At Bundarra station in 1900 white shearers refused to work until Aboriginal shed hands were given a fair wage.[53] Organiser reports published in The Worker made constant reference to the recruitment of Aboriginal shearers and station hands,[54] and a summary of the gains of the labour movement in 1906 noted that "even the Aborigines were taking it up".[55] One report from a 1902 strike at Booberoi noted the important role that Aboriginal workers played and stated that:

> The knock-out to Haley was the unanimous roll up of the aborigines, who are staunch Unionists; and deserve our assistance in other ways. If the whites had been as true to their fellows as the dark skins, Booberoi would be Union today.[56]

An obituary notice for an Aboriginal shearer called "Bundaburra Jack" noted: "Like most aboriginals he was a good Unionist. Bundaburra was always one of the first to nominate for his ticket when an organiser called".[57]

This doesn't mean that there are no examples of hostility towards Aboriginal workers. There were concerns raised about the use of Aboriginal workers as scabs during the 1894 strike in Queensland,

---

51. *Worker* (Brisbane), 7 February 1891, p.2.
52. *Worker* (Brisbane), 17 July 1897, p.6.
53. *The Worker* (Wagga), 20 October 1900, p.7.
54. See *The Worker* (Wagga), 5 October 1901, p.7, 1 November 1902, p.6, 1 October 1904, p.7, and 21 August 1905, p.6, for a few examples.
55. *The Worker* (Wagga), 6 December 1906, p.2.
56. *The Worker* (Wagga), 30 August 1902, p.6.
57. *The Worker* (Wagga), 3 Feb 1909, p.7.

particularly at the North Yanko station, and condemnation of the government giving them temporary free train passes to get to the stations.[58] However the same paper also reported positively on the Aboriginal shearers at the Weilmoringle strike camp who refused to work under a non-union agreement even when the struggle was clearly lost.[59] Another article noted that during the 1894 strike there was a shed in which all the white shearers scabbed and only the two Aboriginal shearers refused to work under a non-union contract. When the two shearers walked out of the shed, *The Worker* reported one yelled out "Well, the only thing I'm sorry for is that I have one drop of white blood in me".[60]

In response to criticism in the daily newspapers that the shearers' union discriminated against Aboriginal workers, David Temple wrote a widely republished reply, which while expressing his racist opposition to migrant groups reveals a different attitude towards Aboriginal workers:

> The bush unionist objects to Chinese, Cingalese, Polynese, Malayese and such, not to the harmless and much injured aboriginal whom if an occasional unionist insults – there are blackguards everywhere – an occasional squatter still more frequently shoots on sight like a dingo. In many of the strike camps were aboriginals who had knocked off with the rest from various stations. At Warri Malaise there were thirty-two whites and as many blacks.[61]

There are even sympathetic articles about Aborigines making more general statements about their dispossession. So one article noted a "well received" speech by Mr Breston, an Aboriginal man, who condemned the government for their treatment of his people and demanded that "the Government should give the aboriginals half the land they had been robbed of".[62] Another explained that a group of

---

58. See *The Worker* (Wagga), 15 September 1894, p.3 and 18 May 1895, p.1.
59. *The Worker* (Wagga), 27 October 1894, p.3.
60. *The Worker* (Wagga), 5 October 1901, p.6.
61. *Worker* (Brisbane), 27 June 1891, p.3.
62. *Worker* (Brisbane), 14 December 1895, p.4.

Aboriginal people were demanding the right to attend the Victorian state parliament on the basis that "as their country had been stolen from them by the white fellows they deserved some consideration".[63]

In 1900 in Breelong, NSW, James "Jimmy" Governor, his brother Joe and another Aboriginal man called Jack Underwood murdered the family of a white station owner for whom the Governor brothers had worked. The three Aboriginal men then went on the run, apparently killing several more people in the process, leading to one of the biggest manhunts in Australian history at this time.[64]

This is how *The Worker* reported on the events:

> Unless the Breelong aboriginals are singularly alert and well mounted, it is not likely that they have committed all the murders which have lately taken place in the Mudgee and Dubbo districts. Indeed, there is reason to believe that this is a preconcerted uprising of the aboriginals against those who have robbed them of their country... But whether these murders are the result of a general rising of aboriginals or committed by two or three blacks only, the moral is the same. The Breelong blacks have charged the whites with taking their country, and say that their crime is caused by a desire for revenge. The charge cannot be rebutted, even though it be no excuse for these murders. We have not only dispossessed them, we have done more than that – we have made these poor benighted savages heirs to all the vices of civilisation and imparted to them little of its protection, none of its guiding, self-restraining influences.

> Therefore, we are responsible for this sudden outburst of savagery. And when these ignorant and misguided men stand manacled in the dock, it would be but justice that we should place alongside of them the Nineteenth Century Christianity whose neglect of our aboriginals has now caused the shedding of much innocent blood and is practically responsible for that now and the sorrow also of many bereaved ones.[65]

---

63. *Worker* (Brisbane), 19 February 1898, p.11.
64. See Biber 2008 for background on these events.
65. *The Worker* (Wagga), 28 July 1900, p.4.

An update on the events at Breelong a week later noted that "the recent aboriginal uprising was caused by their employment at starvation rates and the continual condemnation of their work".[66]

Why did unionised shearers have these attitudes to Aboriginal workers?

First of all they faced a common enemy – the pastoral bosses and the police. As Russell Ward has noted, "It may be doubted whether the police force of any English-speaker country, except Ireland, has ever been more thoroughly unpopular than were those of most Australian colonies in the last century...the popular attitude towards policemen in general was one of hatred and contempt".[67] For the shearers this hatred was hardened during the strikes of the late 1880s and 1890s when the police collaborated with the pastoralists to protect scab labour and break up strike camps. Sometimes the link between the oppressors of the Indigenous and non-Indigenous shearers could be very direct, such as a report that the wife of a anti-unionist station owner also attempted to cover up the murder of Aboriginal people on her land.[68] A review of a book about the role of the Native Mounted Police (NMP) in Queensland in massacring Aboriginal communities ended with the comment:

> We may remind our readers that the police "protection" afforded to the "free" labourers during the shearers' strike was under the command of the most famous inspector of this corps, and that much of interest concerning the working of that branch of the Queensland "force" can be learned by a perusal of Mr. Vogan's book, which is decidedly rough on the up-country squatters and their friends of the NMP.[69]

The most consistently militant sections of the shearers' unions were the more proletarianised and landless workers in the Western districts. For them the argument that Aboriginal people had to be wiped out in order for white men to use the land productively often

---

66. *The Worker* (Wagga), 4 August 1900, p.5.
67. Ward 2003 [1966], pp.154–5.
68. *Worker* (Brisbane), 4 June 1892, p.1.
69. *The Australian Workman*, 25 July 1891, p.2.

fell on deaf ears, seeing as they were forced to work for the small minority of people who actually owned the vast swathes of profitable land. This is why, while unionised shearers were sympathetic to other shearers or Aboriginal people condemning their dispossession, they were usually cynical about colonial elites making similar statements. When the then ex-premier of Queensland, Hugh Nelson, gave a speech lamenting the fact that the "White people had taken their country from the poor aboriginals", the Worker commented bitterly about this "maudlin rubbish", "considering that 70 percent of the people of this country don't own an inch of land between them".[70] Or as one of the delegates at the 1891 ASU conference put it, the "shearers had not robbed them of their country, but the capitalists".[71]

This hatred of a common enemy was then reinforced by the particular place that Aboriginal workers occupied within the structure of the rural workforce. As others have noted, there were specific aspects to Aboriginal labour that made it more likely that European-born workers would have greater sympathy for them than the "foreign aliens" they too often saw as their enemies.[72] The contradictory nature of the Aboriginal worker, as not white but also by their very definition not "foreign", produced an uneasy conundrum. Their relatively small number, due to the impact of the European invasion, made it harder for white workers to imagine them as an invading horde, particularly when their existence wasn't tied to a competing national power, and in the shed the Aboriginal shearer could prove their skill in front of everyone, and was often acknowledged as possessing a natural ability. The effect of this on the minds of shearers often with little, or no, land to their name, finding themselves sometimes hundreds or even thousands of miles away from home, slaving alongside "the original inhabitants of the soil" is the bedrock upon which the articles and resolutions, multi-racial strike camps and respect, whether begrudging or otherwise, was built.

The most human reason behind the attitudes during the 1890s is that the unionists were responding to that same "whispering in

---

70. *Worker* (Brisbane), 13 May 1899, p.9.
71. *Shearers' & General Labourers' Record*, 15 June 189, p.2.
72. In particular Judith Elton in her extensive review of the relationship between the shearers' unions and Aboriginal labour. Elton 2007.

our hearts" that Henry Reynolds argues pricked the guilt of liberal humanitarians and clergymen.[73] Contrary to the stereotyped image of the robotic white worker who only mechanically reacts to his crudest economic needs, many of the accounts of Aboriginal oppression written by shearers are filled with genuine horror at the conditions other humans were forced to live in. In 1891, Walter Bell, a Riverina shearer, went to Western Australia to join the hunt for gold. What he found instead was a land in which all the good prospects were but a fabrication and instead "slavery flourishes". If an Aboriginal refuses to work for a station owner "he is charged with sheep stealing, chained by the neck to others, and despatched to a place named Rott Nest". Bell himself saw five Aboriginal men chained together in just this way and heard that squatters stole young Aboriginal girls and sold them to "mean whites" who were working for them. Bell's letter is a description of a hellscape; it was printed in *The Hummer* with the warning that this is what happens in lands "where the benevolent squatter can run the show for all its worth".[74]

The difference between this and the colonial middle-class humanitarian view is that this sympathy was combined with a class instinct rooted in the ideals of the "brotherhood of labour". The shearing strikes of the 1880s and 1890s sharply divided rural Australian society into opponents and supporters of the shearers' unions. You could be the whitest Australian worker of all time, but if you refused to support the union movement then you were at the very least an idiot, at worst a scab and a traitor, and therefore outside of the labour movement. On the other hand if Aboriginal workers made the decision to support the class struggle then, whatever other ideas shearers could have about them, they were seen as a part of the labour movement.

The particular contradictions of the development of racial politics made it easier for some shearers, in particular the more militant and politically developed unionists, to break through some of the racist barriers of colonial Australia, and begin to build an alternative culture of mutual respect and even solidarity. This culture was limited by other aspects of the shearers' union and the broader social

---

73. Reynolds 1998.
74. *The Hummer*, 19 October 1891, p.7.

context in which it emerged, which was after all a thoroughly racist settler society born out of colonialism and violence. The acceptance by most shearers of the need to exclude "foreign labour" placed certain limits on how far their sympathies for the Aboriginal workers could develop. After all that exclusion was based on the acceptance of a racially hierarchical worldview. In practice and rhetoric such a worldview was adapted in order to allow the Aboriginal worker a place within the movement for the emancipation of labour, but the racism that blinded many shearers to possibilities of solidarity with the Chinese expressed itself in an article mocking the marriage of a white woman to an Aboriginal man,[75] in the paternalism that blighted even the more sympathetic writers and in concerns raised over Aborigines being manipulated into voting for conservative politicians.[76] While it is outside the scope of this article to go into the details, once the shearers' unions began to be incorporated into the capitalist state through arbitration courts and the forming of Labor governments, this negative aspect became more pronounced.

It would be misleading though to think that sympathy towards Aboriginal workers was simply guaranteed or automatic. Militant unionists had to formulate a political attitude towards Aboriginal workers and make arguments to the rest of the shearers about how they should relate to Aboriginal people. At the 1891 ASU conference the most pro-Aboriginal statements were made by left-wing delegates from the most militant branches of the union, such as W Percy from Cobar, H Langwell and Robert Stevenson from Bourke (who moved the original motion on behalf of the Creswick branch). These branches were in the far-flung western division of New South Wales, and as has already been noted it was here that the membership of the union was much more dominated by propertyless workers from outside the area, unlike the central and eastern divisions which had a greater number of shearers who were also small farmers.

The fact that sympathetic attitudes towards Aboriginal workers wasn't automatic is also revealed by looking at the later history of the union in Western Australia. In the north-west of the country there were pastoral stations where a significant section of the

---

75. *The Australian Workman*, 7 December 1895, p.3.
76. *The Worker*, 4 June 1898, p.5 and *The Worker*, 16 June 1898, p.16.

workforce was Aboriginal. However the AWU failed to organise these workers. This failure was criticised by Mick Sawtell, a rank-and-file AWU activist, young socialist and future stalwart of the militant Industrial Workers of the World, who in 1910 wrote a series of letters and articles arguing that the union should launch an organising campaign among the Aboriginal workers on the Pilbara stations. This was discussed at the 1910 AWU conference. However while AWU members from the eastern states raised positive examples of their own work in organising Aboriginal workers, under pressure from the more conservative members from Western Australia, some of whom wanted Aboriginal workers replaced by white workers, the conference passed a vague motion criticising the exploitation of Aboriginal workers in north-western Australia and praising the work of the WA branch. No organising effort seems to have happened, a failure which would have lasting consequences. When the Aboriginal workers in the Pilbara did start to organise themselves in the 1940s this led to significant conflict with the AWU officialdom.[77]

Racism towards other groups, such as non-white foreign workers like the Chinese, was also not unchallengeable. Several historians[78] have already unpacked how anti-Chinese racism was driven by sections of the ruling class and their middle-class allies rather than some natural and inevitable outgrowth of working-class consciousness. A minority of the more militant shearers did try to push against some of the stream of anti-Chinese sentiment, such as Robert Stevenson and the Bourke branch of the ASU (who also strongly

---

77. For the 1910 AWU conference discussion see *The Worker*, 2 February 1910, p.5. For Sawtell's articles see *The Worker*, 16 March 1910, p.5, 4 May 1910, p.5, and 5 January 1911, p.3. For the later history of the AWU and Aboriginal workers in the Pilbara see Scrimgeour 2020, in particular pp.440–3.

Sawtell is an interesting figure. He learnt some Aboriginal languages during his years in the bush before becoming a socialist and then a member of the Industrial Workers of the World, during which he served several stints in prison for his left-wing activism. In 1921 he rejected the "violence" of the Bolshevik revolution and renewed his interest in theosophy. In the 1930s he was a supporter of Aboriginal activism and advised the Communist Party on Aboriginal issues, before becoming a member of the Aboriginal Welfare Board and drawing criticism from Aboriginal activists for his increasingly conservative and paternalistic views. See Roe 2005.

78. See Small n.d. and Griffiths 2006.

backed Aboriginal workers in the 1891 conference). He moved that Chinese members who joined before the 1888 conference should be allowed to retain their membership because of the "need to act fairly towards men who had done the ASU no harm".[79] Stevenson and the Bourke branch were criticised by other branches of the ASU and QSU for being too soft on the Chinese. At the founding conference of the General Labourers Union of Australasia (GLU) set up by the ASU to organise shed-hands, and into which it eventually amalgamated, a delegate called Power from Casterton moved that the union should organise Chinese workers, although his motion was defeated.[80]

Despite some limitations, the common experiences of black and white shearers in the battles of the 1890s positively shaped workers' consciousness for years, and even decades, to come. Aboriginal workers would continue to play an important role within the AWU. In 1913 the Adelaide branch of the AWU reported that out of its 5,000 members, 400 were Aboriginal.[81] Mark Davidson, a Labor MLA, chaired a select committee critical of the abuses of the Aborigines Protection Board in 1937 despite stiff opposition from his own party. When asked why he cared so much about the issue, Davidson reportedly evoked his time working alongside Aboriginal workers as a shearer in Western New South Wales during the 1890s.[82] During the 1891 strike two Aboriginal children, William and Duncan Ferguson, spent their days running about the strike camp at Waddai in the Riverina. "From that time, young Bill Ferguson was tied emotionally to the labour movement."[83] William Ferguson would go on to be an organiser for the AWU and later both the Ferguson brothers would play a prominent role in Aboriginal activism during the 1930s.[84]

This forgotten history challenges the dominant contemporary view that the Australian working class has been hostile to Indigenous workers due to their supposed position as "settlers".[85] Rather than seeking "the intensification of settler expansion and racial

79. Merritt 1986, p.148.
80. Merritt 1986, p.176.
81. *The Worker* (Wagga), 19 February 1913, p.3.
82. *Workers Weekly*, 22 April 1938, p.4.
83. Horner 1974, p.3.
84. Stanbrook and Fieldes 2019.
85. For an overview and critique of this position see Humphreys 2021.

segregation", "through colour bars, boycott campaigns and demands for expulsion",[86] non-Indigenous shearers organised alongside their fellow Indigenous workers in great industrial conflicts and in the process expressed strikingly sympathetic views towards the Indigenous situation – views all the more remarkable considering the context of racism in 1890s colonial society. Together white and black shearers fought against the main forces in society driving Indigenous dispossession and oppression – the pastoral capitalists, the police and the colonial governments. If non-Indigenous shearers actually benefited from Indigenous oppression and settler expansion then this joint struggle would have been impossible. White shearers didn't need to give up their supposed privileges in order to participate in joint struggles with Indigenous shearers; instead they looked to their common interests as workers exploited by the capitalist system. This history reveals not only the actual struggles and attitudes that existed but also the latent possibilities for more developed solidarity between Indigenous and non-Indigenous workers to emerge, as it did throughout the twentieth century in the post-war Aboriginal strikes in the Pilbara and Darwin, and the land rights struggles of the 1960s and 70s.

References

Much of the information in this article comes from newspapers published at the time, in particular *The Worker* published in Wagga, and *Worker* from Queensland. All the articles I quote can be accessed via trove: https://trove.nla.gov.au

Armstrong, Mick 2007, "Burning the *Rodney* – dealing with scabs in the shearers' strikes", Socialist Alternative. https://www.sa.org.au/node/1573

Biber, Katherine 2008, "Besieged at Home: Jimmy Governor's Rampage", *Public Space: The Journal of Law and Social Justice*, 2008, Vol. 2.

Elton, Judith 2007, *Comrades or competition?: Union relations with Aboriginal workers in the South Australian and Northern Territory pastoral industries, 1878–1957*, PhD thesis, University of South Australia.

---

86. Englert 2020, p.12.

Englert, Sai 2020, "Settlers, Workers, and the Logic of Accumulation by Dispossession", *Antipode: A Radical Journal of Geography*, 52 (6). https://doi.org/10.1111/anti.12659

Griffiths, Phillip 2006, T*he making of White Australia: Ruling class agendas, 1876–1888*, PhD thesis, ANU. https://espace.library.uq.edu.au/data/UQ_265385/Griffiths_thesis.pdf

Hone, J Anee 1969, "Chirnside, Thomas (1815–1887)", *Australian Dictionary of Biography*, National Centre of Biography, Australian National University. https://adb.anu.edu.au/biography/chirnside-thomas-3203/text4815

Horner, Jack 1974, *Vote Ferguson for Aboriginal Freedom: a biography*, Australia and New Zealand Book Co.

Humphreys, Jordan 2021, "Capitalism, colonialism and class: A Marxist explanation of Indigenous oppression today", *Marxist Left Review*, 21, Summer. https://marxistleftreview.org/articles/indigenous_oppression/

Lane, Ernie 1993 [1939], *Dawn to Dusk: Reminiscences of a Rebel*, SHAPE (Social History of Australia Publishing Enterprise).

Palmer, Vance 1954, *The Legend of the Nineties*, Melbourne University Press.

Markus, Andrew 1978, "Talka longa mouth: Aborigines and the labour movement 1890–1970", *Who are our enemies? Racism and the Australian working class*, Hale and Iremonger.

Merritt, John 1986, *The Making of the AWU*, Oxford University Press.

O'Malley, Timothy Rory 2009, *Mateship and Money-Making: Shearing in Twentieth Century Australia*, PhD thesis, University of Sydney.

Owen, Chris 2016, *Every Mother's Son is Guilty: Policing the Kimberley Frontier of Western Australia 1882–1905*, University of Western Australia Press.

Reynolds, Henry 1998, *This Whispering in our Hearts*, Allen and Unwin.

Roe, Jill 2005, "Sawtell, Olaf (Michael) (1883–1971)", *Australian Dictionary of Biography,* National Centre of Biography, Australian National University. https://adb.anu.edu.au/biography/sawtell-olaf-michael-13186/text23871.

Scrimgeour, Anne 2020, *On Red Earth Walking: The Pilbara Strike, Western Australia 1946–1949*, Monash University Publishing.

Small, Jerome n.d., "Reconsidering White Australia: Class and racism in the 1873 Clunes Riot", Marxist Interventions. https://sa.org.au/interventions/raceriots.htm

Stanbrook, Gavin and Diane Fieldes 2019, "William Ferguson: The life of an Aboriginal rebel", *Marxist Left Review*, 18, Winter. https://marxistleftreview. org/articles/william-ferguson-the-life-of-an-aboriginal-rebel/

Sullivan, AJ 2005 [1916], "Retrospect of a Labourer's Life, 1872 to 1916", *Hummer*, Australian Society for the Study of Labour History, 4, (4). https:// www.labourhistory.org.au/hummer/vol-4-no-4/retrospect/

Svensen, Stuart 1989, *The shearers' war : the story of the 1891 shearers' strike*, University of Queensland Press.

Ward, Russell 2003 [1966], *The Australian Legend*, Oxford University Press.

Wisely, Mark 2011, *The Anarcho-Syndicalist Platform for Indigenous Rights: A Trans-National study of Settler-colonialism, White Labourism and the International Workers of the World in Australia and South Africa*, PhD thesis, University of Sydney.

NICK EVERETT

Remembering the 1946 Pilbara Aboriginal pastoral workers strike

Nick Everett has taught in the fields of history, politics and social justice and is currently part of a working group organising events to commemorate the 75th anniversary of the Pilbara Strike. He is the author of a chapter in *Radical Perth, Militant Fremantle* (2nd ed, Interventions 2019) on the Perth-based solidarity movement with the strike.

Anne Scrimgeour, *On Red Earth Walking: The Pilbara Aboriginal Strike, Western Australia 1946–1949*, Monash University Publishing, 2020.

ANNE SCRIMGEOUR'S *ON RED EARTH WALKING* is an engaging and thoroughly researched account of the 1946 Pilbara Strike, when hundreds of Aboriginal workers walked off pastoral stations in protest against their slave-like conditions of employment. Not only were Aboriginal workers on the stations denied award wages paid to white workers, but some – commonly female domestic workers – were paid no wages at all. Strikers demanded freedom to leave their employer and the right to elect their own represent- atives: both rights denied to them under the punitive provisions of the Native Administration Act. Drawing upon extensive interviews, including translated Nyangumarta oral history recordings, newspa- per articles and methodical archival research, Scrimgeour's account explores how the strike and labour movement solidarity defeated the mechanisms of colonial control used by pastoralists and the Department of Native Affairs to keep Aboriginal workers subjugated.

On Red Earth Walking spans 27 chapters, beginning with an account of how wealthy "squatter" (pastoralist) families came to hold power over marrngu people, aided by "native protectors" (commonly also police), who were tasked with enforcing legislation that controlled every aspect of Aboriginal people's lives. In subsequent chapters we are introduced to a cast of characters (listed at the end of the book), which includes Indigenous strike leaders, communists and union militants, including the indomitable Don McLeod, as well as politicians, public servants, priests and police. Two strike camps – Twelve-Mile Camp, located outside of Port Hedland, and Moolyella, located inland near Marble Bar – became home to hundreds of strikers and their families. Strike communities cooked and ate together, and established work teams to hunt, gather pearl and prospect for minerals. Self-taught strikers established two schools, one at each camp, and teachers read reports about the strike to camp dwellers. Meanwhile, the Department vigorously attempted to thwart their efforts, arresting and imprisoning strike leaders, denying the strike camps access to ration cards and attempting to lure strikers away from their camps with the promise of education and employment opportunities at a church-run mission. Drawing on interviews she undertook with strikers and family members in the 1990s, Scrimgeour places Aboriginal voices front and centre in her storytelling.

In the 1860s, when European settlers first established sheep stations along the De Grey and Yule rivers, they took control over both Aboriginal land and labour through violence. When marrngu speared sheep for sustenance on lands from which they had been exiled, punitive expeditions soon followed. For those "black-birded" (forcibly recruited) into the pearling industry and those who became station workers, brutal treatment became routine. Sensitive to the criticism the Colonial Office was receiving for such a state of affairs, the British Imperial Government stipulated that, as a condition of Western Australian self-government, £5000 or one percent of state revenue (whichever was the greatest) be allocated to the Aboriginal Protection Board to fund Aboriginal education and welfare. Though this provision was enshrined in Section 70 of the colony's 1889 constitution, by 1897 powerful pastoral interests had successfully agitated for its repeal. The colonial government's Aborigines Department was granted significantly less funding and subsequently tasked with implementing the infamous provisions of the Aborigines Act 1905, which confined Aboriginal people to reserves, denied them freedom of movement and appointed local police officers to serve as native "protectors". Following the Moseley Royal Commission, the 1905 Act was replaced by the Native Administration Act 1936 and the newly formed Department of Native Affairs was granted even more powers of control over Aboriginal people.

Pastoralists were well-represented in the state's parliament, ensuring that the Department of Native Affairs and the police worked to serve their interests. Aboriginal people received rations of tobacco, tea, sugar, flour and meat in return for their labour, but were required to reside in "native camps" close to station homesteads. Typically, these camps were located in dry riverbeds and evacuated during the wet season, when Aboriginal residents were forced to share the shearing shed with the station's sheep. "Repeated displays of violence by the police served to maintain settler dominance over Aboriginal people," explains Scrimgeour (p.27).[1] She cites recollections by pastoral workers of beating and floggings for alleged misdemeanours and dog culls carried out in dawn raids on marrngu camps by police without warning, used as a means of intimidation. Pastoralists sometimes alerted police to the presence of children of mixed Aboriginal and non-Aboriginal parentage, thereby facilitating their removal, and on other occasions acted to prevent such removals. Nonetheless, their actions served to maintain the subordination of their Aboriginal workforce.

The coming of World War II brought significant changes to the Pilbara. Historians have argued that temporary employment opportunities for Aboriginal workers at better rates of pay, both within the army and in jobs normally the preserve of white workers, raised expectations and contributed to the strike. A labour shortage gave Aboriginal workers, especially those of mixed descent, bargaining power and access to award wages and conditions for the first time. Additionally, it has been argued that military personnel from the south brought with them more enlightened views about racial equality.[2] Scrimgeour, however, asserts that it was not

---

1. See also McGrath 1987, pp.107–108.
2. See for example, Davies 1988, p.33 and Wilson 2015, pp.40–42.

temporary conditions of equal pay and status for Aboriginal workers that contributed to the strike. Rather additional barriers in the form of discriminatory wartime restrictions forced a tipping point that gave rise to widespread industrial action.

While Aboriginal pastoral workers were excluded from wartime construction projects, Port Hedland's "mixed-descent Euralian population" as they were then known, were called upon to fill a labour shortage when non-Aboriginal civilians were evacuated south, in March 1942. Some were employed as wharf labourers, unloading munitions and supplies. However, they were treated with deep suspicion and frequently denied enlistment in the armed forces. Following the deployment of large numbers of troops in Port Hedland, Native Affairs Commissioner Francis Bray declared Port Hedland a prohibited area: Aboriginal people were not allowed to enter the town without a pass. The rationale for doing so was an irrational fear of fraternisation between male soldiers and Aboriginal women. In a bold display of defiance, Euralian community leader Lawrence (Pop) Clarke and his sons burnt their passes. According to Clarke's daughter Rose Nowers, "All of these men worked on the wharf all this time and all of a sudden they had to have special passes and yellow tickets". The pass system, she argued, "caused a lot of bad feeling, a lot of ill feeling" (pp.54–55).

Commissioner Bray rejected army proposals to evacuate Port Hedland's Aboriginal population to inland internment camps. Nonetheless, the Department of Native Affairs increased surveillance and control over the Euralian community, imposing a requirement for work permits to be held by employers of Euralians. It was at this time that Don McLeod, who had worked throughout the North West as a wharfie, miner, fencer, well-borer and mechanic, rallied to their cause. He concluded that the repressive measures of the "slave act of 1905" were intended to keep "Blackfellows illiterate, isolated and destitute".[3] The law, in McLeod's view, was set up by pastoralists and politicians to prevent "liberal-minded persons" from working to improve the livelihoods of Aboriginal people.

McLeod, a regular listener of the Anti-Fascist League's radio

---

3.   McLeod 1984, p.17.

show, came to view the struggle against fascism in Europe as linked to the fight for Aboriginal rights at home. After acquiring a copy of the pamphlet *New Deal for the Aborigines*, and corresponding with Communist author Katherine Susanna Prichard, McLeod joined the Australian Community Party in 1944.[4] In the lead-up to the strike, McLeod addressed the party's state conference, telling delegates he had joined the party because it "was the only political party with a policy to fit the situation and the only one honestly prepared to put up a fight."[5] Prichard, Communist Party organiser Graham Alcorn and *Workers' Star* correspondent Joan Williams saw in McLeod an ally to advance the party's program for Aboriginal rights.

In McLeod's account of the strike, *How the West Was Lost*, he recalls the idea of a strike first being canvassed at a meeting of Aboriginal Lawmen from across the state at Skull Springs, on the banks of the Davis River, in 1942. McLeod records that he was the only white man in attendance at the six-week long meeting and that he was delegated to represent the group in negotiations with the Department of Native Affairs, in Perth.[6] According to Scrimgeour, marrngu accounts suggest the Skull Springs meeting did not take place until 1945, following a long period of gestation for the strike idea involving many discussions between McLeod and marrngu workers, and that the strike was incidental to the purpose of the meeting. Nonetheless, McLeod was no doubt persuasive in his discussions with marrngu that strike action could be "a useful weapon" to challenge the power of the pastoralists and the authorities. The Skull Springs meeting must have impressed upon McLeod that marrngu bonds of kinship and culture, and resilient social organisation, could provide a strong foundation for the strike movement. While McLeod gained the respect of marrngu for stand-ing up for their rights, he was just one agent for social change in a wider movement. According to one of the strike leaders, Clancy

---

4. In July 1944, he wrote to CPA member Ernie Thornton, National Secretary of the Federated Iron Workers Association, describing himself as "a Party member undisclosed". Cited in Hess 1994, p.69.
5. Brown 1976, p.123. The state conference, the first since the end of the war, was held in Perth in March 1946.
6. McLeod 1984, pp.40–41.

McKenna (Warntupungkarna), marrngu elders had been discussing the injustices they faced for years. McKenna observed, "McLeod gave us hint about the strike and we took it up" (p.94).

In April 1946, Dooley Bin Bin set off to stations around the Pilbara by foot and by rail with the message, "Strike on 1st May 1946!" The date chosen was both symbolic and strategic: it was International Workers' Day and also the beginning of the shearing season. Yet the strike was far from an immediate success. Some station owners coaxed workers back with an offer of higher wages; others called upon the police to evict strikers and their families. Laurie O'Neill, the Department of Native Affairs' northern inspector and a former Kimberley policeman, threatened to remove strike leaders to other parts of the state. Native Affairs Commissioner Francis Bray later wrote that "natives were warned of the mischievous propaganda of Communist McLeod" and that McKenna was especially targeted "because he was a channel for McLeod's insidious propaganda".[7] Bray and O'Neill were convinced that strike action could be averted if a few bad apples were removed from the barrel.

The state's immediate response was to come down heavily on strike leaders. First McKenna and then Dooley were arrested and charged with "enticement to strike". Their conviction was a foregone conclusion. Both were officially represented by the same Department officials who were seeking their conviction. O'Neill hoped that their arrest would not only serve as a warning to others, but that they could be persuaded to give evidence against McLeod. While McKenna and Dooley served out their sentences in Marble Bar, McLeod was arrested and detained in Port Hedland on the charge of entering a "native camp". The arrests awakened a powerful solidarity movement in the south.

From the strike's commencement, the West Australian Communist Party newspaper *Workers' Star* carried frequent reports on the strike. *Workers' Star* reporter Joan Williams claims these reports were vital in combatting a "news blackout by the West Australian after its first report on the strike".[8] On 19 May, two hundred people attended a meeting on the Perth Esplanade, calling on the Justice

7. McLeod 1984, p.101.
8. Williams 1993, p.128.

Minister Emil Nulsen "to revoke the sentences and free the imprisoned strike leaders" (p.147). A week later, a three hundred-strong
meeting at Perth Town Hall launched the Committee for the Defence
of Native Rights (CDNR). The CDNR obtained support and strike
fund donations from a dozen WA union branches, the ALP, university and women's organisations, as well as the Australian Council of
Trade Unions and federal ministers. A CDNR appeal to the United
Nations alleged that the strike leaders' arrests amounted to "feudal
treatment of Aborigines in Northern Australia" (pp. 155–6). In
London, the Anti-Slavery Society took up the cause.

Throughout the strike, arrests and imprisonment of strikers
and supporters became a frequent occurrence. In August, CDNR
secretary and Anglican minister Rev. Peter Hodge travelled to Port
Hedland to meet with the strikers and, much to his surprise, was
arrested alongside McLeod for visiting an Aboriginal camp. Hodge
was fined, while McLeod was sentenced to three months imprisonment. In October 1946, the WA Court of Criminal Appeal rejected
appeals by McLeod and Hodge against their convictions. However,
a subsequent appeal to the High Court quashed the convictions,
giving the strikers more freedom to organise. This reprieve proved
only temporary. McLeod was arrested in total seven times during
the three-year dispute.[9] McKenna was jailed again in January 1947,
along with ten others, after being charged with preventing several
Warrawagine station hands from working.

Having failed to intimidate the strikers with the strong arm of
the law, authorities attempted to starve the strikers into submission.
The strikers had no union and therefore no established strike fund.
With post-war rationing still in place, essential supplies could only
be purchased with ration coupons. However, these were in the hands
of their station bosses, who insisted that they would be provided
only if the strikers returned to work. Again, the strikers stood firm. A
war of attrition between the parties now ensued. However, the tide
was slowly turning against the pastoralists as community sentiment
began to shift.

---

9.   McLeod records that he was arrested "three times for being within five chains
     of a congregation of natives, three times for inciting natives to leave their lawful
     employment, and once for forgery". McLeod 1984, p.49.

As the 1949 shearing season approached, 32 men were arrested when police intercepted their walk off from Warrawagine station. The men were force marched in chains and handcuffs along the Nullagine and De Grey Rivers before being imprisoned at Marble Bar. Reports of such brutal treatment, giving rise to claims of slavery, sat at odds with the new image the Department was seeking to project. Native Affairs Commissioner Stanley Middleton, appointed in August 1948, had begun to steer the Department's Aboriginal affairs policy in an assimilationist direction. As Scrimgeour puts it: "The task ahead...he believed, was to...guide Aboriginal people from primivism to modernity, from segregation and denigration to inclusion and acceptance into the social and economic life of mainstream Australia society" (p.363).

The Seamen's Union called for the prisoners' immediate release and announced a ban on the shipment of wool from all but two stations that had acceded to strikers' demands. The threat of a wool ban proved persuasive. Middleton's newly appointed deputy, Elliot-Smith, assured McLeod that the wages and conditions negotiated at Mount Edgar and Limestone stations would be applied throughout the Pilbara. Middleton and the minister for native affairs, Ross McDonald, both claimed Elliot-Smith had outstepped his mandate and continued to resist any formal agreement involving McLeod. Nonetheless, the once all-powerful common front of the pastoralists, the Department and police had been decisively weakened. Some Aboriginal pastoral workers now returned to the stations with signed contracts that guaranteed improved wages and conditions. Others remained in self-managed communities, operating mining ventures they had established during and after the dispute.

Scrimgeour argues that through strike action, "marrngu had stepped out of the shadows and made themselves visible" (pp.458–9) and, in so doing, not only won concessions from their employers, but achieved a new sense of independence and self-confidence. Sadly, she passed away in January this year, just before her book's publication. *On Red Earth Walking* is a comprehensive compilation of a lifetime's research and a testament to the power of solidarity between organised labour and an oppressed people struggling for their rights. It shines a light on decades of brutal treatment of Aboriginal workers in Western Australia and explains how their bold defiance opened a new chapter in the struggle for Aboriginal rights.

References

Brown, Max 1976, *The Black Eureka*, Australian Book Society.

Davies, Lloyd 1988, ""Protecting Natives?: The Law and the 1946 Aboriginal Pastoral Workers' Strike", *Papers in Labour History*, 1, pp.31–42.

Hess, Michael 1994, "Black and Red: The Pilbara Pastoral Workers' Strike", *Aboriginal History 18*, (1), pp.65–77.

McGrath, Ann 1987, *Born in the Cattle: Aborigines in Cattle Country*, Allen & Unwin.

McLeod, DW 1984, *How the West Was Lost: The Native Question in the Development of Western Australia*, self-published.

Williams, Justina 1993, *Anger & Love*, Fremantle Arts Centre Press.

Wilson, Deborah 2015, *Different White People: Radical Activism for Aboriginal Rights 1946–1972*, UWA Publishing.

SADIA SCHNEIDER

Lenin embalmed

Sadia Schneider is a trade union activist working in education and has been involved in socialist politics for over a decade. She has written on Marx, Lenin and the state for both *Marxist Left Review* and *Red Flag*.

Hjalmar Jorge Joffre-Eichhorn, Patrick Anderson and Johann Salazar (eds), *Lenin150 (Samizdat)*, 2nd edition, Daraja Press, 2021.

THE RENAISSANCE OF LITERATURE ON LENIN in the last decade has produced many useful insights. Unfortunately, with regard to this book, I can't share the enthusiasm of those on the far left who have reviewed it so far.[1] A few notable exceptions aside, the essays in this collection are frustrating and disappointing. Some of the worst fads and trends of the left find expression here. *Lenin150 (Samizdat)* reveals that striving for novelty often produces its opposite. The book harnesses the unique powers of academic jargon to give a radical gloss to postmodernism, identity politics, Maoism, liberalism and nostalgia for the USSR.

A bad start

The *Introduction* resembles a bad stand-up routine replete with in-jokes. Why, asks editor Hjalmar Jorge Joffre-Eichhorn, does so much interest and controversy surround Lenin so many years after

---

1. Le Blanc 2020; Bambery 2021; Korr 2021.

his death? – "False Consciousness? A strange case of Leninitus? Left-Wing Melancholia? Post-Traumatic Socialist Disorder?" (p.2). To buffer his answer to this question, Joffre-Eichhorn squeezes in references to Vladimir Mayakovksy, Julius Caesar and German pop psychology, which adds words but not substance. On the enduring significance of Lenin, he concludes: "The man Lenin was a winner. He had as the Germans say, the Sieger-Gen, the innate capacity and will to win. And while all this might sounds terribly deterministic and mechanical – sorry Vladimir Ilyich – what I am getting at here is simply the fact that 'Lenin lived, Lenin lives, Lenin will live' has not only a propagandistic and (vaguely) lyrical but also an ontological dimension that I believe should not be reduced to the eternal paying homage to Lenin the actually existing revolutionary, though we may to that too, but rather to make his Sieger-Gen the psycho-material foundation of our own individual and collective DNA, our fighting spirit so to speak" (p.3). This insight has all the sophistication of Nike's "Just do it" minus the concision.

USSR nostalgia

The collection is a collage of USSR kitsch which, judging by the essays, reflects not just the aesthetic but also the political proclivities of many of the contributors. The book is full of nostalgic images of stoic statues of Lenin throughout the former Soviet bloc countries. Joffre-Eichhorn describes these statues as "comforting," while the editor/photographer Johan Salazar can't deny the "Soviet triumphs" in science, sport, infrastructure and the space race (p.306). But why stop there? The US made similar, arguably greater advances in the same period. The Nazis made great strides in infrastructure and medical research.

In the preface, *Breathing for Revolution – Toward an Oxygenic Communism*, the editors confess their stance on the USSR. They are "inclined to defend certain aspects of the 70+ year history of the USSR and other Communist experiments" while acknowledging the "lack of oxygen" (p.xii) – a euphemism for dictatorship. It is correct but insufficient to criticise the absence of democratic rights in the USSR. Stalinism plus parliamentary democracy does not equal socialism. What is missing in the preface and in the rest of the essays is an understanding of Lenin and Stalin as the embodiments of revolution and counter-revolution respectively.

Many of the authors are critical of Stalin's excesses but simultaneously blur the line between Stalinist/Maoist distortions and genuine Marxism.[2] A few, such as Roland Boer in *Lenin and non-antagonistic contradiction*, not only defend but celebrate high Stalinism. Seeing as Roland's bio at the back of the book praises him as "the first foreign national to be appointed to an ongoing position in a School of Marxism Studies in China", I expected thinly veiled Stalinism, and thinly veiled it was. In his introduction, Boer clarifies what he means by "socialism": "[t]he category of non-antagonistic contradictions arose from the practical experience of constructing socialism, initially in the Soviet Union in the 1930s, and then in China, especially through the impetus of Mao Zedong and later in the context of the socialist project of "Reform and Opening-up" led by Deng Xiaoping" (p.103). The highpoints of the socialist tradition for Boer are Russia at the height of Stalin's repression – the "results of the socialist offensive" that led to the "creative period of the 1930s" and the early years of one-party rule in China. "Non-antagonistic contradiction" for Mao and for Boer functions as a twisted theoretical whitewash to argue that a one-party dictatorship lording over the massive exploitation of workers and the peasantry is not necessarily at odds with liberation. It is particularly sickening to have such rubbish published alongside an essay by Leon Trotsky, who fought and was ultimately murdered by Stalin.

Žižek's essay deserves a special mention for combining the most insipid reformism with a high Stalinist fetishisation of state power. In his essay *Lenin? Which Lenin?* Žižek argues that the left has for decades now been "in the trap of oppositionalism". The problem, according to Žižek, is twofold. First, the left should stop fighting the state and focus instead on getting elected. Second, once elected they should be less antagonistic. Žižek chastises the left for lacking vision

---

2. For example Ronald Grigor Suny's essay, *A whole river of blood: Lenin and Stalin*, argues that Stalinism was a "malignant perversion of the aspirations of the original founders and the revolutionary masses who came onto the streets in 1917" (p.258) but then concludes that Stalin was an (unintentional) outgrowth of Lenin's polemical style.

before offering sage advice that if and when elected, leftist govern-ments should make sure to "define a positive role for the private sector".[3] Given the failures of multiple leftist electoral projects of the last few years it's unclear whether Žižek isn't paying attention or has a desire to see history repeated as farce.

Taking Lenin out of context

Readers of this journal would know that we think Lenin has a lot to offer revolutionaries today. But his insights can't simply be dumped on various contemporary situations. Lenin famously argued that the truth is concrete. Taken as isolated proclamations, Lenin's phrases and interventions can be used to justify just about anything.

This is exemplified in Atilio A Boron's essay, *Notes on "Left-wing" Communism: an Infantile Disorder,* which argues that it is ultra-left and aids US imperialism to criticise the Bolivian government from the left. Obviously, the left should oppose the US's constant and belligerent attempts to undermine democratically elected govern-ments in the region. But to argue that it is ultra-left to criticise these long-running capitalist regimes is ludicrous. Lenin's approach to tactical compromises and alliances placed a premium on sharpen-ing, rather than blunting, criticisms. More to the point, *"Left-wing" Communism* was not about giving left cover to reformists. It was an argument about how revolutionaries could win a mass audience in order to defeat them.

In a similar vein Georgy Mamedov uses Lenin's essays on the national question to make the case for "radical identity politics". Mamedov distinguishes between conventional identity politics with its emphasis on "representation" with "revolutionary identity politics" that seeks societal transformation using examples from the 1970s of gay liberation and Marxist feminism as examples of the latter. Mamedov feels the need to marry identity politics and

---

3.   "The majority of radical Leftist thought in recent decades has been caught in the trap of oppositionalism: it adopts as self-evident that true politics is only possible at a distance from the state and its apparatuses" and "Instead of just focusing on antagonism, it is...crucial for a Leftist government today to define a role for the private sector...one should not just antagonise it but also propose a positive vision of its role." (p.292).

Marxism for the same reasons Marxist feminists (whom he quotes favourably) felt the need to do this in the 1970s – he accepts that the USSR was in some way socialist. According to Mamedov, "the experience of actually existing socialist regimes showed that economic transformation on its own does not lead to the transformation of oppositionist social relations..." (p.121). He is talking about Stalinism, not genuine Marxism, when decrying "[t]he stubborn economism of traditional Marxist politics".

While there are politically better and worse iterations of identity politics, the framework is not consistent with Marxism generally or Lenin's approach to oppression specifically – see Sarah Garnham's article in this edition of the journal for a full explanation. Lenin's writings on the national question are not a blueprint for marrying Marxism and identity politics, but a consistent application of revolutionary Marxism. Like Marx, Lenin took seriously questions of oppression not because he sought to "de-privilege" Russian workers but rather the opposite – because he wanted to raise their class consciousness and confidence. Marxists fight with the oppressed and against oppression because we want to see workers take power and oppression divides and weakens us.

Some better contributions

Some better essays stand out. Alain Badiou's *Lenin, Founder of the Modern Meaning of Politics* discusses the significance of Lenin's *April Theses* for advancing a conception of politics that was not centred on managing the institutions of the state, but rather reorganising society along totally new lines. Badiou correctly situates the *April Theses* as crucial to understanding the difference between the February and October revolutions of 1917: "The February revolution...aims only to change the form of the state; politics thereby assumes the first of its two possible meanings". In contrast, Lenin's *Theses* embody politics in the second sense where "the aim of political action must be to transform the organisation of society in its entirety, shattering the economic oligarchy and entrusting production...to the management of all those who work" (p.16).

I share Badiou's opinion regarding the importance of the *April Theses*. However, the idea that these engendered a "new" understanding of politics unique to Lenin is wrong. Marx classically liberated "politics" from its position as an adjunct of states and nation-states. In works like *The Critique of the Philosophy of Right* and *On the Jewish Question,* he advanced a theory of politics that rejected the idea that liberation would be won through the bourgeois state. In developing his April theses, and for his subsequent arguments in *State and Revolution,* Lenin returned to and developed Marx's writings.

Some of the essays seem to be a genuine attempt, with mixed results, to draw on Lenin to grapple with contemporary political questions. Vashna Jagarnath's *Peace, land and bread – We are not going to die of coronavirus, we are going to die of hunger!* and Michael Bri's *Learning from Lenin – and doing it differently* fall into this category. Jagarnath's essay is a highly charged account of the political landscape in South Africa in 2020. Her essay is a powerful polemic against the ruinous role of NGOs, and calls for politics that look to the power of the working class. However, Jagarnath's attempt to graft the slogan "peace, land and bread" onto contemporary South Africa is less successful, suggesting that the key impasse faced by the left is its inability to formulate appropriate slogans.

Michael Brie looks at Lenin's most decisive interventions such as his opposition to the First World War, his initiation of a new International and his theory of the state and imperialism. He tries to translate these into the tasks facing the European left, but his calls to action amount to extremely vague appeals for "new narratives" while cautioning against "extremes": "The European Left...is often driven by an either/or, right-or-wrong mentality. This divides and paralyses us. We need scenarios that do justice to the openness of the situation and at the same time reflect on the concrete possibilities" (p.34). Writing from Germany, where *Die Linke* has continued its drift to the right, one wonders how Brie could think political intransigence is the problem.

Arguably the best essay is Elvira Concheiro Bórquez's *Lenin does not mean Leninism.* In the least equivocal terms, she argues that Lenin's thought is the antithesis of Marxism-Leninism as state ideology. She highlights how Stalin's construction of a cult of Lenin was a conscious process by which he cemented his power and that it involved a complete renunciation of the democratic, anti-dogmatic approach that rendered Lenin such an important figure in the Russian revolution. On this same basis, she points out how Lenin's Marxism broke with the deterministic and reductionist tendencies of the Second International in placing the emphasis on agency and conscious intervention into the historic process. Michael Neocosmos' *Lenin's Turn to the Masses (1921–23)* similarly highlights how even against the backdrop of civil war, increasing isolation and economic ruin Lenin sought at every turn to expand the democratic participation of the masses to combat the developing bureaucratism. Unfortunately he identifies Lenin's democratic legacy with Mao's Cultural Revolution, which mobilised students against workers and intellectuals in service of a factional battle within the CCP.

The last two pieces worth commenting on are Matthieu Renault's *On revolutionary prudence, or the wisdom of Lenin* and Jodi Dean's *Lenin's Desire: Reminiscences of Lenin and the desire of the comrade*. These contributions are symptomatic of the politically better contributions – an interesting, politically astute insight is bookended by wacky digressions that not only fail to add anything but actually obscure the main insight.

Renault's article begins with a rather long tangent of "free word association" where he ponders the connection between the two Beatles songs, *Back in the USSR* and *Dear Prudence*, ending with the very pertinent question "what if the Beatles had established a connection between Gandhi and Lenin?" This thought is left hanging (for good reason) and Renault moves on to argue that Lenin's brilliance lay in a prudence ("*phronesis*") defined by "concrete analysis of a concrete situation" in contrast to the conventional wisdom involving abstract proclamations of truth ("*sophia*"). As Renault points out, Lenin was contemptuous of self-proclaimed "sages" of the petty bourgeoisie; attributing wisdom instead to what the working class acquires in struggle.

Renault's insight loses its utility when he extends it to explain the difference between Lenin and Stalin – "The essential discord between Lenin and Stalin thus ultimately boils down to the difference between *phronesis* and *sophia*" (p.200). According to this tortured reading, Stalin's lack of prudence is to blame for a host of his policies, from his suppression of national minorities to the brutality that characterised the USSR from the late 1920s. Renault returns to the Beatles at the end of the essay, bringing in Jacques Derrida to further elaborate on the significance of the songs and the Gandhi/ Lenin connection – "The circle is complete, the link between *Back in the USSR* and *Dear Prudence* by the Beatles is revealed: Lenin's revolutionary prudence arrives, by strange detours, at Gandhi's *phronesis*" (p.199). Strange detours indeed.

Dean's essay, despite the esoteric title, is actually an argument about the relationship between the revolutionary party and the class. Importing a Lacanian psychoanalytic framework, she suggests that the relationship between the two is mutually constitutive. The role of organisation is not to dictate to the masses from on high but to actualise the agency of the working class as a political subject and vice versa. This argument builds on the correct understanding that Lenin's emphasis on organisation was a product of his faith in the working class, not opposed to it – an argument made by several contributions to *Marxist Left Review*. Although shrouded in somewhat unhelpful Lacanian language of desire and object relations (eg "Lenin's desire is the desire of the proletariat", p.129) her argument cuts against the tendency to see Lenin in terms of his intellectual prowess, but rather as a figure who developed through his intimate engagement with the Russian working class.

It is worth contrasting some of the better literature on Lenin, which includes Neil Harding's *Lenin's Political Thought*, Tom Freeman's *Lenin's Interventionist Marxism* and Paul Le Blanc's *Lenin and the Party*. Each of these books offer slightly different insights and emphases, but what they have in common is an attempt to understand Lenin in context and to draw out his relevance for today in terms of the two interconnected issues that defined him as a thinker – the question of revolutionary organisation and workers' power. Harding's *Lenin's Political Thought* is an expansive and meticulously researched account of Lenin's thought – how it was shaped by and in turn helped shape the traditions of Russian Marxism, the debates and divisions within the RSDLP, the struggles of the working class, the peasantry and developments within global capitalism. Freeman's book covers a shorter period, from 1861–1907, but stands out as a politically relevant contribution. He argues that what distinguished Lenin was his emphasis on conscious political leadership and intervention which was a consistent feature of his approach to party building throughout his life. Freeman highlights the democratic and dynamic character of Lenin's thought, explicitly connecting rather than contrasting this to Lenin's focus on building a vanguard party. In this journal, Sandra Bloodworth's articles underline the abyss separating Lenin's democratic and interventionist Marxism from Second International social democracy and Stalinism.[4]

Conclusion

Many of the essays in *Lenin150* shine a light on Lenin's key insights and interventions and a few of the authors clearly appreciate the richness of Lenin's thought. Unfortunately, for the most part, this understanding is used to conflate Marxism with variants of reformism and Stalinism, which share an obsession with capturing the capitalist state. In rejecting the need to smash the state these distortions are a barrier to the human liberation envisioned by Lenin, Marx, Trotsky, Luxemburg, Gramsci and many others.

The contributors to this collection are overwhelmingly professors and bring with them the worst tropes of academia – jargon obscures meaning, idiosyncrasy takes precedence over substance and obscurity is a virtue. The question that kept arising for me reading this was – how is this relevant? The relevance deficiency applies to this collection in several ways. Esoteric articles such as *What Lenin teaches us about witchcraft*, *A conversation about Lenin and theatre*, *Electric communism: the continued importance of energy to revolution* and *City of Lenin and the socialist life of a river* vindicate the mocking description of the university as "the ivory tower". Then there is the question of relevance with regard to the argument being made – what does Derrida's linguistic musings on the name "USSR" have to do with national liberation? We'll never know because the author doesn't feel compelled to explain. Finally, and

---

4. Sandra Bloodworth, "Lenin vs 'Leninism'", *Marxist Left Review*, 5, Summer 2012; and "Lenin and a theory of revolution for the West", *Marxist Left Review*, 8, Winter 2014.

most importantly, there is the question of relevance to the project of changing the world.

Ironically, this collection seems to be an attempt to make Lenin relevant, to destodgify the left and make it seem fun. This might be entertaining for all involved but what we, the working class and the oppressed need and deserve is political clarity. Theory should help us to better understand the world in order to change it. More than the sum of pithy quotes and polemics, this is what Lenin was about.

References

Bambery, Chris, "*Lenin150 (Samizdat)*: Review", *Counterfire*, March 2021. https://www.counterfire.org/articles/book-reviews/22169-lenin-150-samizdat-book-review

Freeman, Tom 2017, *Lenin's Interventionist Marxism*, Interventions.

Harding, Neil 2009 [1977–78], *Lenin's Political Thought*, Haymarket Books.

Korr, Kevin 2021, "A Patchwork Lenin", *International Socialism*, 170, April. http://isj.org.uk/a-patchwork-lenin/

Le Blanc, Paul 1993, *Lenin and the Revolutionary Party*, Humanities Press.

Le Blanc, Paul 2020, "*Lenin150 (Samizdat)*: Review", Links International Journal of Socialist Renewal, September. http://links.org.au/lenin150-samizdat-lenin-birthday-book